COMPASS

THE SORCERERS' CROSSING

Taisha Abelar is a member of the same informal society of sorcerers that includes Carlos Castaneda.

The Sorcerers' Crossing

Taisha Abelar

PENGUIN COMPASS

PENGUIN COMPASS
Published by the Penguin Group
Penguin Group (USA) Inc., 375 Hudson Street, New York, New York 10014, U.S.A.
Penguin Group (Canada), 90 Eglinton Avenue East, Suite 700, Toronto,
Ontario, Canada M4P 2Y3 (a division of Pearson Penguin Canada Inc.)
Penguin Books Ltd, 80 Strand, London WC2R 0RL, England
Penguin Ireland, 25 St Stephen's Green, Dublin 2, Ireland
(a division of Penguin Books Ltd)
Penguin Group (Australia), 250 Camberwell Road, Camberwell,
Victoria 3124, Australia (a division of Pearson Australia Group Pty Ltd)
Penguin Books India Pvt Ltd, 11 Community Centre, Panchsheel Park,
New Delhi – 110 017, India
Penguin Group (NZ), 67 Apollo Drive, Rosedale, North Shore 0632, New Zealand
(a division of Pearson New Zealand Ltd)
Penguin Books (South Africa) (Pty) Ltd, 24 Sturdee Avenue, Rosebank,
Johannesburg 2196, South Africa

Penguin Books Ltd, Registered Offices: 80 Strand, London WC2R 0RL, England

First published in the United States of America by Viking Penguin, a division of
Penguin Books USA Inc., 1992
Published in Arkana 1993

30   29

THE LIBRARY OF CONGRESS HAS CATALOGUED THE HARDCOVER AS FOLLOWS:
Abelar, Taisha.
The sorcerers' crossing/Taisha Abelar.
p. cm.
ISBN 0-670-84272-9 (hc.)
ISBN 978-0-14-019366-4 (pbk.)
1. Occultism. 2. Abelar, Taisha. I. Title.
BJ1999.A188   1992
133.4'3—dc20   91–39370

Printed in the United States of America
Set in Primer
Designed by Wilma Jane Weichselbaum

With affection for all

who journey into the unknown

Foreword
by
Carlos Castaneda

Taisha Abelar is one of a group of three women that were deliberately trained by some sorcerers from Mexico, under the guidance of don Juan Matus.

I have written at length about my own training under him, but I have never written anything about this specific group, of which Taisha Abelar is a member. It was a tacit agreement among all of those who were under don Juan's tutelage that nothing should be said about them.

For over twenty years we have upheld this agreement. And even though we have worked and lived in close proximity, never have we talked with one another about our personal experiences. In fact, never had there been an opportunity even to exchange our views about what specifically don Juan or the sorcerers of his group did to each one of us.

Such a condition was not contingent upon don Juan's presence. After he and his group left the world, we continued to adhere to it, for we had no desire to use our energy to review any previous agreements. All our available time and energy were employed in validating for ourselves what don Juan had so painstakingly taught us.

Don Juan had taught us sorcery as a pragmatic endeavor by means of which any of us can directly perceive energy. He had maintained that in order to perceive energy in such a fashion, we need freedom from our normal capacity to perceive. To free ourselves and directly perceive energy was a task that took all we had.

It is a sorcerer's idea that the parameters of our normal perception have been imposed upon us as part of our socialization, not quite arbitrarily but laid down mandatorily nonetheless. One aspect of these obligatory parameters is an interpretation system, which processes sensory data into meaningful units and renders the social order as a structure of interpretation.

Our normal functioning within the social order requires a blind and faithful adherence to all its precepts, none of which calls for the possibility of directly perceiving energy. For example, don Juan maintained that it is possible to perceive human beings as fields of energy, like huge, oblong, whitish luminous eggs.

In order to accomplish the feat of heightening our perception, we need internal energy. Thus, the problem of making internal energy available to fulfill such a task becomes the key issue for students of sorcery.

Circumstances proper to our time and place have made it possible now for Taisha Abelar to write about her training, which was the same as mine, and yet thoroughly different. The writing took her a long time, because, first, she had to avail herself of the sorcery means to write. Don Juan Matus himself gave me the task of writing about his sorcery knowledge. And he himself set the mood of this task by saying, "Don't write like a writer, but like a sorcerer." He meant that I had to do it in a state of enhanced awareness, which sorcerers call *dreaming*. It took Taisha Abelar many years to perfect her dreaming to the point of making it the sorcery means to write.

In don Juan's world, sorcerers, depending on their basic temperaments, were divided into two complementary factions: *dreamers* and *stalkers*. Dreamers are those sorcerers who have the inherent facility to enter into states of heightened awareness by controlling their dreams. This facility is developed through training into an art: the art of dreaming. Stalkers, on the other hand, are those sorcerers who have the innate facility to deal with facts and are capable of entering states of heightened awareness by manipulating and controlling their own behavior. Through sorcery training, this natural capability is turned into the art of *stalking*.

Although everybody in don Juan's party of sorcerers had a complete knowledge of both arts, they were arranged in one faction or the other. And Taisha Abelar was grouped with the stalkers and trained by them. Her book bears the mark of her stupendous training as a stalker.

Preface

I have devoted my life to the practice of a rigorous discipline, which, for lack of a more suitable name, we have called sorcery. I am also an anthropologist, having received my Ph.D. in that field of study. I mention my two areas of expertise in this particular order because my involvement with sorcery came first. Usually, one becomes an anthropologist and then one does fieldwork on an aspect of culture—for example, the study of sorcery practices. With me, it happened the other way around: as a student of sorcery I went to study anthropology.

In the late sixties, while I was living in Tucson, Arizona, I met a Mexican woman by the name of Clara Grau, who invited me to stay in her house in the state of Sonora, Mexico. There, she did her utmost to usher me into her world, for Clara Grau was a sorceress, part of a cohesive group of sixteen sorcerers. Some of them were Yaqui Indians; others were Mexicans of various origins and backgrounds, ages and sexes. Most were women. All of them pursued, single-heartedly, the same goal: breaking the perceptual dispositions and biases that imprison us within the boundaries of the normal everyday world and prevent us from entering other perceivable worlds.

For sorcerers, to break such perceptual dispositions enables one to cross a barrier and leap into the unimaginable. They call such a leap "the sorcerers' crossing." Sometimes they refer to it as "the abstract flight," for it entails soaring from the side of the concrete, the physical, to the side of expanded perception and impersonal abstract forms.

These sorcerers were interested in helping me accomplish this abstract flight so that I could join them in their basic endeavors.

For me, academic training became an integral part of my preparation for the sorcerers' crossing. The leader of the sorcerers' group with whom I am associated, the *nagual,* as he is called, is a person with a keen interest in formal academic erudition. Hence, all those under his care had to develop their capacity for the abstract, clear thinking that is acquired only in a modern university.

As a woman, I had an even greater obligation to fulfill this requirement. Women in general are conditioned from early childhood to depend on the male members of our society to conceptualize and initiate changes. The sorcerers that trained me had very strong opinions in this regard. They felt that it is indispensable that women develop their intellects and enhance their capacity for analysis and abstraction in order to have a better grasp of the world around them.

Also, training the intellect is a bona-fide sorcerers' subterfuge. By deliberately keeping the mind occupied in analysis and reasoning, sorcerers are free to explore, unimpeded, other areas of perception. In other words, while the rational side is busy with the formality of academic pursuits, the energetic or nonrational side, which sorcerers call "the double," is kept occupied with the fulfillment of sorcery tasks. In this way, the suspicious and analytic mind is less likely to interfere or even notice what is going on at a nonrational level.

The counterpart of my academic development was the enhancement of my capacity for awareness and perception: together the two develop our total being. Working together as a unit, they took me away from the taken-for-granted life that I had been born into and socialized for as a woman, to a new area of greater perceptual possibilities than what the normal world had in store for me.

This is not to say that solely my commitment to the world of sorcery was enough to assure my success. The pull of the daily world is so strong and sustained that in spite of their most assiduous training, all practitioners find themselves again and again in the midst of the most abject terror, stupidity and indulging, as if they had learned nothing. My teachers warned me that I was no exception. And that only a minute to minute relentless struggle can balance one's natural but stupefying insistence to remain unchanged.

After a careful examination of my final aims, I, in conjunction with my cohorts, arrived at the conclusion that I have to describe my training in order to emphasize to seekers of the unknown the importance of developing the ability to perceive more than we do with normal perception. Such enhanced perception has to be a sober, pragmatic, new way of perceiving. It cannot be, under any condition, merely the continuation of perceiving the world of everyday life.

The events I narrate here depict the initial stages of sorcery training for a stalker. This phase involves the cleansing of one's habitual ways of thinking, behaving and feeling by means of a traditional sorcery undertaking, one which all neophytes need to perform, called "the recapitulation." To complement the recapitulation, I was taught a series of practices called "sorcery passes," involving movement and breathing. And to give these practices an adequate coherence, I was instructed with the accompanying philosophical rationales and explanations.

The goal of everything I was taught was the redistribution of my normal energy, and the enhancement of it, so that it could be used for the out-of-the-ordinary feats of perception demanded by sorcery training. The idea behind the training is that as soon as the compulsive pattern of old habits, thoughts, expectations and feelings is broken by means of the recapitulation, one is indisputably in the position to accumulate enough energy to live by the new rationales provided by the sorcery tradition—and to substantiate those rationales by directly perceiving a different reality.

The Sorcerers' Crossing

1

I had walked to an isolated spot, away from the highway and people, in order to sketch the early morning shadows on the unique lava mountains that fringe the Gran Desierto, in southern Arizona. The dark brown jagged rocks sparkled as bursts of sunlight illuminated their peaks. Strewn on the ground around me were huge chunks of porous rock, remnants of the lava flow from a gigantic volcanic eruption. Making myself comfortable on a large clump of rock and oblivious to anything else, I had sunk into my work, as I often did in that rugged, beautiful place. I had finished outlining the prom-ontories and depressions of the distant mountains when I noticed a woman watching me. It annoyed me no end that someone would disturb my solitude. I tried my utmost to ignore her, but when she moved nearer to look at my work, I turned around in anger to face her.

Her high cheekbones and shoulder-length black hair made her look Eurasian. She had a smooth, creamy complexion, so it was difficult to judge her age; she could have been anywhere between thirty and fifty. She was perhaps two inches taller than I, which would have made her five nine, but with her powerful frame, she looked twice my size. Yet, in her black silk pants and Oriental jacket, she seemed extremely fit.

I noticed her eyes; they were green and sparkling. It was that friendly gleam that made my anger vanish, and I heard myself asking the woman an inane question, "Do you live around here?"

"No," she said, taking a few steps toward me. "I'm on my way to the U.S. border checkpoint at Sonoyta. I stopped to stretch my legs and ended up in this desolate spot. I was so surprised to see someone out here, so far away from everything, that I couldn't help intruding the way I have. Let me introduce myself. My name is Clara Grau."

She extended her hand and I shook it, and without the slightest hesitation I told her that I was given the name Taisha when I was born, but later, my parents didn't think the name was American enough and began calling me Martha, after my mother. I detested that name and decided on Mary instead.

"How interesting!" she mused. "You have three names that are so different. I'll call you Taisha, since it's your birth name."

I was glad she had selected that name. It was the one I had chosen myself. Although at first I had agreed with my parents about the name being too foreign, I had disliked the name Martha so much that I ended up making Taisha my secret name.

In a harsh tone that she immediately concealed behind a benign smile, she bombarded me with a series of statements in the guise of questions, "You're not from Arizona," she began.

I responded to her truthfully, an unusual thing for me to do, accustomed as I was to being cautious with people, especially strangers. "I came to Arizona a year ago to work."

"You couldn't be more than twenty."

"I'll be twenty-one in a couple of months."

"You have a slight accent. You don't seem to be an American, but I can't pinpoint your exact nationality."

"I am an American, but as a child I lived in Germany," I said. "My father is American and my mother, Hungarian. I left home when I went to college and never went back, because I didn't want to have anything more to do with my family."

"I take it you didn't get along with them?"

"No. I was miserable. I couldn't wait to leave home."

She smiled and nodded as if she was familiar with the feeling of wanting to escape.

"Are you married?" the woman asked.

"No. I don't have anyone in the world." I said that with the touch of self-pity I had always had whenever I talked about myself.

She didn't make any comment, but spoke calmly and precisely as if she wanted to put me at ease and at the same time convey as much information about herself as she could with each of her sentences.

As she talked, I put my drawing pencils in my case but without taking my eyes away from her. I didn't want to give her the impression I wasn't listening.

"I was an only child and both my parents are dead now," she said. "My father's family are Mexican from Oaxaca. But my mother's family are Americans of German descent. They are from back east, but now live in Phoenix. I just returned from the wedding of one of my cousins."

"Do you also live in Phoenix?" I asked.

"I've lived half my life in Arizona and the other half in Mexico," she replied. "But for the past years, my home has been in the state of Sonora, Mexico."

I began to zip up my portfolio. Meeting and talking to this woman had so unsettled me that I knew I wouldn't be able to do any more work that day.

"I've also traveled to the Orient," she said, regaining my attention. "There, I learned acupuncture and the martial and healing arts. I've even lived for a number of years in a Buddhist temple."

"Really?" I glanced at her eyes. They had the look of a person who meditated a great deal. They were fiery, and yet tranquil.

"I'm very interested in the Orient," I said, "especially in Japan. I also have studied Buddhism and the martial arts."

"Really?" she said, echoing me. "I wish I could tell you my Buddhist name, but secret names shouldn't be revealed except under the proper circumstances."

"I told you my secret name," I said, tightening the straps of my portfolio.

"Yes, Taisha, you did, and that's very significant to me," she replied with undue seriousness. "But still, right now it's time only for introductions."

"Did you drive here?" I asked, scanning the area for her car.

"I was just going to ask you the same question," she said.

"I left my car about a quarter of a mile back, on a dirt road south of here. Where is yours?"

"Is your car a white Chevrolet?" she asked cheerfully.

"Yes."

"Well, mine is parked next to it." She giggled as if she had said something funny. I was surprised to find her laughter so irritating.

"I've got to go now," I said. "It's been very pleasant meeting you. Good-bye!"

I started to walk to my car, thinking that the woman would remain behind admiring the scenery.

"Let's not say good-bye yet," she protested. "I'm coming with you."

We walked together. Next to my one hundred and ten pounds, the woman was like a huge boulder. Her midsection was round and powerful. She projected the feeling that she could easily have been obese, but she wasn't.

"May I ask you a personal question, Mrs. Grau?" I said, just to break the awkward silence.

She stopped walking and faced me. "I'm not anybody's Mrs.," she snapped. "I am Clara Grau. You can call me Clara, and, yes, go right ahead and ask me anything you wish."

"I take it you're not partial to love and marriage," I commented, reacting to her tone.

For a second, she gave me a fearsome look, but she softened it instantly. "I'm definitely not partial to slavery," she said. "But not only for women. Now, what was it that you were going to ask me?"

Her reaction was so unexpected that I lost track of what I was going to ask and embarrassed myself by staring at her.

"What made you walk all the way to this place in particular?" I asked hurriedly.

"I came here because this is a place of energy." She pointed at the lava formations in the distance. "Those mountains were once spewed forth from the heart of the earth, like blood. Whenever I'm in Arizona, I always make a detour to come here. This place oozes a peculiar earthly energy. Now let me ask you the same question, what made *you* pick this spot?"

"I often come here. It's my favorite place to sketch." I didn't mean it as a joke, but she burst out laughing.

"This detail settles it!" she exclaimed, then continued in a quieter tone. "I'm going to ask you to do something you may consider outlandish or even foolish, but hear me out. I'd like you to come to my house and spend a few days as my guest."

I raised my hand to thank her and say no, but she urged me to reconsider. She assured me that our common interest in the Orient and the martial arts warranted a serious exchange of ideas.

"Where exactly do you live?" I asked.

"Near the city of Navojoa."

"But that's more than four hundred miles from here."

"Yes, it's quite a distance. But it's so beautiful and peaceful there that I'm certain you would like it." She kept silent for a moment as if waiting for my reply. "Besides, I have the feeling that there is nothing definite you're involved in at the moment," she continued, "and you've been at a loss to find something to do. Well, this could be just the thing you've been waiting for."

She was right about my being completely at a loss as to what to do with my life. I had just taken some time off from a secretarial job in order to catch up with my artwork. But I certainly didn't have the slightest desire to be anyone's house guest.

I looked around, searching the terrain for something that would give me an inkling of what to do next. I had never been able to explain where I had gotten the idea that one could get help or clues from the surroundings. But I usually did get help that way. I had a technique, which seemed to have come to me out of nowhere, by means of which I often found options previously unknown to me. I usually let my thoughts wander away as I fixed my eyes on the southern horizon, although I had no idea why I always picked the south. After a few minutes of silence, insights usually came to me to help me decide what to do or how to proceed in a particular situation.

I fixed my gaze on the southern horizon while we walked, and suddenly I saw the mood of my life stretched out before me like the barren desert. I can truthfully say that although I knew that the whole area of southern Arizona, a bit of California and half of the state of Sonora, Mexico, is the Sonoran Desert, I had never before noticed how lonely and desolate this wasteland was.

It took a moment for the impact of my realization that my life was as empty and barren as that desert to register. I had broken off with my family, and I had no family of my own. I didn't even have any prospects for the future. I had no job. I had lived off a small inheritance left to me by the aunt I was named after, but this income had run out. I was utterly alone in the world. The vastness that stretched all around, harsh and indifferent, summoned up in me an overwhelming sense of self-pity. I felt in need of a friend, someone to break the solitude of my life.

I knew it would be foolish to accept Clara's invitation and jump into an unknown situation over which I had no control, but there was something about the directness of her manner and about her physical vitality that aroused in me both curiosity and a feeling of respect. I found myself admiring and even envying her beauty and strength. I thought that she was a most striking and powerful woman, independent, self-reliant, indifferent, yet not hard or humorless. She possessed the exact qualities I had always wanted for myself. But above all, her presence seemed to dispel my barrenness. She made the space around her energetic, vibrant, full of endless possibilities.

Yet still, it was my unbending policy never to accept invitations to people's houses, and certainly not from someone whom I had just met in the wilderness. I had a small apartment in Tucson and to accept invitations meant to me that I had to reciprocate, a thing that I wasn't prepared to do. For a moment, I stood there motionless, not knowing which way to turn.

"Please say that you'll come," Clara urged. "It would mean a great deal to me."

"All right, I suppose I could visit with you," I said lamely, wanting to say the exact opposite.

She looked at me elated and I immediately disguised my panic with a conviviality I was far from feeling. "It'll be good for me to change scenery," I said. "It'll be an adventure!"

She nodded approvingly. "You won't regret it," she said with an air of confidence that helped to dispel my doubts. "We can practice martial arts together."

She delivered a few brisk movements with her hand that were at once graceful and powerful. It seemed incongruous to me that this robust woman could be so agile.

"What specific style of martial arts did you study in the Orient?" I asked, noticing that she easily adopted the stance of a long-pole fighter.

"In the Orient, I studied all the styles, and yet none of them in particular," she replied, with just a hint of a smile. "When we are at my house, I'll be happy to demonstrate them."

We walked the rest of the way in silence. When we reached the place where the cars were parked, I locked my gear in the trunk and waited for Clara to say something.

"Well, let's get started," she said. "I'll lead the way. Do you drive fast or slow, Taisha?"

"At a crawl."

"Me too. Living in China cured me from hurrying."

"May I ask you a question about China, Clara?"

"Of course. I've already said that you may ask anything you want without asking permission first."

"You must have been in China before the Second World War. Isn't that so?"

"Oh, yes. I was there a lifetime ago. I gather that you've never been to mainland China, yourself."

"No. I've only been to Taiwan and Japan."

"Of course things were different before the war," Clara mused. "The line to the past was still intact then. Now everything is severed."

I didn't know why I was afraid to ask her what she meant by her remark, so I asked instead how long would the drive to her house be. Clara was disturbingly vague; she only warned me to be prepared for an arduous trip. She softened her tone and added that she found my courage extremely rewarding.

"To go so nonchalantly with a stranger," she said, "is either utterly foolish or tremendously daring."

"Usually I'm very cautious," I explained, "but this time I'm not myself at all."

This was the truth, and the more I thought about my inexplicable behavior, the greater became my discomfort.

"Please tell me a little more about yourself," she asked pleasantly. As if to put me at ease, she came and stood by the door of my car.

Again I found myself conveying true information about myself. "My mother is Hungarian but from an old Austrian family," I said.

"She met my father in England during the Second World War, when the two of them worked in a field hospital. After the war, they moved to the United States and then they went to South Africa."

"Why did they go to South Africa?"

"My mother wanted to be with her relatives that lived there."

"Do you have any brothers or sisters?"

"I have two brothers, a year apart in age. The oldest is twenty-six now."

Her eyes were focused on me. And with an unprecedented ease, I unburdened painful feelings I had kept bottled up all my life. I told her that I grew up lonely. My brothers never paid attention to me because I was a girl. When I was little, they used to tie a rope around me and hook me to a post like a dog while they ran around the yard and played soccer. All I could do was tug at my rope and watch them having a good time. Later, when I was older, I'd run after them. But by that time they both had bicycles and I could never keep up with them. When I used to complain to my mother, her usual reply was that boys will be boys, and that I should play with dolls and help around the house.

"Your mother raised you in the traditional European way," she said.

"I know it. But that's no consolation."

Once I had started, it seemed that there was no way for me to stop telling this woman more about my life. I said that whereas my brothers went on trips and, later, away to school, I had to stay at home. I wanted to have adventures like the boys, but according to my mother, girls had to learn to make beds and to iron clothes. It's adventure enough to take care of a family, my mother used to say. Women are born to obey. I was on the verge of tears when I told Clara that I had three male masters to serve as far back as I could remember: my father and my two brothers.

"That sounds like an armful," Clara remarked.

"It was terrible. I left home to get as far away from them as I could," I said. "And to have adventures too. But so far, I haven't had all that much fun and excitement. I suppose I just wasn't brought up to be happy and light-hearted."

Describing my life to a total stranger made me extremely anxious.

I stopped talking and looked at Clara, waiting for a reaction that would either alleviate my anxiety or would increase it to the point of making me change my mind and not go with her after all.

"Well, it seems that there's only one thing you know how to do well, so you may as well make the most of it," she said.

I thought she was going to say I could draw or paint, but to my utter chagrin, she added, "All you know how to do is to feel sorry for yourself."

I tightened my fingers on the handle of the car door. "That's not true," I protested. "Who are you to say that?"

She burst out laughing and shook her head. "You and I are very alike," she said. "We've been taught to be passive, subservient and to adapt to situations, but inside we're seething. We're like a volcano ready to erupt, and what makes us even more frustrated is that we have no dreams or expectations except the one of someday finding the right man, who will take us out of our misery."

She left me speechless.

"Well? Am I right? Am I right?" she kept asking. "Be honest, am I right?"

I clenched my hands, getting ready to tell her off. Clara smiled warmly, exuding vigor and a sense of well-being that made me feel that I didn't need to lie or hide my feelings from her.

"Yes, you have me pegged," I agreed.

I had to admit that the only thing that gave meaning to my dreary existence, besides my artwork, was the vague hope that someday I would meet a man who would understand me and appreciate me for the special person I was.

"Maybe your life will change for the better," she said in a promissory tone.

She got into her car and signaled me with her hand to follow her. I became aware then that she had never asked me if I had my passport or enough clothes or money or had other obligations. That didn't frighten or discourage me. I didn't know why, but as I released the handbrake and began moving, I was certain I had made the right decision. Perhaps my life was going to change after all.

2

After more than three hours of continuous driving, we stopped for lunch in the city of Guaymas. As I waited for our food to arrive, I glanced out the window at the narrow street flanking the bay. A group of shirtless boys were kicking a ball; elsewhere, workers were laying bricks at a construction site; others were taking their noon break, leaning against piles of unopened sacks of cement, sipping sodas from bottles. I couldn't help but think that in Mexico everything seemed extra loud and dusty.

"In this restaurant, they serve the most delicious turtle soup," Clara said, regaining my attention.

Just then a smiling waitress with a silver front tooth placed two bowls of soup on the table. Clara politely exchanged a few words with her in Spanish before the waitress hurried off to serve other customers.

"I've never had turtle soup before," I said, picking up a spoon and examining it to see if it was clean.

"You're in for a real treat," Clara said, watching me wipe my spoon with a paper napkin.

Reluctantly, I tasted a spoonful. The bits of white meat floating in a creamy tomato base were indeed delicious.

I took several more spoonfuls of soup, then asked, "Where do they get the turtles?"

Clara pointed out the window. "Right from the bay."

A handsome, middle-aged man sitting at the table next to ours turned to me and winked. His gesture, I thought, was more an attempt at being humorous than a sexual innuendo. He leaned toward me as if we had been addressing him. "The turtle you're eating now was a big one," he said in accented English.

Clara looked at me and raised an eyebrow as if she couldn't believe the audacity of the stranger.

"This turtle was big enough to feed a dozen hungry people," the man went on. "They catch the turtles in the sea. It takes several men to haul one in."

"I suppose they harpoon them like whales," I remarked.

The man deftly moved his chair to our table. "No, I believe they use large nets," he said. "Then they club them to render them unconscious before slitting open their bellies. That way, the meat doesn't get too tough."

My appetite flew out the window. The last thing I wanted was for an insensitive assertive stranger to join us at our table, yet I didn't know how to handle the situation.

"Since we're on the subject of food, Guaymas is famous for its jumbo shrimp," the man continued with a disarming smile. "Let me order some for the two of you."

"I've already done that," Clara said cuttingly.

Just then our waitress returned bringing a plate of the largest shrimp I had ever seen. It was enough for a banquet, certainly much more than Clara and I could possibly eat, no matter how hungry we were.

Our unwanted companion looked at me waiting to be invited to join our meal. If I had been alone, he would have succeeded in attaching himself to me against my will. But Clara had other plans and reacted in a decisive manner. She jumped up with feline agility, loomed over the man and looked straight down into his eyes. "Buzz off, you creep!!" she yelled in Spanish. "How dare you sit at our table. My niece is no frigging whore!"

Her stance was so powerful and her tone of voice so shocking that everything in the room came to a halt. All eyes were focused on our table. The man cowered so pitifully that I felt sorry for him. He just slid out of the chair and half crawled out of the restaurant.

"I know that you're trained to let men get the best of you, just because they're men," Clara said to me after she had sat down again. "You've always been nice to men, and they've milked you for everything you had. Don't you know that men feed off women's energy!"

I was too embarrassed to argue with her. I felt every eye in the room was on me.

"You let them push you around because you feel sorry for them," Clara continued. "In your heart of hearts you're desperate to take care of a man, any man. If that idiot had been a woman, you yourself would never have let her sit down at our table."

My appetite was spoiled beyond repair. I became moody, pensive.

"I see I've hit a sore spot," Clara said with a smirk.

"You made a scene; you were rude," I said reproachfully.

"Definitely," she replied, laughing. "But I also scared him half to death." Her face was so open and she seemed to be so happy that I finally had to laugh, remembering how shocked the man had been.

"I'm just like my mother," I grumbled. "She succeeded in making me a mouse when it comes to men."

The moment I voiced that thought, my depression vanished and I felt hungry again. I polished off almost the whole plate of shrimp.

"There's no feeling comparable to starting a new turn with a full stomach," Clara declared.

A pang of fear made the shrimp sit heavy in my stomach. Because of all the excitement, it hadn't occurred to me to ask Clara about her house. Maybe it was a shack, like the ones I had seen earlier while driving through the Mexican towns. What kind of food would I be eating? Perhaps this was going to be my last good meal. Would I be able to drink the water? I envisioned myself coming down with acute intestinal problems. I didn't know how to ask Clara about my accommodations without sounding insulting or ungrateful. Clara looked at me critically. She seemed to sense my turmoil.

"Mexico is a harsh place," she said. "You can't let your guard down for an instant. But you'll get used to it.

"The northern part of the country is even more rugged than the rest. People flock to the north in search of work or as a stopping place before crossing the U.S. border. They come by trainloads. Some stay, others travel inland in boxcars to work in the huge agricultural enterprises owned by private corporations. But there just isn't enough food or work for everyone, so the majority go as *braceros* to the United States."

I finished every drop of the soup, feeling guilty about leaving anything behind.

"Tell me more about this area, Clara."

"All the Indians here are Yaquis who were relocated in Sonora by the Mexican government."

"Do you mean they have not always been here?"

"This is their ancestral homeland," Clara said, "but in the twenties and thirties, they were uprooted and sent by the tens of thousands to central Mexico. Then in the late forties, they were brought back to the Sonoran Desert."

Clara poured some mineral water into her glass and then filled mine. "It's hard to live in the Sonoran Desert," she said. "As you saw while driving, the land here is rugged and inhospitable. Yet the Indians had no choice but to settle around the shambles of what was once the Yaqui River. There, in ancient times, the original Yaquis built their sacred towns and lived in them for hundreds of years until the Spaniards came."

"Will we drive by those towns?" I asked.

"No. We don't have time. I want to get to Navojoa before dark. Maybe someday we can take a trip to visit these sacred towns."

"Why are those towns sacred?"

"Because for the Indians the location of each town along the river symbolically corresponds to a spot in their mythical world. Like the lava mountains in Arizona, these sites are places of power. The Indians have a very rich mythology. They believe they can step in and out of a dream world at a moment's notice. You see, their concept of reality is not like ours.

"According to the Yaqui myths, those towns also exist in the other world," Clara went on, "and it is from that ethereal realm that they receive their power—they call themselves the people without reason, to differentiate themselves from us, the people with reason."

"What sort of power do they get?" I asked.

"Their magic, their sorcery, their knowledge. All of that comes down to them directly from the dream world. And that world is described in their legends and stories. The Yaqui Indians have a rich, extensive oral history."

I looked around the crowded restaurant. I wondered which of the people sitting at the tables, if any, were Indians, and which were Mexican. Some of the men were tall and wiry, while others were short and stocky. All the people looked foreign to me, and I felt secretly superior and distinctly out of place.

Clara finished the shrimp along with the beans and rice. I felt bloated myself, but in spite of my protests, she insisted on ordering caramel custard for dessert.

"You'd better fill up," she said with a wink. "You never know when you'll have your next meal or what it will consist of. Here in Mexico we always eat the kill of the day."

I knew she was teasing me, and yet I sensed truth in her words. Earlier I had seen a dead donkey hit by a car on the highway. I knew that the rural areas lack refrigeration and therefore people eat whatever meat is available. I couldn't help wondering what my next meal would be. Silently, I decided to limit my stay with Clara to only a couple of days.

In a more serious tone, Clara continued her discussion. "Things went from bad to worse for the Indians here," she said. "When the government built a dam as part of a hydroelectric project, it changed the course of the Yaqui River so drastically that the people had to pack up and settle elsewhere."

The harshness of this kind of life clashed with my own upbringing where there was always enough food and comfort. I wondered if coming to Mexico wasn't the expression of a deep desire, on my part, for a complete change. All my life I had been searching for adventure, yet now that I was in its clutches, a dread of the unknown filled me.

I took a bite of the caramel custard and put out of my mind that dread which had sprouted since meeting Clara in the Arizona desert. I was glad to be in her company. At the moment, I was well-fed on jumbo shrimp and turtle soup, and even though, as Clara herself had intimated, this might be my last good meal, I decided I would have to trust her and allow the adventure to unfold.

Clara insisted on paying the bill. We filled up the cars with gasoline and were on the road again. After driving for several more hours, we arrived at Navojoa. We didn't stop but went through it, leaving the Pan American Highway to turn onto a gravel road heading east. It was midafternoon. I wasn't tired at all; in fact, I had enjoyed the remainder of the trip. The further south we drove, the more a sense of happiness and well-being replaced my habitual neurotic and depressed state.

After more than one hour of a bumpy ride, Clara veered off the road and signaled for me to follow. We coasted on hard ground along a high wall topped by a flowering bougainvillaea. We parked in a clearing of well-packed earth at the end of the wall.

"This is where I live," she called to me as she eased herself out of the driver's seat.

I walked to her car. She looked tired and seemed to have grown bigger. "You look as fresh as when we started," she commented. "Ah, the marvels of youth!"

On the other side of the wall, completely hidden by trees and dense shrubs, loomed a huge house with a tile roof, barred windows and several balconies. In a daze, I followed Clara through a wrought-iron gate, past a brick patio and through a heavy wooden door into the back of the house. The terra-cotta tile floor of the cool, empty hall enhanced the starkness of the whitewashed walls and the dark natural-wood beams of the ceiling. We walked through it into a spacious living room.

The white walls were bordered with exquisitely painted tiles. Two immaculate beige couches and four armchairs were arranged in a cluster around a heavy wooden coffee table. On top of the table were some open magazines in English and Spanish. I had the impression that someone had just been reading them, sitting in one of the armchairs, but had left in a hurry when we entered through the back door.

"What do you think of my house?" Clara asked, beaming proudly.

"It's fantastic," I said. "Who would have thought there'd be such a house way out here in the wilderness?" Then my envious self reared its head and I became utterly ill at ease. It was the kind of house I had always dreamed of owning, yet knew I would never be able to afford.

"You can't imagine how accurate you are in describing this place as fantastic," she said. "All I can tell you about the house is that, like those lava mountains we saw this morning, it is imbued with power. A silent exquisite power runs through it, like an electric current runs through wires."

Upon hearing this, an inexplicable thing happened: my envy disappeared. It vanished totally with the last word she said.

"Now I'll show you to your bedroom," she announced. "And I'll also set up some ground rules you must observe while you're here as my guest.

"Any part of the house which is to the right and to the back of this living room is yours to use and explore, and that includes the grounds. But you must not enter any of the bedrooms, except of course, yours. There you can use anything you want. You can even break things in fits of anger or love them in outbursts of affection. The left side of the house, however, is not accessible to you at any time, in any way, shape or form. So stay out of it."

I was shocked by her bizarre request yet I assured her that I understood perfectly and I would acquiesce to her wishes. My real feelings were that her request was rude and arbitrary. In fact, the more she warned me to stay away from certain parts of the house, the more curious I became to see them.

Clara seemed to have thought of something else and added, "Of course, you can use the living room; you can even sleep here on the sofa if you're too tired or lazy to go to your bedroom. Another part you can't use, however, is the grounds in front of the house and also the main door. It's locked for the time being, so always enter the house through the back door."

Clara didn't give me time to respond. She ushered me down a long corridor past several closed doors, which she said were bedrooms and therefore forbidden to me, to a large bedroom. The first thing I noticed upon entering was the ornate wooden double bed. It was covered with a beautiful crocheted off-white bedspread. Next to a window on the wall facing the back of the house stood a hand-carved, mahogany étagère filled to capacity with antique objects, porcelain vases and figurines, cloisonné boxes and tiny bowls. On the other wall was a matching armoire, which Clara opened. Hanging inside were women's vintage dresses, coats, hats, shoes, parasols, canes; all of them seemed to be exquisite hand-picked items.

Before I could ask Clara where she had gotten those beautiful things, she closed the doors. "Feel free to use anything you wish," she said. "These are your clothes, and this is your room for as long as you stay in this house." She then glanced over her shoulder as if someone else were in the room and added, "And who can tell how long that will be!"

It appeared that she was talking about an extended visit. I felt my palms sweat as I awkwardly told her that I could, at best, stay for only a few days. Clara assured me that I would be perfectly safe with her there. Much safer, in fact, than anywhere else. She added that it would be foolish for me to pass up this opportunity to broaden my knowledge.

"But I've got to look for a job," I said by way of an excuse. "I don't have any money."

"Don't worry about money," she said. "I'll lend you whatever you need or give it to you. It's no problem."

I thanked her for her offer but informed her that I had been brought up to believe that to accept money from a stranger was highly improper, no matter how well-meaning the offer was.

She rebuffed me, saying, "I think what's the matter with you, Taisha, is that you got angry when I requested that you don't use the left side of the house or the main door. I know that you felt I was being arbitrary and excessively secretive. Now you don't want to stay more than a polite day or two. Maybe you even think I'm an eccentric old woman with a few bats in the belfry?"

"No, no, Clara, it's not that. I've got to pay my rent. If I don't find a job soon I won't have any money, and to accept money from anyone is out of the question for me."

"Do you mean that you didn't get offended by my request to avoid certain parts of the house?"

"Of course not."

"Didn't you get curious to know why I made the request?"

"Yes, I was curious."

"Well, the reason is that other people live on that side of the house."

"Your relatives, Clara?"

"Yes. We are a large family. There are, in fact, two families living here."

"Are they both large families?"

"They are. Each has eight members, making sixteen people all together."

"And they all live on the left side of the house, Clara?" In all my life I had never heard of such an odd arrangement.

"No. Only eight live there. The other eight are my immediate family and they live with me on the right side of the house. You are my guest, so you must stay on the right side. It's very important that you understand this. It may be unusual, but it's not incomprehensible."

I marveled at her power over me. Her words put my emotions at ease, but they didn't calm my mind. I understood then that in order to react intelligently in any situation, I needed a conjunction of both: an alarmed mind and unsettled emotions. Otherwise, I remained passive, waiting for the next external impulse to sway me. Being with Clara had made me understand that in spite of my protest to the contrary, in spite of my struggle to be different, independent, I was incapable of thinking clearly or of making my own decisions.

Clara gave me a most peculiar look, as if she were following my unvoiced thoughts. I tried to mask my confusion by hurriedly saying, "Your house is beautiful, Clara. Is it very old?"

"Of course," she said, but didn't explain whether she meant that it was a beautiful house or that it was very old. With a smile she added, "Now that you've seen the house—that is, half of it—we have a little business to take care of."

She removed a flashlight from one of the cabinets, and from the armoire she took out a padded Chinese jacket and a pair of hiking boots. She told me that I had to put them on after we had a snack, because we were going for a walk.

"But we just got here," I protested. "Won't it be dark soon?"

"Yes. But I want to take you to a look-out point in the hills from where you can see the entire house and grounds. It's best to first see the house at this time of the day. We all had our first glimpse of it in the twilight."

"Who do you mean when you say 'we'?" I asked.

"The sixteen people that live here, naturally. All of us do exactly the same things."

"All of you have the same professions?" I asked, unable to hide my surprise.

"Good gracious, no," she said, bringing her hand to her face as she laughed. "I mean that whatever any one of us has to obligatorily do, the rest of us have to do too. Each one of us had to first see the house and grounds in the twilight, so that is the time you must view it, too."

"Why are you including me in this, Clara?"

"Let's just say, for now, it's because you are my guest."

"Am I going to meet your relatives later on?"

"You'll get to know all of them," she assured me. "At the moment, there is no one in the house except the two of us, and a guard dog."

"Are they away on a trip?"

"Exactly, all of them have left for an extended journey and here I am, guarding the house with the dog."

"When are you expecting them back?"

"It'll be a matter of weeks yet, maybe even months."

"Where did they go?"

"We are always on the move. Sometimes I leave for months at a time and someone else stays behind to look after the property."

I was about to ask again where they went, but she answered my question. "They all went to India," she said.

"All fifteen of them?" I asked incredulously.

"Isn't that remarkable? It'll cost a fortune!" She said that in a tone of voice that was such a caricature of my inner feelings of envy that I had to laugh in spite of myself. Then the thought struck me that it wouldn't be safe to be alone in such a remote, empty house with only Clara for company.

"We are alone but there's nothing to fear in this house," she said with a curious finality. "Except maybe the dog. When we return from our walk, I'll introduce you to him. You've got to be very calm to meet him. He'll see right through you and attack if he senses any hostility or that you're afraid."

"But I am afraid," I blurted out. I was already starting to shake.

I hated dogs ever since I was a child, when one of my father's Doberman pinschers jumped on me and pushed me to the ground. The dog didn't actually bite me, she just growled and showed me her pointed teeth. I screamed for help, for I was too terrified to move. I was so frightened I wet my pants. I still remember how my brothers made fun of me when they saw me, calling me a baby that should be wearing diapers.

"I don't like dogs one bit, myself," Clara said, "but the dog we have is not really a dog. He is something else."

She had sparked my interest, but that didn't dispel my sense of foreboding.

"If you want to freshen up first, I'll accompany you to the outhouse, just in case the dog is prowling around," she said.

I nodded. I was tired and irritable; the impact of the long drive had finally caught up with me. I wanted to wash the dust of the road from my face and comb the tangles out of my stringy hair.

Clara led me through a different corridor, then out to the back. There were two small buildings some distance from the main house.

"That's my gymnasium," she said, pointing at one of them. "It is off limits to you too. Unless I care to invite you in someday."

"Is that where you practice martial arts?"

"It is," Clara said dryly. "The other building is the outhouse.

"I'll wait for you in the living room, where we can have some sandwiches. But don't bother about fixing your hair," she said, as if noticing my preoccupation, "there are no mirrors here. Mirrors are like clocks: they record the passage of time. And what's important is to reverse it."

I wanted to ask her what she meant by reversing time, but she prodded me toward the outhouse. Inside, I found several doors. Since Clara hadn't made any stipulations about the left and right sides of this building, and since I didn't know where the toilet was, I explored all of it. On one side of the central hall, there were six small water closets, each with a low wooden toilet the height for squatting. What made them unusual was that I didn't notice the distinct odor of a septic tank, nor the overpowering stench of lime-filled dirt holes. I could hear water running underneath the wooden toilets, but I couldn't tell how or from where it was led in.

On the other side of the hall, there were three identical beautifully tiled rooms. Each contained a free-standing antique tub and a long chest on top of which sat a pitcher filled with water and a matching porcelain basin. There were no mirrors in those rooms, or any stainless-steel fixtures on which I could have caught my reflection. In fact, there was no plumbing at all.

I poured water into a basin, splashed my face with it, then ran my wet fingers through my tangled hair. Instead of using one of the soft white Turkish towels for fear I would dirty it, I wiped my hands with some tissues that were in a box on the chest. I took several deep breaths and rubbed my tense neck before going out to face Clara again.

I found her in the living room arranging flowers in a blue and white Chinese vase. The magazines that had been open earlier were neatly stacked and next to them was a plate of food. She smiled when she saw me.

"You look as fresh as a daisy," she said. "Have a sandwich. Soon it'll be twilight. We have no time to lose."

3

After I had gobbled down half of a ham sandwich, I hurriedly put on the jacket and boots Clara had given me and we left the house, each carrying a heavy-duty flashlight. The boots were too tight and the left one rubbed against my heel. I was certain I was going to get a blister. But I was glad I had the jacket, for the evening was cold. I pulled up the collar and fastened the toggle at the neck.

"We are going to walk around the grounds," Clara said. "I want you to see this house from a distance and in the twilight. I'll be pointing out things for you to remember, so pay close attention."

We followed a narrow trail. In the distance, I could see the dark, jagged silhouette of the eastern mountains against the purple sky. When I commented on how sinister they looked, Clara replied that the reason those mountains seemed so ominous was because their ethereal essence was ancient. She told me that everything in the realms of the visible and invisible has an ethereal essence, and that one must be receptive to it in order to know how to proceed.

What she said reminded me of my tactic of looking at the southern horizon to gain insights and direction. Before I could ask her about it, she continued talking about the mountains and trees and the ethereal essence of rocks. It seemed to me that Clara had internalized Chinese culture to the point that she spoke in riddles, the way enlightened men were depicted in Oriental literature. I became aware, then, that at an underlying level, I had been humoring her all day. This was an odd feeling, for Clara was the last person I would want to treat in a condescending manner. I was used to humoring weak or overbearing people at my job or in school, but Clara was neither weak nor overbearing.

"That is the place," Clara said, pointing to a level clearing on higher ground. "You'll be able to see the house from there."

We left the trail and walked to the flat area she had pointed out. From there we had a breath-taking view of the valley below. I could see a large clump of tall green trees surrounded by darker brown areas, but not the house itself, for it was completely camouflaged by the trees and shrubs.

"The house is perfectly oriented according to the four directions," Clara said, pointing to a mass of greenery. "Your bedroom is on the north side, and the forbidden part of the house is on the south side. The main entrance is to the east; the back door and the patio area are to the west."

Clara pointed with her hand where all those sections were, but for the life of me, I couldn't see them; all I was able to make out was the dark green patch.

"You'd need X-ray vision to see the house," I grumbled. "It's totally hidden by trees."

"And very important trees, too," Clara said amiably, ignoring my disagreeable mood. "Every one of those trees is an individual being with a definite purpose in life."

"Doesn't it go without saying that every living being on this earth has a definite purpose?" I said, peeved.

Something in the enthusiastic way that Clara was showing off her property annoyed me. The fact that I couldn't see what she was pointing at made me even more irritable. A strong gust of wind made my jacket balloon at my waist, and then the thought occurred to me that my irritation might be born out of sheer envy.

"I didn't mean it to sound trivial," Clara apologized. "What I wanted to say was that everything and everyone in my house is there for a specific reason. And that includes the trees, myself and of course, also, you."

I wanted to change the subject, so for lack of anything better to say, I asked, "Did you buy this house, Clara?"

"No. We inherited it. It has been in the family for generations, although given the turmoils Mexico has been through, the house has been destroyed and rebuilt many times."

I realized that I felt most at ease when I asked simple, direct questions, and Clara gave me direct answers. Her discussion about ethereal essences had been so abstract that I needed the respite of talking about something mundane. But to my chagrin, Clara cut our commonplace exchange short and lapsed into her mysterious insinuations again.

"That house is the blueprint of all the actions of the people who live there," she said almost reverently. "Its best feature is that it's concealed. It is there for anyone to see, but no one sees it. Keep this in mind. It's very important!"

How could I not remember it, I thought. For the past twenty minutes I had been straining my eyes in the semidarkness to see the house. I wished I had a pair of binoculars so that I could have satisfied my curiosity. Before I could comment, Clara began walking down the hill. I would have liked to stay there a while longer by myself, to breathe in the fresh night air. But I was afraid I would not be able to find my way back in the dark. I made a mental note to return to that spot during the day and determine for myself whether it was really possible to see the house the way Clara had said.

On our return trek, we were at the back entrance of her property in no time at all. It was pitch black; I could see only the small area illuminated by our flashlights. She beamed hers onto a wooden bench and told me sit and take off my boots and jacket, then hang them on the rack next to the door.

I was famished. Never in my life could I remember being so hungry, yet I thought it would be rude to ask Clara outright whether or not we were going to eat dinner. Perhaps she expected that the sumptuous meal we had in Guaymas would last us for the day. Yet judging from Clara's size, she was not one that would skimp on food.

"Let's go to the kitchen and see what we can find to eat," she volunteered. "But first, I'm going to show you where the dynamo is kept and how to turn it on."

She guided me with her flashlight along a path leading around a wall to a brick shed, roofed with corrugated steel. The shed housed a small diesel generator. I knew how to turn it on because I had lived in a house in the country that had a similar generator in case of electrical failure. When I pulled the lever, I noticed from the shed window that only one side of the main house and part of the hall seemed to be wired for electric lights; they were lit while everything else remained in darkness.

"Why didn't you wire the whole house?" I asked Clara. "It doesn't make sense to leave most of the house dark." On an impulse, I added, "If you like, I can wire it for you."

She looked at me, surprised. "Is that right? Are you sure you wouldn't burn the place down?"

"Positive. They used to tell me at home that I'm a wizard with wires. I worked as an electrician's apprentice for a while, until the electrician started getting fresh with me."

"What did you do?" Clara asked.

"I told him where he could shove his wires, and quit."

Clara let out a guttural laugh. I didn't know what she found humorous, that I worked as an electrician or that one had made passes at me.

"Thanks for the offer," Clara said after regaining her voice. "But the house is wired exactly the way we want it. We use electricity only where it's needed."

I surmised that it was needed mostly in the kitchen and that this must be the part of the house that had light. Automatically I started toward the area that was lit. Clara tugged at my sleeve to stop me.

"Where are you going?" she asked.

"To the kitchen."

"You're heading the wrong way," she said. "This is rural Mexico; neither the kitchen nor the bathroom is inside the main house. What do you think we have? Electric refrigerators and gas stoves?"

She led me along the side of the house, past her gymnasium to another small building I hadn't seen before. It was almost totally hidden by pungent flowering trees. The kitchen was actually one enormous room, with a terra-cotta tile floor, freshly whitewashed walls and a bright row of track lights overhead. Someone had gone to a great deal of trouble installing modern fixtures. But the appliances were old—in fact, they looked like antiques. On one side of the room stood a gigantic iron wood-burning stove that, surprisingly, seemed to be lit. It had a foot bellow and an exhaust pipe that vented through a hole in the ceiling. On the other side of the room, there were two long picnic-style tables, with benches placed on either side. And next to them was a work table with a three-inch-thick butcher-block top. The surface of the wood looked used, as if it had seen a lot of chopping.

Hanging from strategically placed hooks along the walls were baskets, iron pots and pans and a variety of cooking utensils. The whole place had the look of a rustic but comfortable well-stocked kitchen that one sees featured in certain magazines.

On the stove were three earthen pots with lids. Clara told me to sit down at one of the tables. She went to the stove and, with her back toward me, busied herself, stirring and ladling. In a few minutes, she had placed a meal of meat stew, rice and beans in front of me.

"When did you prepare all this food?" I asked, genuinely curious, for she had had no time in which to do it.

"I just whipped all this up and put it on the stove before we left," she said lightly.

How gullible does she think I am? I thought. This food must have taken hours to prepare. She laughed self-consciously at my stare of disbelief.

"You're right," she said as if she wanted to give up the pretense. "There's a caretaker that prepares food for us sometimes."

"Is the caretaker here now?"

"No, no. The caretaker must have been here in the morning, but is gone now. Eat your food and don't worry about such unimportant details as where it came from."

Clara and her house are full of surprises, was the thought that crossed my mind, but I was too tired and hungry to ask any more questions or to ponder about anything that wasn't immediate. I ate voraciously; the jumbo shrimp I had stuffed myself with at lunch was totally gone and forgotten. For someone who was a finicky eater, I was wolfing down my food. As a child, I had always been too nervous to relax and enjoy our meals. I was always anticipating all the dishes I would have to wash afterward. Every time one of my brothers used an extra plate or a needless spoon, I'd cringe. I was certain that they deliberately used as many dishes as they could just so I would have more to wash up. On top of that, at every meal, my father would take the opportunity to argue with my mother. He knew her manners prevented her from leaving the table until everyone had finished eating. So he poured out to her all his complaints and grievances.

Clara said that it wouldn't be necessary for me to wash dishes, although I offered my help. We went to the living room, one of the rooms she apparently felt needed no electricity, for it was pitch black. Clara lit a gasoline lantern. I had never in my life seen the light of such a lamp. It was bright and eerie, yet at the same time soft and mellow. Shimmering shadows were everywhere. I felt I was in a dream world, far from the reality lit up by electric lights. Clara, the house, the room all seemed to belong to another time, to a different world.

"I promised you that I would introduce you to our dog," Clara began, sitting down on the couch. "The dog is an authentic member of the household. You must be very careful with what you feel or say around him."

I sat down next to her. "Is it a sensitive, neurotic dog?" I asked, dreading the encounter.

"Sensitive, yes. Neurotic, no. I seriously think this dog is a highly evolved creature, but being a dog makes it difficult, if not impossible, for that poor soul to transcend the idea of the self."

I laughed out loud at the preposterous notion of a dog having an idea of itself. I confronted Clara with the absurdity of her statement.

"You're right," she conceded. "I shouldn't use the word 'self.' I should rather say, he is lost in feeling important."

I knew that she was poking fun at me. My laughter became more guarded.

"You may laugh, but I'm actually quite serious," Clara said in a low tone. "I'll let you be the judge." She leaned closer and lowered her voice to a whisper. "Behind his back, we call him *sapo*, which means 'toad' in Spanish, because he looks like a huge toad. But don't you dare call him that to his face; he'll attack you and rip you to shreds. Now, if you don't believe me or if you're daring or stupid enough to try it and the dog gets mad, there's only one thing you can do."

"What's that?" I asked, humoring her again, although this time with a genuine touch of fear.

"You say very quickly that I am the one who looks like a white toad. He loves to hear that."

I wasn't about to fall for her tricks. I thought I was too sophisticated to believe such nonsense. "You've probably trained your dog to react negatively to the word *sapo*," I argued. "I've had experience with dog training. I'm certain dogs aren't intelligent enough to know what people are saying about them. Let alone get offended by it."

"Then let's do the following," Clara proposed. "Let me introduce you to him, then we'll look in a zoology book for pictures of toads and comment on them. Then at one point you say to me, very quietly, 'He certainly looks like a toad,' and we'll see what happens."

Before I could accept or reject her proposition, Clara went out through a side door and left me alone. I assured myself that I had the situation well under control and that I wouldn't let this woman talk me into believing absurdities, such as dogs in possession of a highly evolved consciousness.

I was giving myself a mental pep talk to be more assertive, when Clara came back with the hugest dog I had ever seen. It was a male dog, massive, with fat paws the size of coffee saucers. His hair was lustrous, black; he had yellow eyes with the look of someone bored to death with life. His ears were rounded and his face bulged and wrinkled on the sides. Clara was right, he had a definite resemblance to a giant toad. The dog came right up to me and stopped, then looked at Clara as if waiting for her to say something.

"Taisha, may I introduce you to my friend Manfred. Manfred, this is Taisha."

I felt like extending my hand and shaking its paw, but Clara gave me a don't-do-it signal with a movement of her head. "Very pleased to meet you, Manfred," I said trying not to laugh or sound afraid.

The dog moved closer and began to sniff my crotch. Disgusted, I jumped back. But at that instant, he turned around and hit me with his hindquarters, directly behind my knee joint so that I lost my balance. The next thing I knew, I was on my knees, then on all fours on the floor and the beast was licking the side of my face. Then before I could get up or even roll over, the dog farted right in my nose.

I jumped up screaming. Clara was laughing so hard she couldn't talk. I could have sworn that Manfred was laughing too. He was so elated that he had propped himself behind Clara, and was looking at me askance, scratching the floor with his huge front paws.

I was so outraged that I yelled, "Damn you, stinking toad-dog!"

In one instant, the dog jumped and rammed me with his head. I fell backward onto the floor with the dog on top of me. His jaw was only inches from my face. I saw a look of fury in his yellow eyes. The smell of his foul breath was enough to make anyone vomit, and I was definitely close to it. The louder I screamed for Clara to get that damn dog off me, the more ferocious became his snarls. I was about to faint from fright, when I heard Clara yell above the dog's growls and my screams, "Tell him what I told you, tell him quickly."

I was too terrified to speak. Exasperated, Clara tried to move the dog off me by pulling him by his ears, but this only enraged the beast more.

"Tell him! Tell him what I said!" Clara yelled.

In my terror, I couldn't remember what I was supposed to say. Then as I was about to pass out, I heard my voice screeching, "I'm sorry. Clara is the one who looks like a toad."

Instantly the dog stopped his snarling and moved off my chest. Clara helped me up and guided me to the couch. The dog followed beside us as if he were giving her a hand. Clara had me drink some warm water, which made me even more nauseous. I barely reached the outhouse before I became violently ill.

Later, when I was resting in the living room, Clara suggested that we look at the book about toads with Manfred to give me a chance to reiterate that it was Clara who looked like a white toad. She said that I had to erase any confusion from Manfred's mind.

"Being a dog makes him very petty," she explained. "Poor soul! He doesn't want to be that way, he just can't help it. He flares up whenever he feels someone is making fun of him."

I told her that in my state, I was a poor subject for further experiments in dog psychology. But Clara insisted that I play it out to the end. As soon as she opened the book, Manfred came over to look at the pictures. Clara teased and joked about how strange toads looked, that some of them were even downright ugly. I held up my end and played along. I said the word "toad," and the Spanish word "*sapo*," as often and as loudly as I could in the context of our absurd conversation. But there was no reaction from Manfred. He seemed as bored as he was the first time I laid eyes on him.

When, as we had agreed upon, in a loud voice I said that Clara certainly looked like a white toad, Manfred immediately began wagging his tail and showed signs of true animation. I repeated the key phrase several times, and the more I repeated it, the more excited the dog became. I had then a flash of insight and said that I was a skinny toad, working her way to being just like Clara. At that, the dog jumped up as if prodded by an electric shock. And when Clara said, "You're carrying this a bit too far, Taisha," I truly thought Manfred was so elated that he couldn't take it any longer. He ran out of the room.

I leaned back against the couch dazed. Down in the depth of me, and in spite of all the circumstantial evidence supporting it, I still couldn't believe that a dog could react to a derogatory nickname the way Manfred had.

"Tell me, Clara," I said, "what is the trick? How did you train your dog to react that way?"

"What you saw is not a trick," she replied. "Manfred is mysterious, an unknown being. There is only one man in the world who can call him *sapo* or *sapito*, little toad, to his face without inciting his wrath. You'll meet that man one of these days. He's the one who's responsible for Manfred's mystery. So he's the only person who can explain it to you."

Clara stood up abruptly. "You've had a long day," she said, handing me the gasoline lantern. "I think it's time for you to go to bed."

She took me to the room she had assigned to me. "You'll find everything you need inside," she said. "The chamber pot is under the bed, in case you are afraid to go to the outhouse. I hope you'll be comfortable."

With a pat on my arm, she disappeared down the dark corridor. I had no idea where her bedroom was. I wondered if it could perhaps be in the wing of the house I was not allowed to set foot in. She had said good night in such a strange fashion that for a moment I just stood there holding on to the doorknob, inferring all sorts of things.

I entered my room. The gasoline lantern splashed shadows everywhere. On the floor was a pattern of swirls cast from the vase of flowers that had been in the living room, which Clara must have brought in and set on the table. The carved wood chest was a mass of shimmering grays; the posts of the bed were lines that curved up the wall like snakes. Instantly I grasped the reason for the presence of the mahogany étagère filled with figurines and cloisonné objects. The light of the lantern had completely transformed them, creating a fantasy world. Cloisonné and porcelain are not suited for electric lights, was the thought that came to mind.

I wanted to explore the room, but I was bone tired. I set the lantern on a small table next to the bed and undressed. Laid over the back of a chair was a white muslin nightgown, which I put on. It seemed to fit, at least it didn't drag on the floor.

I climbed into the soft bed and lay with my back propped against the pillows. I didn't douse the lantern immediately; I became intrigued watching the surreal shadows. I remembered that as a child, I used to play a game at bedtime: I would count how many shadow objects I could recognize on the walls of my room.

The breeze from the half-open window made the shadows on the walls flutter. In my exhausted state, I imagined I could see shapes of animals, trees and flying birds. Then in a mass of gray light I saw the faint outline of a dog's face. It had rounded ears and a flat, wrinkled snout. It seemed to be winking at me. I knew it was Manfred.

Strange feelings and questions began to flood my mind. How could I ever arrange the events of the day? I couldn't explain any of them to my satisfaction. The one thing that was most remarkable was that I knew for certain that my last remark—that I was a skinny toad on my way to being like Clara—had established a bond of empathy between Manfred and myself. I also knew for certain that I couldn't think of him as an ordinary dog, and that I was no longer afraid of him. In spite of my disbelief, he seemed to possess a special intelligence that made him aware of what Clara and I were saying.

The wind suddenly made the curtains open, dissolving the shadows in an array of shimmering fluff. The dog's face began to merge with the other markings on the wall that I fancied to be charms that would give me the power to meet the night.

How remarkable, I thought, that the mind can project its experiences onto a blank wall, as if it were a camera that had stored endless footage of film.

The shadows flickered as I lowered the wick of the lantern and the last bit of light faded from the room, leaving me in pitch blackness. I wasn't afraid of the darkness. The fact that I was in a strange bed, in a strange house didn't distress me. Earlier, Clara had said this was my room, and after being in it for only a short while, I felt completely at home. I had a strong feeling that I was protected.

As I stared at the blackness in front of me, I noticed the air in the room become effervescent. I remembered what Clara had said about the house being charged with an imperceptible energy, like an electric current flowing through wires. I hadn't been aware of it earlier because of all the activity. But now, in absolute silence, I distinctly heard a mild humming sound. Then I saw the minutest bubbles jumping all around the room at a tremendous speed. They were frantically bumping into one another, giving off a buzzing sound like the drone of thousands of bees. The room, the entire house seemed to be charged with a subtle electric current that filled my very being.

4

"Did you sleep well?" Clara asked me as I entered the kitchen.

She was about to sit down at the table to eat. I noticed there was a place set for me, although she hadn't told me the night before at what time breakfast would be.

"I slept like a bear," I said truthfully.

She asked me to join her and dished some spicy shredded meat onto my plate. I told her that waking up in an unknown bed had always been a difficult moment for me. My father had changed jobs often and the family had to move to wherever there was a position available. I dreaded the morning jolt of awakening disoriented in a new house. But that dread hadn't materialized this time. The feeling I had upon awakening was that the room and the bed had always been mine.

Clara listened intently and nodded. "That's because you are in harmony with the person to whom the room belongs," she said.

"Whose room is it?" I asked, curious.

"You'll find out some day," she said, placing a hefty portion of rice next to the meat on my plate. She handed me a fork. "Eat up. You'll need all your strength today."

She didn't let me talk until I had finished everything on my plate.

"What are we going to do?" I asked as she put the dishes away.

"Not we," she corrected me. "You will be going to a cave to begin your recapitulation."

"My what, Clara?"

"I told you last night that everything and everyone in this house has a reason for being here, including you."

"Why am I here, Clara?"

"Your reason for being here has to be explained to you in stages," she said. "On the simplest level, you're here because you like it here, regardless of what you may think. A second, and more complex, reason is that you're here to learn and practice a fascinating exercise called the recapitulation."

"What is this exercise? What does it consist of?"

"I'm going to tell you about it when we get to the cave."

"Why can't you tell me now?"

"Bear with me, Taisha. I can't answer all your questions at this point, because you don't have enough energy yet to handle the answers. Later on, you yourself will realize why it's so difficult to explain certain things.

"Put on your hiking boots, and let's go now."

We left the house and climbed the low hills toward the east, following the same trail we had taken the previous night. After a short hike, I spotted the flat clearing on high ground that I had intended to revisit. Without waiting for Clara to take the initiative, I headed toward it, for I was eager to find out if I could see the house during the daytime.

I peered down into a bowllike depression squeezed between hills and covered with green foliage. But although it was clear and sunny, I couldn't see any signs of the buildings. One thing was evident; there were more huge trees than I remembered seeing at night.

"Surely you can recognize the outhouse," Clara said. "It's that reddish spot by that clump of mesquite trees." I jumped inadvertently, for I had been so absorbed gazing into the valley that I hadn't heard Clara come up behind me.

To help direct my attention, she pointed to a particular section of the greenness below. I thought of telling her, out of politeness, that I was seeing it, the way I always agreed with people, but I didn't want to start my day by humoring her. I kept silent. Besides, there was something so exquisite in that hidden valley that it took my breath away. I stared at it so totally absorbed that I became drowsy; leaning against a boulder, I let whatever was in the valley carry me away. And it did transport me. I felt that I was at a picnic ground where a party was going full force. I heard the laughter of people . . .

My reverie ended when Clara lifted me to my feet by my armpits.

"My goodness, Taisha!" she exclaimed. "You're stranger than I thought. For a moment there, I thought I'd lost you."

I wanted to tell her what I dreamt because I was certain that I had dozed off for an instant. But she didn't seem interested and started walking away.

Clara had a firm and purposeful stride, as if she knew exactly where she was going. I, on the other hand, walked aimlessly behind her trying to keep up without stumbling. We walked in total silence. After a good half hour, we were by a particular formation of rocks I was certain we had passed earlier.

"Weren't we here before?" I asked, breaking the silence.

She nodded. "We're going in circles," she admitted. "Something is stalking you and if we don't lose it, it will follow us to the cave."

I turned around to see if someone was behind us; I could distinguish only the shrubs and the twisted branches of trees. I hurried to catch up with Clara and tripped over a stump. Startled, I shrieked as I fell forward. With incredible speed, Clara caught me by the arm and broke my fall by placing her leg in front of me.

"You're not very good at walking, are you," she commented.

I told her I had never been a good outdoor person, that I grew up believing hiking and camping were for country folks, unsophisticated backwoods people, but not for educated urbanites. Walking in the foothills of the mountains was not an experience I found enjoyable. And except for the view of her property, scenery that others would find breathtaking left me indifferent.

"Just as well," Clara said. "You're not here to look at the scenery. You have to keep your mind on the trail. And watch out for snakes."

Whether there were snakes in the area or not, her admonition certainly kept my attention on the ground. As we continued walking, I became increasingly out of breath. The boots Clara had equipped me with were like lead weights on my feet. I had a hard time lifting my thighs to put one foot in front of the other.

"Is this nature walk really necessary?" I finally asked.

Clara stopped in her tracks and faced me. "Before we can talk about anything meaningful, you'll have to be at least aware of your elaborate entourage," she said. "I'm doing my best to help you do just that."

"What are you talking about?" I demanded. "What entourage?" My habitual moodiness had gotten hold of me again.

"I'm referring to your barrage of habitual feelings and thoughts, your personal history," Clara explained. "Everything that makes you into what you think you are, a unique and special person."

"What's wrong with my habitual feelings and thoughts?" I asked. Her incomprehensible assertions were definitely annoying me.

"Those habitual feelings and thoughts are the source of all our troubles," she declared.

The more she spoke in riddles, the greater became my frustration. At that moment, I could have kicked myself for succumbing to this woman's invitation to spend some time with her. It was a delayed reaction. Fears that had been kindling inside me now flared up full force. I imagined that she might be a psychopath who at any moment might pull out a knife and kill me. On second thought, having been trained in martial arts as she obviously had been, she wouldn't need a knife. One kick from her muscular leg could have been the end of me. I was no match for her. She was older than I, but infinitely more powerful. I saw myself ending up as just another statistic, a missing person never heard from again. I deliberately slowed down my pace to increase the distance between us.

"Don't get into such a morbid frame of mind," Clara said, definitely intruding into my thoughts. "By bringing you here, all I wanted to do was to help prepare you to face life with a little more grace. But it seems that all I succeeded in doing is to start a landslide of ugly suspicions and fears."

I felt genuinely embarrassed for having had such morbid thoughts. It was bewildering how she had been so absolutely right about my suspicions and fears, and how she had with one stroke soothed my internal turmoil. I wished it would have been possible for me to apologize and reveal to her what was going through my mind, but

I wasn't prepared to do that; it would have put me at even more of a disadvantage. "You have a strange power to soothe the mind, Clara," I said instead. "Did you learn to do this in the Orient?"

"It's no great feat," she admitted, "not because your mind is easy to soothe, but because all of us are alike. To know you in detail, all I have to do is to know myself. And this, I promise you, I do.

"Now, let's keep on walking. I want to reach the cave before you collapse completely."

"Tell me again, Clara, what are we going to do in that cave?" I asked, unwilling to start walking again.

"I'm going to teach you unimaginable things."

"What unimaginable things?"

"You'll know soon," she said, looking at me with wide eyes.

I craved more information, but before I could engage her in conversation, she was already halfway up the next slope. I dragged my feet and followed her for another quarter of a mile or so until we finally sat down by a stream. There, the foliage of the trees was so dense I could no longer see the sky. I took off the boots. I had a blister on my heel.

Clara picked up a hard-pointed stick and poked my feet in between the big and the second toe. Something like a mild current of electricity shot up my calves and ran along my inner thighs. Then she made me kneel on all fours and, taking each foot at a time, turned my soles up and poked me at the point just below the protuberance of my big toe. I yelled with pain.

"That wasn't so bad," she said in the tone of someone accustomed to treating sick people. "Classical Chinese doctors used to apply that technique to jolt and revive the weak or to create a state of unique attention. But today such classical knowledge is dying out."

"Why is that, Clara?"

"Because the emphasis on materialism has led man to move away from esoteric pursuits."

"Is that what you meant when you told me in the desert that the line to the past was severed?"

"Yes. A great upheaval always brings about deep changes in the energy formation of things. Changes that are not always for the better."

She ordered me to place my feet into the stream and feel the smooth rocks along the bottom. The water was ice cold and made me shiver involuntarily.

"Move your feet at the ankles in a clockwise circle," she suggested. "Let the running water draw away your fatigue."

After a few minutes of circling my ankles, I felt refreshed but my feet were nearly frozen.

"Now try to feel all your tension flow down to your feet, then throw it out with a sideward snap of your ankles," Clara said. "This way you'll also get rid of the coldness."

I continued flicking the water with my feet until they were numb. "I don't think this is working, Clara," I said, pulling my feet out.

"That's because you're not directing the tension away from you," she said. "Flowing water takes away tiredness, coldness, illness and every other unwanted thing, but in order for this to happen, you must intend it. Otherwise, you can flick your feet until the stream runs dry with no results."

She added that if one did the exercise in bed, one would have to use the imagination to visualize a running stream.

"What exactly do you mean by 'intend it'?" I asked, drying my feet with the sleeves of the jacket. After a vigorous rubbing, they finally warmed up.

"*Intent* is the power that upholds the universe," she said. "It is the force that gives focus to everything. It makes the world happen."

I couldn't believe that I was listening to her every word. Some major change had definitely taken place, transforming my habitual bored indifference into a most unusual alertness. It wasn't that I understood what Clara was saying, because I didn't. What struck me was the fact that I could listen to her without fretting or becoming distracted.

"Can you describe this force more clearly?" I asked.

"There's really no way to talk about it, except metaphorically," she said. She brushed the ground with the sole of her shoe, sweeping dry leaves aside. "Underneath the dry leaves is the ground, the enormous earth. Intent is the principle underneath everything."

Clara put her cupped hands in the water and splashed her face. I again marveled that her skin had no wrinkles. This time I commented on her youthful appearance.

"The way I look is a matter of keeping my inner being in balance with the surroundings," she said, shaking the water off her hands. "Everything we do hinges on that balance. We can be young and vibrant, like this stream, or old and ominous like the lava mountains in Arizona. It's up to us."

I surprised myself by asking her, as if I believed what she was saying, if there was a way I could gain that balance.

She nodded. "You most certainly can," she said. "And you will, by practicing the unique exercise I'm going to teach you: the recapitulation."

"I can't wait to practice it," I said excitedly, putting on my boots. Then for no explicable reason, I became so agitated that I jumped up and said, "Shouldn't we be on our way again?"

"We've already arrived," Clara announced, and pointed to a small cave on the side of a hill.

As I gazed at it, my excitement drained out of me. There was something ominous and foreboding about the gaping hole, but inviting, too. I had a definite urge to explore it, yet at the same time I was afraid of what I might find inside.

I suspected we were somewhere in the proximity of her house, a thought I found comforting. Clara informed me that this was a place of power, a spot the ancient geomancers from China, the practitioners of *feng-shui,* would have undoubtedly picked as a temple site.

"Here, the elements of water, wood and air are in perfect harmony," she said. "Here, energy circulates in abundance. You'll see what I mean when you get inside the cave. You must use the energy of this unique spot to purify yourself."

"Are you saying that I have to stay here?"

"Didn't you know that in the ancient Orient, monks and scholars used to retreat to caves?" she asked. "Being surrounded by the earth helped them to meditate."

She urged me to crawl inside the cave. Daringly, I eased myself in, putting all thoughts of bats and spiders out of my mind. It was dark and cool, and there was room for only one person. Clara told me to sit cross-legged, leaning my back against the wall. I hesitated, not wanting to dirty my jacket, but once I leaned back, I was relieved to be able to rest. Even though the ceiling was close to my head and the ground pressed hard against my tailbone, it wasn't claustropho-bic. A mild, almost imperceptible current of air circulated in the cave. I felt invigorated, just as Clara had said I would. I was about to take off my jacket and sit on it when Clara, squatting at the mouth of the cave, spoke.

"The apex of the special art I want to teach you," she began, "is called the abstract flight, and the means to achieve it we call the recapitulation." She reached inside the cave and touched the left and right sides of my forehead. "Awareness must shift from here to here," she said. "As children, we can easily do this, but once the seal of the body has been broken through wasteful excesses, only a special manipulation of awareness, right living and celibacy can restore the energy that has drained out, energy needed to make the shift."

I definitely understood everything she said. I even felt that aware-ness was like a current of energy that could go from one side of the forehead to the other. And I visualized the gap in between the two points as a vast space, a void that impedes the crossing.

I listened intently as she continued talking. "The body must be tremendously strong," she said, "so that awareness can be keen and fluid in order to jump from one side of the abyss to the other in the blink of an eye."

As she voiced her statements, something extraordinary happened. I became absolutely certain that I would be staying with Clara in Mexico. What I wanted to feel was that I would be returning to Arizona in a few days; but what I actually felt was that I would not be going back. I also knew that my realization was not merely the acceptance of what Clara had had in mind from the start, but that I was powerless to resist her intentions because the force that was maneuvering me was not hers alone.

"From now on, you have to lead a life in which awareness has top priority," she said, as if she knew I had made the tacit commitment of remaining with her. "You must avoid anything that is weakening and harmful to your body or your mind. Also, it is essential, for the time being, to break all physical and emotional ties with the world."

"Why is that so important?"

"Because before anything else, you must acquire unity."

Clara explained that we are convinced that a dualism exists in us;

the mind is the insubstantial part of ourselves, and the body is the concrete part. This division keeps our energy in a state of chaotic separation, and prevents it from coalescing.

"Being divided is our human condition," she admitted. "But our division is not between the mind and the body, but between the body, which houses the mind or the self, and the double, which is the receptacle of our basic energy."

She said that before birth, man's imposed duality doesn't exist, but that from birth on, the two parts are separated by the pull of mankind's intent. One part turns outward and becomes the physical body; the other, inward and becomes the double. At death the heavier part, the body, returns to the earth to be absorbed by it, and the light part, the double, becomes free. But unfortunately, since the double was never perfected, it experiences freedom for only an instant, before it is scattered into the universe.

"If we die without erasing our false dualism of body and mind, we die an ordinary death," she said.

"How else can we die?"

Clara peered at me with one eyebrow raised. Rather than answer my question, she revealed in a confiding tone that we die because the possibility that we could be transformed hasn't entered our conception. She stressed that this transformation must be accomplished during our lifetime, and that to succeed in this task is the only true purpose a human being can have. All other attainments are transient, since death dissolves them into nothingness.

"What does this transformation entail?" I asked.

"It entails a total change," she said. "And that is accomplished by the recapitulation: the cornerstone of the art of freedom. The art I am going to teach you is called the art of freedom. An art infinitely difficult to practice, but even more difficult to explain."

Clara said that every procedure she was going to teach me, or every task she might ask me to perform, no matter how ordinary it might seem to me, was a step toward fulfilling the ultimate goal of the art of freedom: the abstract flight.

"What I'm going to show you first are simple movements that you must do daily," she continued. "Regard them always as an indispensable part of your life.

"First, I'll show you a breath that has been a secret for generations.

This breath mirrors the dual forces of creation and destruction, of light and darkness, of being and not-being."

She told me to move outside of the cave, then directed me, by gentle manipulation, to sit with my spine curved forward and to bring my knees to my chest as high as I could. While keeping my feet on the ground, I was to wrap my arms around my calves and firmly clasp my hands in front of my knees or, if I wished, I could clasp each elbow. She gently eased my head down until my chin touched my chest.

I had to strain the muscles of my arms to keep my knees from pushing out sideways. My chest was constricted and so was my abdomen. My neck made a cracking sound as I tucked my chin in.

"This is a powerful breath," she said. "It may knock you out or put you to sleep. If it does, return to the house when you wake up. By the way, this cave is just behind the house. Follow the path and you'll be there in two minutes."

Clara instructed me to take short, shallow breaths. I told her that her request was redundant since that was the only way I could breathe in that position. She said that even if I only partially released the arm pressure I was creating with my hands, my breath would return to normal. But this wasn't what she was after. She wanted me to continue the shallow breaths for at least ten minutes.

I stayed in that position for perhaps half an hour, all the while taking shallow breaths as she had instructed. After the initial cramping in my stomach and legs subsided, the breaths seemed to soften my insides and dissolve them. Then after an excruciatingly long time, Clara gave me a push that made me roll backward so I was lying on the ground, but she didn't permit me to release the pressure of my arms. I felt a moment of relief when my back touched the ground, but it was only when she instructed me to unclasp my hands and stretch out my legs that I felt complete release in my abdomen and chest. The only way of describing what I felt is to say that something inside me had been unlocked by that breath and had been dissolved or released. As Clara had predicted, I became so drowsy that I crawled back inside the cave and fell asleep.

I must have slept for at least a couple of hours in the cave; and judging from the position I was lying in when I woke up, I hadn't moved a muscle. I believed that that was probably because there wasn't any room in the cave for me to toss and turn in my sleep, but it could also have been because I was so totally relaxed, I didn't need to move.

I walked back to the house, following Clara's directions. She was on the patio, sitting in a rattan armchair. I had the impression that another woman had been sitting there with her, and when she heard me coming, she had quickly gotten up and left.

"Ah, you look much more relaxed now," Clara said. "That breath and posture does wonders for us."

Clara said that if this breath is performed regularly, with calmness and deliberation, it gradually balances our internal energy.

Before I could tell her how invigorated I felt, she asked me to sit down because she wanted to show me one other body maneuver crucial for erasing our false dualism. She asked me to sit with my back straight and my eyes slightly lowered, so that I would be gazing at the tip of my nose.

"This breath should be done without the constraints of clothing," she began. "But rather than having you strip naked in the patio in broad daylight, we'll make an exception. First, you inhale deeply, bringing in the air as if you were breathing through your vagina. Pull in your stomach and draw the air up along your spine, past the kidneys, to a point between the shoulder blades. Hold the air there for a moment, then raise it even further up to the back of the head, then over the top of your head to the point between your eyebrows."

She said that after holding it there for a moment, I was to exhale through the nose, as I mentally guided the air down the front of my body, first to the point just below the navel, and then to my vagina, where the cycle had begun.

I began to practice the breathing exercise.

Clara brought her hand to the base of my spine, then traced a line up my back, over my head, and gently pressed the spot between my eyebrows. "Try to bring the breath here," she said. "The reason you keep your eyes halfway open is so that you can concentrate on the bridge of your nose as you circulate the air up your back and over your head to this point; and also so you can use your gaze to guide the air down the front of your body, returning it to your sexual organs."

Clara said that circulating the breath in such a fashion creates an impenetrable shield that prevents outside disruptive influences from piercing the body's field of energy; it also keeps vital inner energy from dispersing outwardly. She stressed that the inhalation and exhalation should be inaudible, and that the breathing exercise could be done while one is standing, sitting or lying down, although in the beginning it is easier to do it while sitting on a cushion or on a chair.

"Now," she said, pulling her chair closer to mine, "let's talk about what we began discussing this morning: the recapitulation."

A shiver went through me. I told her that although I had no conception of what she was talking about, I knew it was going to be something monumental and I wasn't sure I was prepared to hear it. She insisted that I was nervous because some part of me sensed that she was about to disclose perhaps the most important technique of self-renewal. Patiently she explained that the recapitulation is the act of calling back the energy we have already spent in past actions. To recapitulate entails recalling all the people we have met, all the places we have seen and all the feelings we have had in our entire lives—starting from the present, going back to the earliest memories—then sweeping them clean, one by one, with the sweeping breath.

I listened, intrigued, although I couldn't help feeling that what she said was more than nonsensical to me. Before I could make any comments at all, she firmly took my chin in her hands and instructed me to inhale through the nose as she turned my head to the left, and then exhale as she turned it to the right. Next, I was to turn my head to the left and right in a single movement without breathing. She said that this is a mysterious way of breathing and the key to the recapitulation, because inhaling allows us to pull back energy that we lost, while exhaling permits us to expel foreign, undesirable energy that has accumulated in us through interacting with our fellow men.

"In order to live and interact, we need energy," Clara went on. "Normally, the energy spent in living is gone forever from us. Were it not for the recapitulation, we would never have the chance to renew ourselves. Recapitulating our lives and sweeping our past with the sweeping breath work as a unit."

Recalling everyone I had ever known and everything I had ever felt in my life seemed to me an absurd and impossible task. "That can take forever," I said, hoping that a practical remark might block Clara's unreasonable line of thought.

"It certainly can," she agreed. "But I assure you, Taisha, you have everything to gain by doing it and nothing to lose."

I took a few deep breaths, moving my head from left to right, imitating the way she had shown me to breathe in order to placate her and let her know I had been paying attention.

With a wry smile, she warned me that recapitulating is not an arbitrary or capricious exercise. "When you recapitulate, try to feel some long stretchy fibers that extend out from your midsection," she explained. "Then align the turning motion of your head with the movement of these elusive fibers. They are the conduits that will bring back the energy that you've left behind. In order to recuperate our strength and unity, we have to release our energy trapped in the world and pull it back to us."

She assured me that while recapitulating, we extend those stretchy fibers of energy across space and time to the persons, places and events we are examining. The result is that we can return to every moment of our lives and act as if we were actually there.

This possibility sent shivers through me. Although intellectually I was intrigued by what Clara was saying, I had no intention of returning to my disagreeable past, even if it was only in my mind. If nothing else, I took pride in having escaped an unbearable life situation. I was not about to go back and mentally relive all the moments I had tried so hard to forget. Yet Clara seemed to be so utterly serious and sincere in explaining the recapitulation technique to me that, for a moment, I put my objections aside, and concentrated on what she was saying.

I asked her if the order in which one recollects the past matters. She said that the important point is to re-experience the events and feelings in as much detail as possible and to touch them with the sweeping breath, thereby releasing one's trapped energy.

"Is this exercise part of the Buddhist tradition?" I asked.

"No, it isn't," she replied solemnly. "This is part of another tradition. Someday, soon, you'll find out what that tradition is."

5

I didn't see Clara again until the following morning at breakfast. The previous afternoon, in the middle of our conversation on the patio, she suddenly had a vacant, far-away look as if she had caught sight of something or someone at the side of the house. She hurriedly got up and excused herself, leaving me to ponder the importance of all the things she had said.

As we sat to eat our morning meal of shredded meat and rice, I told Clara that on my return trip from the cave yesterday, I had confirmed her statement that it was only a short distance from the house. "Why did we really meander so much to get there, Clara?" I asked.

Clara burst out laughing. "I was trying to get you to take off your boots, so we passed by the stream," she replied.

"Why did I have to take off my boots? Was it because of my blister?"

"It wasn't your blister," Clara said emphatically. "I needed to poke very crucial points on the soles of your feet to awaken you from your lifelong lethargy. Otherwise, you would have never listened to me."

"Aren't you exaggerating, Clara? I would have listened to you even if you didn't poke my feet."

She shook her head and gave me a knowing smile. "All of us were brought up to live in a sort of limbo where nothing counts except petty, immediate gratifications," she said. "And women are the masters of that state. Not until we recapitulate can we overcome our upbringing. And talking about recapitulating . . ."

Clara noticed my pained expression and laughed.

"Do I have to go back to the cave, Clara?" I interrupted, anticipating what I thought she was going to tell me. "I'd much rather stay here with you. If you pose for me, I can make a few sketches of you, and then paint your portrait."

"No, thank you," she said, uninterested. "What I am going to do is give you some preliminary instructions on how to proceed with the recapitulation."

When we had finished eating, Clara handed me a writing pad and pencil. I thought she had changed her mind about my sketching her portrait. But as she pushed the writing materials toward me, she said that I should begin making a list of all the people I had met, starting from the present and going back to my earliest memories.

"That's impossible!" I gasped. "How on earth am I going to remember everyone I've ever come into contact with from day one?"

Clara moved the plates aside to give me room to write.

"Difficult, true, but not impossible," she said. "It's a necessary part of the recapitulation. The list forms a matrix for the mind to hook on to."

She said that the initial stage of the recapitulation consists of two things. The first is the list, the second is setting up the scene. And setting up the scene consists of visualizing all the details pertinent to the events that one is going to recall.

"Once you have all the elements in place, use the sweeping breath; the movement of your head is like a fan that stirs everything in that scene," she said. "If you're remembering a room, for example, breathe in the walls, the ceiling, the furniture, the people you see. And don't stop until you have absorbed every last bit of energy you left behind."

"How will I know when I've done that?" I asked.

"Your body will tell you when you've had enough," she assured me. "Remember, intend to inhale the energy that you left in the scene you're recapitulating, and intend to exhale the extraneous energy thrust into you by others."

Overwhelmed by the task of making the list and beginning to

recapitulate, I couldn't think at all. A perverse and involuntary reaction of my mind was to go absolutely blank; then a deluge of
thoughts flooded in, making it impossible for me to know where to
start. Clara explained that we must start the recapitulation by first
focusing our attention on our past sexual activity.

"Why do you have to begin there?" I asked suspiciously.

"That's where the bulk of our energy is caught," Clara explained.
"That's why we must free those memories first!"

"I don't think my sexual encounters were all that important."

"It doesn't matter. You could have been staring up at the ceiling
bored to death, or seeing shooting stars or fireworks—someone still
left his energy inside you and walked off with a ton of yours."

I was totally put off by her statement. To go back to my sexual
experiences now seemed repugnant. "It's bad enough," I said, "to
relive my childhood memories. But I won't hash up what happened
with men."

Clara looked at me with a raised eyebrow.

"Besides," I argued, "you'll probably expect me to confide in you.
But really, Clara, I don't think what I did with men is anyone's
business."

I thought I had made my point. Clara resolutely shook her head
and said, "Do you want those men you had to continue feeding from
your energy? Do you want those men to get stronger as you get
stronger? Do you want to be their source of energy for the rest of
your life? No. I don't think you understand the importance of the
sexual act or the scope of the recapitulation."

"You're right, Clara. I don't understand the reason for your bizarre
request. And what's this business of men getting stronger because
I'm their source of energy? I'm nobody's source or provider. I promise
you that."

She smiled and said that she had made a mistake in forcing a
confrontation of ideologies at this time. "Bear with me," she begged.
"This is a belief I have chosen to uphold. As you progress with your
recapitulation, I will tell you about the origin of this belief. Suffice
it to say that it is a critical part of the art I'm teaching you."

"If it's as important as you claim, Clara, perhaps you'd better tell
me about it now," I said. "Before we go any further with the recapitulation, I'd like to know what I'm getting into."

"All right, if you insist," she said, nodding.

She poured some camomile tea into our mugs and added a spoonful of honey to hers.

In the authoritative voice of a teacher enlightening a neophyte, she explained that women, more so than men, are the true supporters of the social order, and that to fulfill this role, they have been reared, uniformly the world over, to be at the service of men.

"It makes no difference whether they are bought right off the slave block, or they are courted and loved," she stressed. "Their fundamental purpose and fate is still the same: to nourish, shelter and serve men."

Clara looked at me, I believed, to assess if I was following her argument. I thought I was, but my gut reaction was that her entire premise seemed wrong.

"That may be true in some cases," I said, "but I don't think you can make such sweeping generalizations to include all women."

Clara disagreed vehemently. "The diabolical part of women's servile position is that it doesn't appear to be merely a social prescription," she said, "but a fundamental biological imperative."

"Wait a minute, Clara," I protested. "How did you arrive at that?"

She explained that every species has a biological imperative to perpetuate itself, and that nature has provided tools in order to ensure that the merging of female and male energies takes place in the most efficient way. She said that in the human realm, although the primary function of sexual intercourse is procreation, it also has a secondary and covert function, which is to ensure a continual flow of energy from women to men.

Clara put such a stress on the word "men" that I had to ask, "Why do you say it as if it were a one-way street? Isn't the sexual act an even exchange of energy between male and female?"

"No," she said emphatically. "Men leave specific energy lines inside the body of women. They are like luminous tapeworms that move inside the womb, sipping up energy."

"That sounds positively sinister," I said, humoring her.

She continued her exposition in utter seriousness. "They are put there for an even more sinister reason," she said, ignoring my nervous laughter, "which is to ensure that a steady supply of energy reaches the man who deposited them. Those lines of energy, established through sexual intercourse, collect and steal energy from the female body to benefit the male who left them there."

Clara was so adamant in what she was saying that I couldn't joke about it but had to take her seriously. As I listened, I felt my nervous smile turn into a snarl. "Not that I accept for a minute what you're saying, Clara," I said, "but just out of curiosity, how in the world did you arrive at such a preposterous notion? Did someone tell you about this?"

"Yes, my teacher told me about it. At first, I didn't believe him either," she admitted, "but he also taught me the art of freedom, and that means that I learned to *see* the flow of energy. Now I know he was accurate in his assessments, because I can see the wormlike filaments in women's bodies for myself. You, for example, have a number of them, all of them still active."

"Let's say that's true, Clara," I said uneasily. "Just for the sake of argument, let me ask you why should this be possible? Isn't this one-way energy flow unfair to women?"

"The whole world is unfair to women!" she exclaimed. "But that's not the point."

"What is the point, Clara? I know I'm missing it."

"Nature's imperative is to perpetuate our species," she explained. "In order to ensure that this continues to take place, women have to carry an excessive burden at their basic energy level. And that means a flow of energy that taxes women."

"But you still haven't explained why this should be so," I said, already becoming swayed by the force of her convictions.

"Women are the foundation for perpetuating the human species," Clara replied. "The bulk of the energy comes from them, not only to gestate, give birth and nourish their offspring, but also for ensuring that the male plays his part in this whole process."

Clara explained that ideally this process ensures that a woman feeds her man energetically through the filaments he left inside her body, so that the man becomes mysteriously dependent on her at an ethereal level. This is expressed in the overt behavior of the man returning to the same woman again and again to maintain his source of sustenance. That way, Clara said, nature ensures that men, in addition to their immediate drive for sexual gratification, set up more permanent bonds with women.

"These energy fibers left in women's wombs also become merged with the energy makeup of the offspring, should conception take place," Clara elaborated. "It may be the rudiments of family ties, for the energy from the father merges with that of the fetus, and enables the man to sense that the child is his own. These are some of the facts of life a girl's mother never tells her. Women are reared to be easily seduced by men, without the slightest idea of the consequences of sexual intercourse in terms of the energy drainage it produces in them. This is my point and this is what is not fair."

As I listened to Clara talk, I had to agree that some of what she said made sense to me at a deep bodily level. She urged me not just to agree or disagree with her, but to think this through and evaluate what she had said in a courageous, unprejudiced and intelligent manner.

"It's bad enough that one man leaves energy lines inside a woman's body," Clara went on, "although that is necessary for having offspring and ensuring their survival. But to have the energy lines of ten or twenty men inside her feeding off her luminosity is more than anyone can bear. No wonder women can never lift up their heads."

"Can a woman get rid of those lines?" I asked, more and more convinced that there was some truth to what Clara was saying.

"A woman carries those luminous worms for seven years," Clara said, "after which time they disappear or fade out. But the wretched part is that when the seven years are about to be up, the whole army of worms, from the very first man a woman had to the very last one, all become agitated at once so that the woman is driven to have sexual intercourse again. Then all the worms spring to life stronger than ever to feed off the woman's luminous energy for another seven years. It really is a never-ending cycle."

"What if the woman is celibate?" I asked. "Do the worms just die out?"

"Yes, if she can resist having sex for seven years. But it's nearly impossible for a woman to remain celibate like that in our day and age, unless she becomes a nun, or has money to support herself. And even then she still would need a totally different rationale."

"Why is that, Clara?"

"Because not only is it a biological imperative that women have sexual intercourse, but it is also a social mandate."

Clara gave me then a most confusing and distressing example. She said that since we are unable to see the flow of energy, we may be needlessly perpetuating patterns of behavior or emotional interpretations associated with this unseen flow of energy. For instance, for society to demand that women marry or at least offer themselves to men is wrong, as it is wrong for women to feel unfulfilled unless they have a man's semen inside them. It is true that a man's energy lines give them purpose, make them fulfill their biological destinies: feeding men and their offspring. But human beings are intelligent enough to demand of themselves more than merely the fulfillment of the reproduction imperative. She said that, for example, to evolve is an equal if not a greater imperative than to reproduce; and that, in this case, evolving entails the awakening of women to their true role in the energetic scheme of reproduction.

She then turned her argument to the personal level and said that I had been reared, like every other woman, by a mother who regarded as her primary function raising me to find a suitable husband so I would not have the stigma of being a spinster. I was really bred, like an animal, to have sex, no matter what my mother chose to call it.

"You, like every other woman, have been tricked and forced into submission," Clara said. "And the sad part is that you're trapped in this pattern, even if you don't intend to procreate."

Her statements were so distressing that I laughed out of sheer nervousness. Clara wasn't fazed at all. "Perhaps all this is true, Clara," I said, trying not to sound condescending. "But in my case, how can remembering the past change anything? Isn't it all water under the bridge?"

"I can only tell you that to wake up, you must break a vicious circle," she countered, her green eyes assessing me curiously.

I reiterated that I didn't believe in her theories about diabolic biological imperatives or vampirelike males leeching off women's energy, and argued that just sitting in a cave remembering isn't going to change anything.

"There are certain things I just don't want to think about ever again," I snapped and banged my fist on the kitchen table. I stood up ready to leave and told her that I didn't want to hear any more about the recapitulation, the list of names or any biological imperatives.

"Let's make a deal," Clara said, with the air of a merchant getting ready to cheat a customer. "You're a fair person; you like to be honorable. So I'll propose that we reach an agreement."

"What kind of an agreement?" I asked with mounting anxiety.

She tore off a sheet from the writing pad and handed it to me. "I want you to write and sign a promissory voucher stating that you're going to try the recapitulation exercise for one month only. If, after a month, you don't notice any increase in energy, or any improvement in how you feel toward yourself or toward life in general, you will be free to go back home, wherever home is. If this turns out to be the case, you can simply write off the entire experience as the bizarre request of an eccentric woman."

I sat down again to calm myself. As I took a few sips of tea, the thought struck me that it was the least I could do after all the trouble Clara had gone to for me. Besides, it was apparent that she wasn't going to let me off the hook that easily. I could always go through the motions of recapitulating my memories. After all, who is to know if, in the cave, I did the visualization and breathing, or if I just daydreamed or took a nap?

"It's only one month," she said sincerely. "You won't be signing your life away. Believe me, I'm really trying to help you."

"I know that," I said. "But why would you bother doing all this for me? Why me, Clara?"

"There is a reason," she replied, "but it's so farfetched that I can't spring it on you now. The only thing I can tell you is that by helping you, I'm fulfilling a worthy purpose: paying off a debt. Would you accept my repaying a debt as a reason?"

Clara looked at me so hopefully that I picked up the pencil and wrote the voucher, deliberately fussing over the wording so that there would be no confusion about the one-month time frame. She bargained with me for not including in that month the time it took me to draw up the list of names. I agreed and made an addendum to that effect; then, in spite of my better judgement, I signed it.

6

It took weeks of brain-racking work to compile the list. I hated myself for having let Clara talk me into not including that time in the voucher. During those long days, I worked in absolute solitude and silence; I only saw Clara at breakfast and at dinner, which we ate in the kitchen; but we hardly spoke. She would rebuff all my attempts at cordial conversation, saying that we would talk again when I had finished my list. When I had completed it, she put down her sewing and immediately accompanied me to the cave. It was four o'clock in the afternoon, and according to Clara, early morning and late afternoon were the most propitious times to begin such a vast undertaking.

At the entrance of the cave, she gave me some instructions.

"Take the first person on your list and work your memory to recall everything you experienced with that person," Clara said, "from the moment you two met to the last time you interacted. Or, if you prefer, you can work backward, from the last time you had dealings with that person to your first encounter."

Armed with the list, I went to the cave every day. At first, recapitulating was painstaking work. I couldn't concentrate, for I dreaded dredging up the past. My mind would wander from what I considered to be one traumatic event to the next, or I would simply rest or daydream. But after a while, I became intrigued with the clarity and detail that my recollections were acquiring. I even began to be more objective about experiences I had always considered to be taboo.

Surprisingly, I also felt stronger and more optimistic. Sometimes, as I breathed, it was as if energy were oozing back into my body, causing my muscles to become warm and to bulge. I became so involved in my recapitulation task that I didn't need a whole month to prove its worth. Two weeks after the starting time stipulated in the voucher, while we were eating dinner, I asked Clara to find someone to move me out of my apartment and to put my things in storage. Clara had suggested this option to me several times before, but each time I had refused her offer, for I was not ready to make the commitment. Clara was delighted with my request.

"I'll have one of my cousins do it," she volunteered. "She'll take care of everything. I don't want any worries to keep you from concentrating."

"Now that you mention it, Clara," I said, "there is one other thing that's been bothering me."

Clara waited for me to speak. I told her that I found it very odd that our meals were always ready, although I had never seen her cooking or preparing food.

"That's because you're never in the house during the day," Clara said matter-of-factly. "And at night, you retire early."

It was true that I spent most of my time in the cave. When I did go back to the house, it was to have a meal in the kitchen, and afterward, I stayed in my room because the size of the house intimidated me. It was enormous. It didn't look abandoned, for it was filled to capacity with furniture, books and various decorative objects made of ceramic, silver or cloisonné. Every room was clean and dust-free, as if a maid came regularly to tidy up. Yet the house seemed empty because there were no people in it. Twice Clara had disappeared on mysterious errands that she refused to discuss; during those times, the only other living being in the house beside myself was Manfred. And those were also the times when Manfred and I hiked into the hills overlooking the house. I had mapped the house and its grounds from an observation point I thought I had found myself. I didn't want to admit, at that time, that Manfred had guided me to it.

From my private promontory, I spent hours trying to figure out the orientation of the house. Clara had indicated that it followed the cardinal points. But when I checked it with a compass, the house seemed to be on a slightly different alignment. The grounds around the house were most disturbing, for they defied any accurate mapping I tried to devise. I could see from my observation post that the grounds seemed much more extensive than when measured from the house itself. Clara had forbidden me to set foot in the front part of the house—the east—as well as the south side. But I had calculated, by walking around the periphery of the house, that the two areas were identical to the west and north sides, to which I had access. However, when seen from a distance, they weren't identical at all, and I was at a loss to explain the discrepancy.

I gave up trying to pin down the layout of the house and grounds and began placing my attention on another mysterious problem: Clara's relatives. Although she constantly referred to them in an oblique manner, I had not yet seen hide nor hair of them.

"When are your relatives coming back from India?" I asked Clara point-blank.

"Soon," she replied. She picked up her rice bowl with one hand and held it the way the Chinese do. I had never seen her use chopsticks before and marveled at the incredible precision with which she manipulated them. "Why are you so concerned with my relatives?" she asked.

"To tell you the truth, Clara, I don't know why, but I'm very curious about them," I said. "I've been having unsettling feelings and thoughts in this huge house."

"Do you mean that you don't like the house?"

"On the contrary, I love it. It's just so big and haunting."

"What kind of thoughts and feelings unsettle you?" she asked, putting down her bowl.

"Sometimes I think I see people in the hallway, or I hear voices. And I'm always under the impression that someone is watching me, but when I look around, there isn't anyone there."

"There's more to this house than meets the eye," Clara admitted, "but that shouldn't engender fear or worry. There is magic in this house, in the land, in the mountains around this entire area. That's the reason we chose to live here. In fact, that's also the reason you decided to live here yourself, even though you don't have the slightest inkling of that being the reason for your choice. But this is the way it should be. You bring your innocence to this house and the house with all the intent it stores turns it into wisdom."

"It all sounds very beautiful, Clara, but what exactly does it mean?"

"I always talk to you with the hope that you will understand me," Clara said with a note of disappointment. "Every one of my relatives, who, I assure you, will come into contact with you sooner or later, will speak to you in the same way. So don't think that we're talking nonsense just because you don't understand us."

"Believe me, Clara, I don't think that at all, and I am grateful that you are trying to help me."

"It's the recapitulation that's helping you, not me," Clara corrected me. "Have you noticed any strange things about the house, other than what you have already told me?"

I told her about the disparity between my visual assessments of the house from the observation post and from the ground.

She laughed until she was coughing.

"I have to adjust my behavior to this new development," Clara said when she could talk again.

"Can you explain to me why the grounds seem to be lopsided, and why I get such different compass readings when I'm down here than when I'm up on the hill?" I asked.

"I certainly can; but it won't make any sense to you. What's more, you may even get frightened."

"Does it have to do with the compass, Clara? Or is it me? Am I crazy or what?"

"It has to do with you, of course; you're the one making those measurements; but it's not that you're crazy; it's something else."

"What is it, Clara? Tell me. This whole thing is giving me the creeps. It's as if I were in a science fiction movie where nothing is real and anything can happen. I hate that genre!"

Clara didn't seem willing to divulge anything more. Instead she asked, "Don't you like the unexpected?"

I told her that having male siblings had been so devastating for me that I became jaded, and as a matter of principle, I hated everything they liked. They watched *Twilight Zone* on television and raved about it. To me, it was a most manipulative and contrived show.

"Let's see how I can put this," Clara conceded. "First of all, this is definitely not a science fiction house. It's rather a house of extraordinary intent. The reason why I can't explain its discrepancies is because I can't explain to you yet what intent is."

"Please don't talk in riddles, Clara," I begged. "It's not only frightening, but plainly infuriating."

"In order for you to understand this delicate matter, I have to talk in a roundabout way," Clara said. "So let me first tell you about the man who was directly responsible for my being here in this house, and indirectly responsible for my relation with you. His name was Julian and he was the most exquisite being you could ever encounter. He found me one day when I had lost my way in those mountains in Arizona and he brought me here to this house."

"Wait a minute, Clara, I thought you said that this house has been in your family for generations," I reminded her.

"Five generations, to be exact," she replied.

"How can you make two contradictory statements with such nonchalance?"

"I'm not contradicting myself. It's you who are interpreting things without a proper foundation. The truth is that this house has been in my family for generations. But my family is an abstract family. It's a family in the same manner this house is a house, and Manfred is a dog. But you already know that Manfred isn't a real dog; nor is this house real, like any other house. Do you see what I mean?"

I wasn't in the mood for Clara's riddles. For a while, I sat quietly, hoping that she would change the subject. Then I felt guilty for brooding and being short-tempered. "No, I don't see what you mean," I finally said.

"In order for you to understand all this, you have to change," Clara said patiently. "But then, that's precisely why you are here: to change. And to change means that you will be able to succeed in making the abstract flight, at which time everything will be clear to you."

At my desperate urging, she explained that this unimaginable flight was symbolized by moving from the right side of the forehead to the left, but what it really meant was bringing the ethereal part of us, the double, into our daily awareness.

"As I've already explained to you," she went on, "the body–mind dualism is a false dichotomy. The real division is between the physical body, which houses the mind, and the ethereal body or the double, which houses our energy. The abstract flight takes place when we bring our double to bear on our daily lives. In other words, the moment our physical body becomes totally conscious of its energetic ethereal counterpart, we have crossed over into the abstract, a completely different realm of awareness."

"If it means I'll have to change first, I seriously doubt I'll ever be able to make that crossing," I said. "Everything seems so deeply ingrained in me that I feel I'm set for life."

Clara poured some water into my cup. She put down the ceramic pitcher and looked at me squarely. "There is a way to change," she said. "And by now you are up to your ears in it; it's called the recapitulation."

She assured me that a deep and complete recapitulation enables us to be aware of what we want to change by allowing us to see our lives without delusion. It gives us a moment's pause in which we can choose to accept our usual behavior or to change it by intending it away, before it fully entraps us.

"And how do you intend something away?" I asked. "Do you just say, 'Begone, Satan!'?"

Clara laughed and took a sip of water. "To change, we need to meet three conditions," she said. "First, we must announce out loud our decision to change so that intent will hear us. Second, we must engage our awareness over a period of time: We can't just start something and give it up as soon as we become discouraged. Third, we have to view the outcome of our actions with a sense of complete detachment. This means we can't get involved with the idea of succeeding or failing.

"Follow these three steps and you can change any unwanted feelings and desires in you," Clara assured me.

"I don't know, Clara," I said skeptically. "It sounds so simple the way you put it."

It wasn't that I didn't want to believe her, it was just that I had always been practical; and from a practical point of view, the task of changing my behavior was staggering in spite of her three-fold program.

We finished our meal in complete silence. The only sound in the kitchen was the constant dripping of water as it passed through a limestone filter. It gave me a concrete image of the gradual cleansing process of recapitulating. Suddenly, I had a surge of optimism. Perhaps it was possible to change oneself, to become purified, drop by drop, thought by thought, just like the water passing through the filter.

Above us, the bright track lights cast eerie shadows on the white tablecloth. Clara put down her chopsticks and began curling her fingers as if she were making shadow pictures on the tablecloth. At any moment I expected her to do a rabbit or a turtle.

"What are you doing?" I asked, breaking the silence.

"This is a form of communication," she explained, "not with people though, but with that force we call intent."

She extended her little and index fingers, then made a circle by touching her thumb to the tips of the two remaining fingers. She told me that this was a signal to trap the attention of that force and to allow it to enter the body through the energy lines that end or originate in the fingertips.

"Energy comes through the index and little finger if they are extended like antennae," she explained, showing me the gesture again. "Then the energy is trapped and held in the circle made by the other three fingers."

She said that with this specific hand position, we can draw sufficient energy into the body to heal or strengthen it, or to change our moods and habits.

"Let's go to the living room, where we can be more comfortable," Clara said. "I don't know about you, but this bench is beginning to hurt my bottom."

Clara stood up and we walked across the dark patio, through the back door and hall of the main house, into the living room. To my surprise, the gasoline lamp had already been lit and Manfred was asleep curled up next to an armchair. Clara made herself comfortable in that chair, which I had always taken to be her favorite. She picked up a piece of embroidery that she had been working on and carefully added a few more stitches, passing the needle through the cloth and pulling it out with a graceful sweeping motion of her hand. Her eyes were steadfast, intent on her work.

To me it was so unusual to see this strong woman doing needlework, that I glanced over curiously to see if I could catch a glimpse of her handicraft. Clara noticed my interest and held up the cloth for me to see. It was a pillowcase with embroidered butterflies perched on colorful flowers. It was too gaudy for my taste.

Clara smiled as if she sensed my critical opinion of her work.

"You might tell me that my work is sheer beauty or that I'm wasting my time," she said, taking another stitch, "but that wouldn't affect my inner serenity. This attitude is called 'knowing your worth.' " She asked a rhetorical question that she answered herself. "And what do you think my worth is? Absolutely zero."

I told her that in my opinion she was magnificent, truly a most inspiring person. How could she say that she had no worth?

"It's all very simple," Clara explained. "As long as the positive and negative forces are in balance, they cancel each other out and that means that my worth is zero. It also means that I cannot possibly be upset when someone criticizes me, nor can I be pleased when someone praises me."

Clara held up a needle and, in spite of the dim light, she quickly threaded it. "Chinese sages of ancient times used to say that in order to know your worth, you have to slip through the eye of the dragon," she said, pulling the two ends of the thread together.

She said that those sages were convinced that the boundless unknown is guarded by an enormous dragon whose scales shine with a dazzling light. They believed that the courageous seekers who dare to approach the dragon are awed by its blinding glare, by the power of its tail that with the minutest flicker crushes anything in its way, and by its burning breath that turns to ashes everything within its reach. But they also believed that there is a way to slip by that unapproachable dragon. Clara said that they were confident that by merging with the dragon's intent, one can become invisible and go through the dragon's eye.

"What does that mean, Clara?" I asked.

"It means that through the recapitulation, we can become empty of thought and desire, which for those ancient seers meant to become one with the dragon's intent, therefore invisible."

I picked up an embroidered cushion, another sample of Clara's work, and tucked it behind my back. I took several deep breaths to clear my mind. I wanted to understand what she was saying. But her insistence in using Chinese metaphors made it all the more confusing to me. Yet there was such an urgency in everything she said, that I felt it would be my loss if I didn't at least try to understand her.

Watching Clara embroidering, I was suddenly reminded of my mother. Perhaps it was that memory that induced in me a monumental sadness, a longing that had no name; or perhaps it was listening to what Clara had said; or just being in her empty, hauntingly beautiful house, under that eerie light of the gasoline lamp. Tears flooded my eyes and I began to weep.

Clara jumped up from her chair and stood beside me. She whispered in my ear so loudly that it sounded like a shout, "Don't you dare to give in to self-pity in this house. If you do, this house will reject you; it'll spit you out, just like you spit out an olive pit."

Her admonition had the proper effect on me. My sadness instantly vanished. I dried my eyes and Clara continued talking as if nothing had happened.

"The art of emptiness was the technique practiced by Chinese men of wisdom who wanted to go through the dragon's eye," she said, taking her seat again. "Today, we call it the art of freedom. We feel it's a better term because that art really leads to an abstract realm where humanness doesn't count."

"Do you mean, Clara, that it is an inhuman realm?"

Clara put her embroidery down in her lap and looked at me. "What I mean is that almost everything we have heard about this realm, from sages and seers who sought it, smacks of human concerns. But we, the ones who practice the art of freedom, have found out from firsthand experience that this is an inaccurate portrayal. In our experience, whatever is human in that realm is so unimportant that it is lost in the vastness."

"Wait a minute, Clara. What about that group of legendary personages called the Chinese immortals? Didn't they achieve freedom in the way you mean it?"

"Not in the way we mean it," Clara said. "Freedom to us is being free from humanness. The Chinese immortals were caught in their myths of immortality, of being wise, of having liberated themselves, of coming back to earth to guide others along the way. They were scholars, musicians, possessors of supernatural powers. They were righteous and whimsical, very much like the classical Greek gods. Even nirvana is a human state, in which bliss is being free from the flesh."

Clara had succeeded in making me feel completely forlorn. I told her that all my life I had been accused of lacking human warmth and understanding. In fact, I had been told that I was the coldest creature anyone could ever come across. Now Clara was saying that freedom was being free from human compassion. And I had always felt I was missing something crucial by not possessing it.

I was on the verge of tears of self-pity again, but Clara came again to my rescue. "Being free from humanness doesn't mean such an idiotic thing as not possessing warmth or compassion," she said.

"Even so, freedom the way you describe it is inconceivable to me, Clara," I insisted. "I'm not sure I would want any part of it."

"And I'm sure I want every part of it," she retorted. "Although my mind cannot conceive it either, believe me, it does exist! And believe me, too, that someday you'll be saying to someone else whatever I am saying to you now about it. Perhaps you'll even be using the same words." She winked at me as if she knew for certain that this was going to happen.

"As you continue to recapitulate, the entrance of the realm where humanness doesn't count will appear to you," Clara went on. "That will be the invitation for you to go through the dragon's eye. This is what we call the abstract flight. It actually entails crossing a vast chasm into a realm that cannot be described because man isn't the measure of it."

I became numb with dread. I didn't dare take Clara lightly, for she always meant what she said. The thought of losing my humanness, such as it was, and jumping into a chasm was more than frightening. I was about to ask her if she knew when that entrance was going to appear to me, but she continued her explanation.

"The truth of the matter is that the entrance is in front of us all the time," Clara said, "but only those whose minds are still and whose hearts are at ease can see or feel its presence."

She explained that to call it an entrance was not metaphorical because it actually appears sometimes as a plain door, a black cavern, a dazzling light or anything conceivable, even a dragon's eye. She said that, in this respect, the metaphors of China's early sages were not farfetched at all.

"Another thing the ancient Chinese seekers believed was that invisibility is the corollary of having attained a calm indifference," she said.

"What is a calm indifference, Clara?"

Instead of answering me directly, she asked if I had ever seen the eyes of fighting cocks.

"I've never seen a fighting cock in my life," I told her.

Clara explained that the look in the eyes of a fighting cock is not the look found in the eyes of ordinary people or animals, for those eyes mirror warmth, compassion, rage, fear.

"The eyes of a fighting cock are filled with none of these," Clara informed me. "Instead, they reflect an indescribable indifference, something also found in the eyes of beings who have made the great crossing. For instead of looking outwardly at the world, they have turned inwardly to gaze at that which is not yet present.

"The eye that gazes inwardly is immovable," Clara went on. "It reflects not human concerns or fears, but the vastness. Seers who have gazed at the boundless have attested that the boundless stares back with a cold, unyielding indifference."

7

One afternoon just before dark, Clara and I were taking the long scenic route to the house from the cave when she suggested that we sit and rest in the shade of some trees. We were watching the shadows that the trees cast on the ground, when suddenly a gust of wind made the leaves quiver. The leaves began to shimmer in a flurry of light and dark, causing ripples in the patterns on the ground. When the wind passed, the leaves once again became still and so did the shadows.

"The mind is like these shadows," Clara said softly. "When our breathing is even, our minds are still. If it is erratic, the mind quivers like stirred leaves."

I tried to notice if my breathing was even or disturbed but I honestly couldn't tell.

"If your breath is agitated, your mind becomes restless," Clara continued. "To quiet the mind, it's best to begin by quieting your breathing." She told me to keep my back erect and to concentrate on my breathing until it was soft and rhythmic, like that of an infant.

I pointed out that if a person is physically active as we had just been, hiking over hills, one's breathing couldn't possibly be as soft as an infant's, who just lies around and does nothing. "Besides," I said, "I don't know how infants breathe. I haven't been around many of them, and when I was, I didn't pay attention to their breathing."

Clara moved closer and put one hand on my back and the other on my chest. To my dismay, she pressed until I was so constricted that I felt I was going to suffocate. I tried to move away but she held me down with an iron grip. To compensate, my stomach began moving in and out rhythmically as air again entered my body.

"This is how infants breathe," she said. "Remember the sensation of your stomach popping out, so you can reproduce it regardless of whether you are walking, exercising or lying around doing nothing. You probably won't believe this, but we are so civilized that we have to relearn how to breathe properly."

She removed her hands from my chest and back. "Now let the breath rise to fill your chest cavity," she instructed. "But don't let it flood your head."

"There is no way for the air to get into my head," I laughed.

"Don't take me so literally," she scolded. "When I say air, I'm really talking about energy derived from the breath, which enters the abdomen, the chest and then the head."

I had to laugh at her seriousness. I braced myself for another barrage of Chinese metaphors.

She smiled and winked. "My seriousness is a corollary of my size," she said with a chuckle. "We big people are always more serious than petite jovial ones. Isn't that right, Taisha?"

I didn't know why she was including me when she talked of big people. I was at least two inches shorter than her and a good thirty-five pounds lighter. I thoroughly resented being called big, and even more so her intimation that I was overly serious. But I didn't voice this because I knew she would make an issue out of it and tell me to do a deep recapitulation on the subject of my size.

Clara looked at me as if to gauge my reaction to her statement. I smiled and pretended it hadn't fazed me in the least. Upon seeing my attentiveness, she became serious again and continued to explain that our emotional well-being is directly linked to the rhythmic flow of our breathing.

"The breathing of a person who is upset," she said, leaning closer, "is rapid and shallow and is localized in the chest or head. The breathing of a relaxed person sinks to the abdomen."

I tried to lower my breathing to my stomach so that Clara wouldn't suspect that I had been upset. But she smiled knowingly and added, "It's harder for big people to breath from the abdomen because their center of gravity is just a bit higher. It's therefore even more important that we remain calm and unperturbed."

She went on to explain that the body is divided into three main chambers of energy: the abdomen, chest and head. She touched my stomach just below my navel, then my solar plexus and then the center of my forehead. She explained that these three points are the key centers of the three chambers. The more relaxed the mind and body are, the more air a person can take into each of the three body divisions.

"Infants take in a vast amount of air for their size," Clara said. "However, as we grow older we become constricted, especially around the lungs, and we take in less air."

Clara took a deep breath before continuing. "Since emotions are directly linked to the breath," she said, "a good way to calm ourselves is by regulating our breathing. For example, we can train ourselves to absorb more energy by deliberately elongating each breath we take."

She stood up and asked me to observe her shadow carefully. I noticed that it was perfectly still. Then she told me to stand and look at my own shadow. I couldn't help detecting a slight quiver, like the shadow of the trees when the leaves were touched by a breeze.

"Why is my shadow shaking?" I asked. "I thought I was standing perfectly still."

"Your shadow quivers because the winds of emotion are blowing through you," Clara replied. "You're more quiet than when you first began to recapitulate, but there is still a great deal of agitation left inside you."

She told me to stand on my left leg with my right leg raised and bent at the knee. I wobbled as I tried to keep my balance. I marveled that she stood on one leg as easily as she had stood on two, and her shadow was absolutely motionless.

"You seem to have a hard time keeping your balance," Clara noted, setting down her leg and raising the other one. "That means that your thoughts and feelings are not at ease, and neither is your breathing."

I raised my other leg to try the exercise again. This time my balance was better, but when I saw how still Clara's shadow was, I experienced a sudden pang of envy and I had to lower my leg to keep from falling.

"Whenever we have a thought," Clara explained, setting down her leg again, "our energy moves in the direction of that thought. Thoughts are like scouts; they cause the body to move along a certain path.

"Now, look at my shadow again," she ordered. "But try not to regard it as merely my shadow. Try to see into the essence of Clara as shown in her shadow-picture."

Immediately I tensed. I was on trial and my performance was going to be evaluated. My childhood competitive feelings of having to outdo my brothers surfaced.

"Don't tense up," Clara said sternly. "This is not a contest. This is merely a delight. Do you understand? A delight!"

I had been thoroughly conditioned to react to words. The word "delight" threw me into total confusion, and finally into panic. She's not using the word correctly, was all I could think. She must mean something else. But Clara repeated the word over and over, as if she wanted it to sink in.

I kept my eyes on her shadow. I had the impression that it was beautiful, serene, full of power. It wasn't merely a dark area, it seemed to have depth, intelligence and vitality. Then suddenly I thought I saw Clara's shadow move independent of any movement of Clara's body. The movement was so incredibly fast that it almost went unnoticed. I waited, holding my breath, peering at it, pouring on it all my attention. Then it happened again, and this time I was certainly prepared for it. It quivered and then stretched, as if its shoulders and chest had suddenly been inflated. The shadow seemed to have come alive.

I let out a shriek and jumped up. I shouted to Clara that her shadow was alive. I was ready to run away, terrified that the shadow would run after me, but Clara restrained me by holding my shoulder.

When I had calmed down enough to talk again, I told her what I had seen, all the while keeping my eyes averted from the ground for fear of catching another glimpse of Clara's sinister shadow.

"To see the movement of shadows means that you have obviously freed a huge portion of energy with your recapitulation," Clara remarked.

"Are you sure I didn't just imagine this, Clara?" I said, hoping she would say I had.

"It was your intent that made it move," she said authoritatively.

"But don't you think that recapitulating also disturbs the mind?" I asked. "I must be very disturbed in order to see shadows moving by themselves."

"No. The purpose of the recapitulation is to break basic assumptions we have accepted throughout our lives," Clara explained patiently. "Unless they are broken, we can't prevent the power of remembering from clouding our awareness."

"What exactly do you mean by the power of remembering, Clara?"

"The world is a huge screen of memories; if certain assumptions are broken," she said, "the power of remembering is not only held in check, but even canceled out."

I didn't understand what she was saying and I resented her being so obscure.

"It probably was the wind that stirred the dirt on which your shadow was projected," I said, offering a reasonable explanation.

Clara shook her head. "Try looking at it again and find out for sure," she suggested.

I felt goose bumps on my arms. Nothing was going to make me stare at her shadow again.

"You insist that shadows of people don't move by themselves," Clara said, "because that's what your ability to remember tells you. Do you remember ever seeing them move?"

"No. I certainly do not."

"There you are. But what happened to you just now is that your normal ability to remember was held in check for an instant and you saw my shadow move."

Clara shook a finger at me and chuckled. "And it wasn't the wind stirring the dirt, either," she said. Then she hid her head with her arm, as if she were a timid child. It struck me as odd that even though she was a grown woman, she never looked ridiculous performing childish gestures.

"I have news for you," Clara continued. "You've seen shadows move before as a child, but then you were not yet rational so it was all right to see them move. As you grew up, your energy was harnessed by social constraints, and so you forgot you had seen them moving, and only remember what you think is permissible to remember."

I was trying to appreciate the scope of what Clara was saying when I suddenly remembered that, as a child, I used to see shadows wiggle and twist on the sidewalks, especially on hot, clear days. I always thought they were trying to pull themselves free from people they belonged to. It terrified me to see the shadows curl sideways to peek behind them. It always seemed odd that adults would be so totally oblivious of their shadows' antics.

When I mentioned this to Clara, she concluded that my being terrified was a product of the conflict between what I really saw, and what I had already been told was possible and permissible to see.

"I don't think I follow you, Clara," I said.

"Try to imagine yourself as a giant memory warehouse," she suggested. "In that warehouse, someone other than yourself has stored feelings, ideas, mental dialogues and behavior patterns. Since it is your warehouse, you can go in there and rummage around any time you want and use whatever you find there. The problem is that you have absolutely no say over the inventory, for it was already established before you came into possession of the warehouse. Thus you are drastically limited in your selection of items."

She added that our lives seem to be an uninterrupted time line because in our warehouses the inventory never changes. She stressed that unless this storehouse is cleared out, there is no way for us to be what we really are.

Overwhelmed by my memories and by what Clara was explaining, I sat down on a large rock. From the corner of my eye, I saw my shadow and experienced a jolt of panic as I asked myself, What if my shadow wouldn't quite sit the way I do? "I can't take this, Clara," I said, jumping up. "Let's go back to the house."

Clara ordered me to stay put. "Calm the mind," she said, staring at me, "and the body too will become tranquil; otherwise you're going to burst."

Clara held her left hand in front of her body with the wrist resting just above the navel; her palm faced sideways, the fingers pressed together, pointed downward to the ground. She told me to adopt this hand position and gaze at the tip of my middle finger. I looked over the bridge of my nose, which forced me to look downward while slightly crossing my eyes. She explained that to gaze fixedly in that manner places our awareness outside of us onto the ground, thus diminishing our inner agitation.

Then she said I was to inhale deeply, pointing at the ground, intending to get from it a sparkle of energy, like a drop of glue, on my middle finger. Next, I was to rotate my hand up at the wrist until the base of my thumb touched my breastbone. I was to gaze at the tip of my middle finger for a count of seven and then shift my awareness immediately to my forehead, to a spot in between the eyes and just above the bridge of the nose. This shift, she said, must be accompanied by the intent of transferring the sparkle of energy from the middle finger to that spot between the eyes. If the transfer is accomplished, a light appears on the dark screen behind the closed eyes. She said that we can send this luminous spot of energy to any part of our body to counteract pain, disease, apprehension or fear.

She then moved her hand and gently pressed my solar plexus. "If you need a quick surge of energy, as you do now, do the power breath I am about to show you and I guarantee that you will feel recharged."

I watched Clara do a series of short inhalations and exhalations through her nose in rapid succession, vibrating her diaphragm. I imitated her and after twenty or so breaths, contracting and relaxing my diaphragm, I felt warmth spreading throughout my midsection.

"We're going to sit here doing the power breath and gazing at the light behind the eyes," she said, "until you're no longer frightened."

"I wasn't really that scared," I lied.

"You didn't see yourself," Clara retorted. "From where I'm sitting, I saw someone who was just about to faint."

She was absolutely right. Never had I experienced such total fright as when I saw Clara's shadow stretching itself out. Lost memories had surfaced from such forgotten depths that, for a second or two, I had felt I was actually a child again.

I held my palm sideways and gazed at my fingertip the way Clara had recommended. I kept my eyes fixed, and then shifted my attention to the center of my forehead. I didn't see any light, but I gradually became calm.

It was almost dark. I could see Clara's silhouette outlined beside me. Her voice was soothing; she said, "Let's remain here for a while longer to allow that sparkle of energy to settle in your body."

"Did you learn this technique in China, Clara?" I asked.

She shook her head. "I told you that I had a teacher here in Mexico," she said, then added reverently, "My teacher was an extraordinary man who dedicated his life to learning and then teaching us the art of freedom."

"But isn't this method of breathing Oriental in origin?"

She seemed to deliberate before answering me. I thought her hesitation was due to her desire to remain secretive.

"Where did your teacher learn it?" I probed. "Was he also in China?"

"He learned everything he knew from his teacher," Clara said evasively.

When I asked her to tell me more about her teacher and what he had taught her, Clara apologized for not being at liberty to discuss the subject further at this time.

"In order to understand it," she explained, "you need to acquire a special kind of energy, which at the moment you don't have."

She patted my hand. "Don't rush things," she said sympathetically. "We intend to teach you all we know. So why the hurry?"

"I'm always so intrigued when you say 'we,' Clara, because I get the impression that there are other people in the house, and I begin to see and hear things that my reason tells me can't possibly be true."

Clara laughed until I thought she was going to fall off the boulder on which she sat. Her sudden and exaggerated outburst annoyed me even more than her refusal to tell me about her teacher.

"You don't know how funny your dilemma is to me," she said by way of an explanation. "It proves to me, just like when you saw the shadows moving, that you're freeing your energy. You are beginning to empty your warehouse. The more items of your inventory you discard, the more you make room for other things."

"Like what?" I said, still annoyed. "Seeing shadows move and hearing voices?"

"Perhaps," she said vaguely. "Or you might even see the people the shadows and voices belong to."

I wanted to know what people she was referring to, but she refused to say any more about it. Abruptly she stood up and announced that she wanted to get back to the house to turn on the generator before it got too dark.

8

I hadn't seen Clara for three days; some mysterious errand was keeping her away. It was her habit now, without a word of warning, to leave me alone in the house for days at a time with only Manfred for company; and although I had the whole house to myself, I never dared to venture beyond the living room, my bedroom, Clara's gymnasium, the kitchen and of course the outhouse. There was something about Clara's house and grounds, especially when Clara was away, that filled me with an irrational fear. The result was that when I was alone, I kept a strict routine, which I found comforting.

I used to wake up around nine, make my breakfast in the kitchen on a hot plate because I still didn't know how to light the woodburning stove, pack a light lunch, then go to the cave to recapitulate or take a long hike with Manfred. I would return in the late afternoon to practice kung fu forms in Clara's martial arts gymnasium. It was a big hall with a vaulted ceiling, a varnished wooden floor and a standing black-lacquer rack on which a variety of martial arts weapons were displayed. Along the wall opposite the door was a raised platform covered with straw mats. I had once asked Clara what the platform was for. She had said it was where she did her meditation.

I had never seen Clara meditate because whenever she went into the building by herself, she always locked the door. Every time I had asked her what kind of meditation she practiced, she had refused to elaborate on it. The only thing I ever found out was that she called it "dreaming."

Clara had allowed me free access to her gymnasium whenever she wasn't using it herself. When I was alone in the house, I gravitated to that room, finding there emotional solace for it was imbued with Clara's presence and power. It was there that she taught me a most intriguing style of kung fu. I had never been interested in Chinese martial arts because my Japanese karate teachers had always insisted that its movements were too elaborate and cumbersome to be of any practical value. Systematically they ran down the Chinese styles and elevated their own, saying that although karate had its roots in the Chinese styles, its forms and applications were thoroughly altered and perfected in Japan. Ignorant of martial arts, I believed my teachers and totally discounted all other styles. Consequently, I didn't know what to make of Clara's kung fu style. In spite of my ignorance, one thing was obvious: she was an indisputable master of it.

After working out for an hour or so in Clara's gymnasium, I would change clothes and go to the kitchen to eat. Invariably, my food would be there, set on the table, but I was always so famished after exercising that I just wolfed down whatever had been prepared without speculating how it got there.

Clara had told me, when I questioned her about it, that when she was gone, the caretaker came to the house to cook my meals. He must have also done the laundry, for I would find my clothes neatly folded in a pile at the door of my bedroom; all I had to do was iron them.

One evening, after a heavy workout, while Manfred looked on growling critically from time to time, I had such a surplus of energy that I decided to break my routine and return to the cave in the darkness to continue recapitulating. I was in such a hurry to get there that I forgot to bring my flashlight. It was a cloudy night, yet despite the total darkness, I didn't stumble on anything along the path. I got to the cave and recapitulated, visualizing and breathing in memories of all my karate instructors and every demonstration and tournament I had participated in. It took me most of the night, but when I had finished I felt thoroughly cleansed of the prejudices that I had inherited from my teachers as part of my training.

The following day Clara still hadn't returned, so I went to the cave a bit later than usual. On my way home, as a deliberate exercise, I tried walking on the same path I walked every day, only this time I kept my eyes shut to simulate darkness. I wanted to see if I could walk without stumbling, because it had only occurred to me later that it had been very unusual to have walked all the way to the cave the night before without tripping. As I walked in daylight but with my eyes shut, I fell several times over stumps and rocks, and badly bruised my shin.

I was on the living room floor putting bandages on my abrasions when Clara unexpectedly walked in the door. "What happened to you?" she asked with a look of surprise. "Were you and the dog fighting?"

At that very instant, Manfred ambled into the room. I was convinced that he had understood what Clara had said. He barked gruffly, as if offended. Clara stood in front of him, bowed slightly from the waist, the way an Oriental student bows to his master, and voiced a most convoluted bilingual apology. She said, "I am extremely sorry, my dear *señor,* for having spoken so lightly about your irreproachable behavior and your exquisite manners and, above all, your superior consideration that makes you *un señor entre señores, el más ilustre entre todos ellos*—a lord among lords, the most illustrious of them all."

I was absolutely bewildered. I thought Clara had lost her mind during her three days' absence. I had never heard her speaking like this before. I wanted to laugh, but her serious expression made my laugh stick in my throat.

She was about to begin another barrage of apologies when Manfred yawned, looked at her bored, turned around and left the room.

Clara sat down on the couch, her body shaking with muffled laughter. "When he's offended, the only way to get rid of him is to bore him to death with apologies," she confided.

I had hoped that Clara would tell me where she had been for the past three days. I waited for a moment in case she would bring up the subject of her absence, but she didn't. I told her that while she was gone, Manfred had come every day to visit me at the recapitulation cave. It was as if he went there from time to time to check if I was all right.

Again I wanted Clara to say something about the nature of her trip, but instead she said without surprise, "Yes, he's very solicitous, and extremely considerate of others. Therefore he expects the same treatment from them, and if he even suspects that he's not getting it, he becomes rabid. When he's in that mood, he's deadly dangerous. Remember that night he nearly snapped your head off when you called him a toad-dog?"

I wanted to change the subject. I didn't like to think of Manfred as a mad dog. Over the past months, he had become more a friend than a beast. He was such a friend that the unsettling certainty he was the only one who truly understood me had taken possession of me.

"You haven't said what happened to your legs," Clara reminded me.

I told her about my failed attempt at walking with my eyes shut. I explained that I had had no difficulty walking in the dark the night before.

She looked at the scratches and welts on my legs and patted my head as if I were Manfred. "Last night, you weren't making a project out of walking," she said. "You were determined to get to the cave, so your feet automatically took you there. This afternoon, you were consciously trying to replicate last night's walking, but you failed miserably because your mind got in the way." She thought for a moment then added, "Or perhaps you weren't listening to the voice of the spirit that could have guided you safely."

She puckered up her lips in a childish gesture of impatience when I told her that I hadn't been aware of any voices, but that sometimes in the house, I thought I heard strange whisperings, although I was convinced that that was only the wind blowing through the empty hallway.

"We've agreed that you weren't going to take anything I say literally, unless I tell you beforehand to do so," Clara reminded me sternly. "By emptying your warehouse, you are changing your inventory. Now there is room for something new, such as walking in darkness. So I thought that perhaps there might also be room for the voice of the spirit."

I was trying so hard to figure out what Clara was saying that my forehead must have been furrowed. Clara sat down in her favorite chair and patiently began to explain what she meant.

"Before you came to this house, your inventory had nothing on dogs being more than dogs. But then you met Manfred and meeting him forced you to modify that part of your inventory." She shook her hand like an Italian and said, "*Capisce?*"

"You mean Manfred is the voice of the spirit?" I asked, dumbfounded.

Clara laughed so hard that she could barely speak. "No, it's not quite what I mean. It's something more abstract," she mumbled.

She suggested I take out my mat from the closet. "Let's go to the patio and sit under the zapote tree," she said, getting some salve from a cabinet. "The twilight is the best time to listen for the voice of the spirit."

I unrolled my mat under the huge tree covered with peachlike green fruits. Clara massaged some salve into my bruised skin. It hurt fearsomely, but I tried not to wince. When she had finished, I noticed that the biggest welt had almost disappeared. She leaned back and propped her back against the thick tree trunk.

"Everything has a form," she began, "but besides the outer shape, there is an inner awareness that rules things. This silent awareness is the spirit. It is an all-encompassing force that manifests itself differently in different things. This energy communicates with us."

She told me to relax and to take deep breaths because she was going to show me how to exercise my inner hearing. "For it is with the inner ear," she said, "that one is able to discern the spirit's biddings.

"When you breathe, allow the energy to flow out of your ears," she continued.

"How do I do that?" I asked.

"When you exhale, fix your attention on the openings of your ears and use your intent and your concentration to direct the flow."

She monitored my attempts for a while, correcting me as I went along. "Exhale through your nose with your mouth closed and the tip of your tongue touching your palate," she said. "Exhale noiselessly."

After a few attempts, I could feel my ears pop and my sinuses clear. Then she instructed me to rub the palms of my hands together until they were hot and to place them over my ears with my fingertips almost touching, at the back of my head.

I did as she instructed. Clara suggested I massage my ears using a gentle circular pressure; then, with my ears still covered and my index fingers crossed over the middle fingers, I was to repeatedly tap behind each ear by snapping my index fingers in unison. As I flicked my fingers, I heard a sound like a muffled bell reverberating inside my head. I repeated the tapping eighteen times as she had instructed. When I removed my hands I noticed I could distinctly hear the faintest sounds in the surrounding vegetation, while before, everything had been undifferentiated and muffled.

"Now, with your ears clear, perhaps you'll be able to hear the voice of the spirit," Clara said. "But don't expect a shout from the treetops. What we call the voice of the spirit is more of a feeling. Or it can be an idea that suddenly pops into your head. Sometimes it can be like a longing to go somewhere vaguely familiar, or a longing to do something also vaguely familiar."

Perhaps it was the power of her suggestion that made me hear a soft murmur around me. As I began paying closer attention to it, the murmur turned into human voices speaking in the distance. I could distinguish women's crystalline laughter, and a man's voice, a rich baritone, singing. I heard the sounds as if the wind was carrying them to me in spurts. I strained to make out what the voices were saying, and the more I listened to the wind, the more elated I became. Some ebullient energy inside me made me jump up. I was so happy that I wanted to play, to dance, to run around like a child. And without realizing what I was doing, I began to sing and leap and twirl around the patio like a ballerina until I had completely exhausted myself.

When I finally came to sit down next to Clara, I was perspiring, but it was not a healthy physical sweat. It was more like the cold sweat of exhaustion. Clara too was out of breath, from laughing at my antics. I had succeeded in making an utter fool of myself, jumping and cavorting around the patio.

"I don't know what came over me," I said, at a loss for an explanation.

"Describe what happened," Clara said in a serious tone. When I refused out of embarrassment, she added, "Otherwise, I'll be forced to view you as being a bit . . . well, batty in the belfry, if you know what I mean."

I told her that I had heard the most haunting laughter and singing, and that it actually drove me to dance around.

"Do you think I'm going crazy?" I asked, concerned.

"If I were you, I wouldn't worry about it," she said. "Your cavorting was a natural reaction to hearing the voice of the spirit."

"It was not a voice; it was lots of voices," I corrected her.

"There you go again, the literal-minded Miss Perfect," she scoffed. She explained that literal-mindedness is a major item of our inventory, and that we have to be aware of it to bypass it. The voice of the spirit is an abstraction that has nothing to do with voices, and yet we may at times hear voices. She said that in my case, since I was raised a devout Catholic, my own way of readapting my inventory would be to turn the spirit into a sort of guardian angel; a kind, protective male that watches over me.

"But the spirit is not anybody's guardian," she went on. "It is an abstract force, neither good nor evil. A force that has no interest whatsoever in us, but that nevertheless responds to our power. Not to our prayers, mind you, but to our power. Remember that, the next time you feel like praying for forgiveness!"

"But isn't the spirit kind and forgiving?" I asked, alarmed.

Clara said that sooner or later I was going to discard all my preconceptions about good and evil, God and religion, and think only in terms of a completely new inventory.

"Do you mean good and evil don't exist?" I asked, armed with the ready-made barrage of logical arguments about free will and the existence of evil I had learned throughout my years of Catholic schooling.

Before I could even begin to present my case, Clara said, "This is where my companions and I differ from the established order. I've told you that for us freedom is to be free from humanness. And that includes God, good and evil, the saints, the Virgin and the Holy Ghost. We believe that a nonhuman inventory is the only possible freedom for human beings. If our warehouses are going to remain filled to capacity with the desires, feelings, ideas and objects of our human inventory, where is our freedom then? Do you see what I mean?"

I understood her, but not as clearly as I would have liked to, partly because I was still resisting the idea of relinquishing my humanness, and also because I hadn't yet recapitulated all the religious preconceptions handed down to me by the Catholic school system. I was also accustomed to never thinking of anything that didn't pertain to me directly.

As I tried to find flaws with her reasoning, Clara jolted me out of my mental speculations with a tap on my ribs. She said that she was going to show me another exercise for stopping thoughts and for feeling energy lines. Otherwise I would be doing what I had always done: be enthralled with the idea of myself.

Clara told me to sit in a cross-legged position and lean sideways as I inhaled, first to the right, then to the left, and to feel how I was being pulled by a horizontal line extending out of the opening of my ears. She said that, surprisingly, the line didn't sway with the motion of one's body but remained perfectly horizontal, and that this was one of the mysteries she and her cohorts had uncovered.

"Leaning in this manner," she explained, "moves our awareness —which normally is always directed to the front—to the side."

She ordered me to loosen my jaw muscles by chewing and swallowing saliva three times.

"What does this do?" I asked, swallowing with a gulp.

"The chewing and swallowing brings some of the energy lodged in the head down to the stomach, lessening the load on the brain," she said with a chuckle. "In your case, you should do this maneuver often."

I wanted to get up and walk around because my legs were falling asleep. But Clara demanded that I remain seated for a while longer and practice this exercise.

I leaned to both sides, trying as hard as I could to feel that elusive horizontal line, but I couldn't feel it. I did manage, however, to stop my thoughts from their usual avalanche. Perhaps an hour passed, sitting in total silence without any thoughts at all. Around us, I could hear crickets chirping and leaves rustling, but no more voices were brought by the wind. For a while I listened to Manfred's barking coming from his room at the side of the house. Then, as if moved by an unvoiced command, thoughts rushed in my mind again. I became aware of their complete absence and how peaceful total silence had been.

My restless body movements must have cued Clara, for she began to speak again. "The voice of the spirit comes from nowhere," she continued. "It comes from the depth of silence, from the realm of not-being. That voice can only be heard when we are absolutely quiet and balanced."

She explained that the two opposing forces that move us, male and female, positive and negative, light and dark, have to be kept in balance so that an opening is created in the energy that surrounds us: an opening through which our awareness can slip. It is through this opening in the energy encompassing us that the spirit manifests itself.

"Balance is what we are after," she went on. "But balance doesn't only mean an equal portion of each force. It also means that as the portions are made equal, the new, balanced combination gains momentum and begins to move by itself."

Clara searched my face in the darkness, I felt, for signs of comprehension. Finding none, she said almost cuttingly, "We are not that intelligent, are we?"

I felt my whole body tense at her remark. I told her that in all my life nobody had ever accused me of not being intelligent. My parents, my teachers had always praised me for being one of the brightest students in the class. When it came to report cards, I nearly made myself ill by studying to make sure I had better grades than my brothers.

Clara sighed and listened patiently to my lengthy reaffirmation of my intelligence. Before I had exhausted my arguments to convince her that she was wrong, she conceded, "Yes, you are intelligent, but everything you've said refers only to the world of everyday life. More than intelligent, you are studious, industrious and cunning. Wouldn't you agree?"

I had to agree with her in spite of myself, because my own reason told me that if I had truly been as intelligent as I claimed, I wouldn't have had to nearly kill myself studying.

"In order to be intelligent in my world," Clara explained, "you must be able to concentrate, to fix your attention on any concrete thing as well as on any abstract manifestation."

"What kind of abstract manifestations are you talking about, Clara?" I asked.

"An opening in the energy field around us is an abstract manifestation," she said. "But don't expect to feel it or see it in the same manner you feel and see the concrete world. Something else takes place."

Clara stressed that for us to fix our attention on any abstract manifestation, we have to merge the known with the unknown in a spontaneous amalgamation. In this way, we can engage our reason yet at the same time be indifferent to it.

Clara told me then to stand up and walk around. "Now that it's dark, try walking without looking at the ground," she said. "Not as a conscious exercise, but as a sorcery *not-doing*."

I wanted to ask her to explain what she meant by a sorcery notdoing, but I knew that if she did, I would be consciously thinking about her explanation and gauging my performance against this new concept, even if I wasn't sure what it meant. I did recall, however, that she had used the term "not-doing" before, and in spite of my reluctance to ask questions, I still tried to remember what she had told me about it. For me, knowledge, even if it was minimal and faulty, was better than none for it gave me a sense of control, whereas no knowledge left me feeling completely vulnerable.

"Not-doing is a term that comes to us from our own sorcery tradition," Clara went on, obviously aware of my need for explanations. "It refers to everything that is not included in the inventory that was forced upon us. When we engage any item of our forced inventory, we are *doing*; anything that is not part of that inventory is *not-doing*."

Any degree of relaxation I had achieved was abruptly disrupted by the statement she had just made.

"What did you mean, Clara, when you referred to your tradition as sorcery?" I demanded.

"You catch every detail when you want to, Taisha. No wonder your ears are so big," she said laughing, but didn't answer me right away.

I stared at her, waiting for her reply. Finally she said, "I wasn't going to tell you about this yet, but since it slipped out, let me just say that the art of freedom is a product of sorcerers' intent."

"What sorcerers are you talking about?"

"There have been people here in Mexico, and there still are, who are concerned with final questions. My magical family and I call them sorcerers. From them we have inherited all the ideas I am acquainting you with. You already know about the recapitulation. Not-doing is another of those ideas."

"But who are these people, Clara?"

"You'll know all there is to know about them soon," she assured me. "For now, let's just practice one of their not-doings."

She said that not-doing at this particular moment would be, for example, to force myself to trust the spirit implicitly by letting go of my calculating mind. "Don't just pretend to trust while secretly harboring doubts," Clara warned me. "Only when your positive and negative forces are in perfect accord will you be capable of either feeling or seeing the opening in the energy around you or walking with your eyes closed and be assured of success."

I took a few deep breaths and began walking, not looking at the ground but with my hands outstretched in front of me in case I bumped into things. For a while I kept stumbling, and on one occasion I tripped over a potted plant and would have fallen had Clara not grabbed my arm. Gradually I began to stumble less and less, until I had no trouble walking smoothly. It was as if my feet could see clearly everything on the patio and knew exactly where to step and where not to step.

9

One afternoon while recapitulating in the cave, I fell asleep. Upon awakening, I found a pair of beautifully polished crystals lying on the ground next to me. For a while I deliberated whether or not to touch them, for they looked quite ominous. They were about five inches long and perfectly translucent. Their tips had been fashioned into a sharp point, and they seemed to shine with a light of their own. When I saw Clara walking toward the cave, I carefully slid the crystals onto my palm and crawled out the cave to show them to her.

"Yes, they are exquisite." She nodded as if she recognized them.

"Where did they come from?" I asked.

"They were left here for you by someone who's watching you very closely," she said, putting down a bundle she was carrying.

"I didn't see anyone leave them."

"That person came while you were dozing off. I warned you not to fall asleep during your recapitulation."

"Who came while I was dozing? One of your relatives?" I asked excitedly. I laid the fragile crystals down on a pile of leaves and put on my shoes. Clara had advised me never to wear shoes while recapitulating because, by constricting the feet, they impede the circulation of energy.

"If I told you who left the crystals, it wouldn't make any sense to you or it might even frighten you," she said.

"Try me. After seeing your shadow move, I don't think anything can frighten me."

"All right, if you insist," she said, untying her bundle. "The person who's watching you is a master sorcerer, with very few equals on this earth."

"You mean a real sorcerer? One who does evil things?"

"I mean a real sorcerer, but not one who does evil things. He is a being who shapes and molds perception the way you might paint a picture with your brushes. But that doesn't mean that he is arbitrary. When he manipulates perception with his intent, his behavior is impeccable."

Clara compared him to the Chinese master painters who were said to have painted dragons so lifelike that when they put in the pupils as the finishing touch, the dragons flew right off the wall or the screen on which they had been painted. In the low tone of a meaningful disclosure, Clara said that when a consummate sorcerer is ready to leave the world, all he has to do is manipulate perception, intend a door, step through it and disappear.

The deep passion, expressed in her voice, made me uneasy. I sat down on a large flat rock and, holding the crystals, I tried to fathom who the master sorcerer might be. Since the day I arrived, I hadn't talked to anyone but Clara and Manfred, simply because there was no one else around. There wasn't any sign of the caretaker Clara had mentioned, either. I was about to remind her that she and Manfred were the only beings I had seen since my arrival, when I recalled that there had been one other person I had seen: a man who seemed to have appeared out of nowhere one morning when I was sketching some trees near the cave. He was squatting in a clearing about a hundred feet from where I was. The cold was making me shiver and also made me focus my attention on his green windbreaker. He had on beige trousers and the typical wide-brimmed straw hat of northern Mexico. I couldn't see his features because he wore his hat tilted over his face, but he seemed muscular and limber.

He was facing sideways; I could see him fold his arms across his chest. Then he turned his back to me and, to my utter amazement, brought his hands all the way around his back where he touched his fingertips. Then he stood up and walked away, disappearing into the bushes.

I quickly sketched his squatting posture, then put down my drawing pad and tried to imitate what he had done; but no matter how I stretched my arms and contorted my shoulders, I couldn't touch my fingers behind my back. I continued squatting with my arms wrapped around me. In a moment, I had stopped shivering and felt warm and comfortable in spite of the cold.

"So you've already seen him," Clara remarked when I had told her about the man.

"Is he the master sorcerer?"

Clara nodded and reached into her bundle to hand me a tamale she had brought for my meal. "He's very limber," she said. "It's nothing for him to dislodge his shoulder joints then ease them into place again. If you continue your recapitulation and store enough energy, he may teach you his art. The time you saw him, he just showed you how to fight the cold with a specific posture: squatting with the arms wrapped around the chest."

"Is that some form of yoga?"

Clara shrugged. "Perhaps your paths will cross again and he'll answer that question himself. In the meantime, I'm sure these crystals will help you to clarify things inside you."

"What exactly do you mean by that, Clara?"

"What aspect of your life were you recapitulating before you fell asleep?" she asked, ignoring my question.

I told Clara that I had been remembering how I hated to do chores at home. It seemed to take me forever to wash the dishes. What made it worse was that all the while I could see my brothers playing ball outside the kitchen window. I envied them for not having to do housework and loathed my mother for making me do it. I felt like smashing all her precious plates, but of course I couldn't.

"How do you feel now, recapitulating all this?"

"I feel like smacking all of them, my mother included. I can't bring myself to forgive her."

"Perhaps the crystals will help you rechannel your intent and your trapped energy," Clara said softly.

Driven by a strange urge, I slid the crystals between my index and middle fingers. The crystals fit comfortably, as if they were attached to my hands.

"I see you already know how to hold them," she remarked. "The master sorcerer instructed me that if I saw that you could hold them correctly by yourself, I was to show you one indispensable movement that you can do with these crystals."

"What kind of movement, Clara?"

"A movement of power," she said. "I'll explain more about its origin and purpose later. For now, let me just show you how it's done."

She told me to firmly press the crystals between my index and middle fingers. Helping me from behind, she gently made me extend my arms in front of me at the height of my shoulders, and rotated them in a counterclockwise direction. She had me begin making large circles that became increasingly smaller until the movement stopped and the crystals became two dots pointed into the distance; their extended imaginary lines converged at a spot on the horizon.

"When you make the circles, be sure to keep your palms facing each other," she corrected me. "And always begin by making large, smooth circles. This way you gather energy that you can then focus onto whatever you want to affect, regardless of whether it is an object, a thought or a feeling.

"How will pointing the crystals affect them?" I asked.

"To move the crystals and point them the way I showed you takes the energy out of things," she explained. "The effect is like defusing a bomb. This is exactly what you want to do at this stage of your training. So never under any circumstance rotate your arms in a clockwise direction while holding the crystals.

"What would happen if I rotated them in that direction?"

"You would not only make a bomb, but you would light the fuse and cause a gigantic explosion. A clockwise movement is for charging things, for gathering energy for any enterprise. We'll save that movement for a later occasion, when you are stronger."

"But isn't that what I need now, Clara? To gather energy? I feel so depleted."

"Of course you need to gather energy," she agreed, "but right now you must do it by demolishing your indulgence in absurdities. There is plenty of energy you can harness simply by not doing the things you are accustomed to, like complaining, or feeling sorry for yourself or worrying about things that can't be changed. Defusing these concerns will give you a positive, nurturing energy that will help to balance and heal you.

"On the other hand, the energy you would gather by moving the crystals in a clockwise direction is a virulent kind of energy, a devastating blast that you won't be able to withstand at the moment. So promise me that you will not under any circumstances attempt to do it."

"I promise, Clara. But it sounds rather tempting."

"The master sorcerer that gave you these crystals is watching your progress," she warned. "So you must not misuse them."

"Why is this master sorcerer interested in watching me?" There was a tinge of morbid curiosity in my question. I was uneasy, yet I felt flattered that a man would go to the trouble of observing me, even if it was from a distance.

"He has designs on you," Clara replied casually.

My alarm was instantaneous. I clenched my hand into a fist and jumped up indignantly.

"Don't be so stupid and leap to the wrong conclusion," Clara said, annoyed. "I assure you, nobody is trying to get in your pants. You really do need to recapitulate your sexual encounters in depth, Taisha, so you can get rid of your absurd suspicions."

Her tone, devoid of all feeling, and her vulgar choice of words were somehow sobering. I sat down again and mumbled an apology.

She put a finger to her lips. "We are not involved in ordinary pursuits," she assured me. "The sooner you get that straight, the better. When I speak of designs, I mean sublime designs; maneuvers for a daring spirit. In spite of what you think, you are very daring. Look at where you are now. Every day you sit for hours alone in a cave recapitulating your life away. That takes courage."

I confessed that whenever I thought how I had followed her and was now living in her house as if it were the most natural thing in the world, I became totally alarmed.

"It has always baffled me," she said, "yet I've never asked you outright what made you accompany me so willingly? I would not have done it myself."

"My parents and brothers always told me that I'm crazy," I admitted. "I suppose that must be the reason. Some strange emotion is bottled up inside me, and because of it, I always end up doing weird things."

"Such as what, for instance?" Her sparkling eyes urged me to confide in her.

I hesitated. There were dozens of things I could think of, each a traumatic event that stood out as a milestone to mark a moment when my life turned—always for the worse. I never talked about these catastrophes, although I was painfully aware of them, and during the past months of intensive recapitulating, many of them had become even more poignant and vivid.

"Sometimes I do silly things," I said, not wanting to go into detail.

"What do you mean by silly things?" Clara probed.

After more prompting on her part, I gave her an example and told her about an experience I had had not too long before in Japan, where I had gone to participate in an international karate tournament. There, in Tokyo's Budokan, I had disgraced myself in front of tens of thousands of people.

"Tens of thousands of people?" she echoed me. "Aren't you exaggerating a bit?"

"Definitely not!" I said. "The Budokan is the largest auditorium in the city and it was packed!" Recalling the incident, I felt my hands clenching and my neck tensing. I didn't want to continue. "Isn't it better just to let sleeping dogs lie?" I asked. "Besides, I've already recapitulated my karate experiences."

"It's important that you talk about your experience," Clara insisted. "Perhaps you didn't visualize it clearly enough or breathed it in thoroughly. It still seems to have a hold over you. Just look at you, you're breaking out in a nervous sweat."

To appease her, I described how my karate teacher had once let it slip that he thought women were lower than dogs. To him, women had no place in the world of karate and especially not in tournaments. That time, in the Budokan, he wanted only his male students to go on stage to perform. I told him that I hadn't come all the way to Japan just to sit on the sidelines and watch the all male team competing. He warned me to be more respectful, but instead I became so angry that I did something disastrous.

"What exactly did you do?" Clara inquired.

I told her that I became so enraged, I climbed onto the central platform, grabbed the gong from the master of ceremonies, struck it myself and formally announced my name and the name of the karate routine I was going to demonstrate.

"And did they give you a grand applause?" Clara asked, grinning.

"I flubbed it," I said, near tears. "In the middle of the long sequence of movements, my mind went blank. I forgot what came next. All I saw was a sea of faces staring at me in disapproval. Somehow, I managed to get through the rest of the form and left the stage in a state of shock.

"To take matters into my own hands, and to disrupt the program the way I did, was bad enough, but to forget my form in front of thousands of spectators was the ultimate insult to the Karate Federation. I brought shame to myself, my teachers and I suppose to women in general."

"What happened afterward?" Clara asked, trying to suppress a chuckle.

"I was expelled from the school, there was talk of revoking my black belt and I never practiced karate again."

Clara burst out laughing. I, on the other hand, was so moved by my shameful experience that I began to weep. On top of that, I was doubly embarrassed for having revealed it to Clara.

Clara shook my shoulders to jolt me. "Do the sweeping breath," she said. "Breathe in now."

I moved my head from right to left, breathing in the energy that was still hopelessly caught in the exhibition hall. As I brought my head back to the right again, I exhaled all the embarrassment and self-pity that had enveloped me. I moved my head repeatedly, doing one sweeping breath after the other until all my emotional turmoil was released. Then I moved my head from right to left and back again without breathing, thereby severing all ties with that particular moment of my past. When I had finished, Clara scanned my body then nodded.

"You are vulnerable because you feel important," she declared, handing me an embroidered handkerchief to blow my nose. "All that shame was caused by your misguided sense of personal worth. Then by bungling your performance, as you were bound to do, you added more insult to your already injured pride."

Clara was silent for a moment, giving me time to collect myself. "Why did you quit practicing karate?" she finally asked.

"I just got tired of it and all the hypocrisy," I snapped.

She shook her head. "No. You quit because no one paid any attention to you after your misadventure, and you didn't get the recognition you thought you deserved."

In all honesty, I had to admit Clara was right. I had believed I deserved recognition. Every time I committed one of my wild, impulsive acts, it had been to boost my self-image or to compete with someone in order to prove that I was better. A sense of sadness and dejection enveloped me. I knew that in spite of all my breathing and recapitulating, there was no hope for me.

"Your inventory is changing very naturally and harmoniously," Clara said, tapping my head lightly. "Don't worry so much. Just concentrate on recapitulating, and everything else will take care of itself."

"Perhaps I need to see a therapist," I said. "Although, isn't recapitulating a kind of psychotherapy?"

"Not at all," Clara disagreed. "The people who first devised the recapitulation lived hundreds, if not thousands, of years ago. So you certainly shouldn't think of this ancient renewing process in terms of modern psychoanalysis."

"Why not?" I said. "You have to admit that going back to your childhood memories and the emphasis on the sexual act sounds like what psychoanalysts are interested in, especially the ones with a Freudian twist."

Clara was adamant. She stressed that the recapitulation is a magical act in which intent and the breath play indispensable roles.

"Breathing gathers energy and makes it circulate," she explained. "It is then guided by the preestablished intent of the recapitulation, which is to free ourselves from our biological and social ties.

"The intent of the recapitulation is a gift bestowed on us by those ancient seers who devised this method and passed it on to their descendants," Clara continued. "Each person performing it has to add his or her own intent to it, but that intent is merely the desire or need to do the recapitulation. The intent of its end result, which is total freedom, was established by those seers of ancient times. And because it was set up independently from us, it is an invaluable gift."

Clara explained that the recapitulation reveals to us a crucial facet of our being: the fact that for an instant, just before we plunge into any act, we are capable of accurately assessing its outcome, our chances, motives and expectations. This knowledge is never to our convenience or satisfaction, so we immediately suppress it.

"What do you mean by that, Clara?"

"I mean that you, for example, knew for a split second that it would be a deadly mistake to jump onto the stage of the auditorium and disrupt the performance, but you immediately suppressed that certainty for various reasons. You also knew, for a moment, that you had stopped practicing karate because you felt offended at not being praised or given recognition. But you instantly covered up that knowledge with another, more self-enhancing explanation: that of being fed up with the hypocrisy of others."

Clara said that this moment of direct knowing was called "the seer" by the people who first formulated the recapitulation, because it allows us to directly see into things with unclouded eyes. Yet in spite of the clarity and accuracy of the seer's assessments, we never pay attention to it or give the seer a chance to make itself heard. Through a continual suppression, we stifle its growth and prevent it from developing its full potential.

"In the end, the seer inside us is filled with bitterness and hatred," Clara went on. "The ancient men of wisdom who invented the recapitulation believed that since we never stop subduing the seer, it finally destroys us. But they also assured us that by means of the recapitulation, we can allow the seer to grow and unfold as it was meant to do."

"I never realized what the recapitulation was really about," I said.

"The purpose of the recapitulation is to grant the seer the freedom to see," Clara reminded me. "By giving it range, we can deliberately turn the seer into a force that is both mysterious and effective, a force that will eventually guide us to freedom instead of killing us.

"This is the reason why I always insist that you tell me what you find out through your recapitulation," Clara said. "You must bring the seer to the surface and give it the chance to speak and tell what it sees."

I had no problem understanding or agreeing with her. I knew perfectly well that there is something inside me that always knows what's what. I also knew that I suppress its capacity to advise, because what it tells me is usually contrary to what I expect or want to hear.

A momentary insight I had to share with Clara was that the only time I ever invoked the seer's guidance was when I looked at the southern horizon and deliberately sought its help, although I had never been able to explain why I did that.

"Someday all that will be explained to you," she promised. But from the way she was grinning, I deduced that she didn't want to say any more about it.

Clara suggested I return to the cave for a few more hours, then come to the house and take a nap before dinner. "I'll send Manfred to fetch you," she offered.

I declined. I couldn't have possibly gone back into the cave that day. I was too exhausted. Revealing to Clara my embarrassing moments, and having to fend off her personal attacks, had left me emotionally drained. For an instant, my attention was caught by light being reflected on one of the crystals. Focusing my attention on the crystals calmed me. I asked Clara if she knew the reason why the master sorcerer had given me the crystals. She replied that he hadn't actually given them to me, but that he had, rather, recovered them on my behalf.

"He found them in a cave in the mountains. Someone must have left them there ages ago," she said gruffly.

Her impatient tone made me think that she didn't want to talk about the master sorcerer either, so I asked her instead, "What else do you know about these crystals?"

I held one up to the sunlight to see its translucence.

"The use of crystals was the domain of sorcerers of ancient Mexico," Clara explained. "They are weapons used to destroy an enemy."

Hearing that gave me such a jolt I nearly dropped one of the crystals. I tried to give them to Clara to hold, wanting nothing more to do with them, but Clara refused to take them.

"Once you hold crystals like these in your hands, you can't pass them on," she reprimanded me. "It's not right; in fact, it's dangerous. These crystals must be treated with infinite care. They are a gift of power."

"I'm sorry," I said, "I didn't mean any disrespect, I just became frightened when you said they were used as weapons."

"Formerly, they were, but not today," she clarified. "We've lost the knowledge of how to turn them into weapons."

"Was there such a knowledge in ancient Mexico?"

"There certainly was! It's part of our tradition," she declared. "Just as in China, where there were ancient beliefs so farfetched that they have turned into legends, here in Mexico we also have our share of beliefs and legends."

"But how is it that nobody knows very much about what went on in ancient Mexico, while everybody is aware of the beliefs and practices of ancient China?"

"Here in Mexico, there were two cultures that collided head on: the Spaniards and the Indians," Clara explained. "We know everything about ancient Spain but not ancient Mexico simply because the Spaniards were the victors and tried to obliterate Indian traditions. But in spite of their systematic and relentless efforts, they didn't succeed completely."

"What were the practices associated with the crystals?" I asked.

"It is believed that sorcerers of ancient times used to hold the mental image of their enemy while in a state of intense and pinpointed concentration, a unique state that is nearly impossible to attain and certainly impossible to describe. In such condition of mental and physical awareness, they would manipulate that image until they found its center of energy."

"What did those sorcerers do with their enemy's image?" I asked, driven by morbid curiosity.

"They used to look for an opening, localized usually in the area of the heart, like a tiny vortex around which energy circulates. As soon as they found it, they would point at it with their dartlike crystals."

At the mention of pointing with the crystals at the image of an enemy, I began to shiver. In spite of my discomfort, I felt compelled to ask Clara what happened to the person whose image was being manipulated by the sorcerers.

"Perhaps his body withered," she offered. "Or maybe the person met with an accident. It is believed that those sorcerers themselves never knew exactly what would happen, although if their intent and power were strong enough, they would be assured of success in destroying their enemy."

More than ever I wanted to put the crystals down, but in the light of what Clara had said, I didn't dare profane them. I wondered why on earth anyone would want to give them to me.

"Magical weapons were terribly important at one time," Clara continued. "Weapons such as crystals became an extension of the sorcerer's own body. They were filled with energy that could be channeled and projected outward across time and space."

Clara said that the ultimate weapon, however, is not a crystal dart, a sword or even a gun, but the human body. For it can be turned into an instrument capable of gathering, storing and directing energy.

"We can regard the body either as a biological organism or as a source of power," Clara explained. "It all depends on the state of the inventory in our warehouse; the body can be hard and rigid or soft and pliant. If our warehouse is empty, the body itself is empty, and energy from infinity can flow through it."

Clara reiterated that in order to empty ourselves, we have to sink into a state of profound recapitulation and let energy flow through us unimpeded. Only in quiescence, she stressed, can we give the seer in us full reign or can the impersonal energy of the universe turn into the very personal force of intent.

"When we have emptied ourselves sufficiently of our obsolete and encumbering inventory," she went on, "energy comes to us and gathers itself naturally; when enough of it coalesces, it turns into power. Anything can announce its presence: a loud noise, a soft voice, a thought that isn't yours, an unexpected surge of vigor or well-being."

Clara emphasized that in the final analysis, it made no difference whether power descends on us in a state of wakefulness or in dreams;

it is equally valid in both cases, the latter being, however, more elusive and potent.

"What we experience in wakefulness, in terms of power, should be put into practice in dreams," she continued, "and whatever power we experience in dreams should be used while we are awake. What really counts is being aware, regardless of whether one is awake or asleep." She repeated it, peering at me, "What counts is being aware."

Clara was silent for a moment, then she told me something I considered to be completely irrational. She said, "Being aware of time, for example, can make a man's life span several hundred years."

"That's absurd," I said. "How can a man live that long?"

"Being aware of time is a special state of awareness that prevents us from aging quickly and dying in a few decades," Clara explained. "There is a belief, handed down from the ancient sorcerers, that if we would be able to use our bodies as weapons—or, put in modern terms, if we would empty our warehouses—we would be able to slip out of the world to roam elsewhere."

"Where would we go?" I asked.

Clara looked at me in surprise, as if I ought to know the answer. "To the realm of not-being, to the shadows' world," she replied.

"It is believed that once our warehouse is empty, we would become so light that we could soar through the void and nothing would hinder our flight. Then we could return to this world youthful and re-newed."

I shifted on the uncomfortable rock numbing my tailbone. "But this is just a belief, isn't it, Clara?" I asked. "A legend handed down from ancient time."

"At this moment, it is just a belief," she acknowledged. "But moments, like all things, are known to change. Nowadays, more than ever, man needs to renew himself and experience emptiness and freedom."

For a moment I wondered what it would be like to be as vaporous as a cloud and float up into the air, with nothing to bar my coming and going. Then I mentally returned to earth again and felt obliged to say, "All this talk about being aware of time and passing into the shadows' world, Clara, is impossible for me to accept or to understand. It isn't part of my tradition or, as you put it, it isn't part of the inventory in my warehouse."

"No, it isn't," Clara agreed. "This is sorcery!"

"Do you mean to say that sorcery still exists and is practiced today?" I asked.

Clara suddenly got up and grabbed her bundle. "Don't ask me any more about it," she said flatly. "Later on, you'll find out whatever you want to know, but from someone who is more capable of explaining these things than I."

10

Clara sat on the rattan armchair at the edge of the patio, brushing her shiny black hair. Then she arranged it with her fingers until everything was in place. When she had finished grooming herself, she brought her left palm to her forehead and stroked it in a circular fashion. Then she moved her hand over the top of her head and down the back of her neck, after which she flicked her wrists and fingers in the air. She repeated this stroking and flicking sequence several more times.

I was fascinated watching her movements. There was nothing careless or haphazard about them. She performed them with intense concentration, as if she were engaged in a most important task.

"What are you doing?" I asked, breaking the silence. "Are you giving yourself some sort of a facial massage?"

Clara glanced over at me, sitting on the matching armchair, imitating her movements. "This circular stroking prevents wrinkles from forming on the forehead," she said. "It may appear like a facial massage to you, but it isn't. These are sorcery passes, movements of the hand that are designed to gather energy for a specific purpose."

"What specific purpose is that?" I asked, flicking my wrists the way she had done.

"The purpose of these sorcery passes is to keep one looking youthful by preventing wrinkles from forming," she said. "The purpose has been decided beforehand, not by me or by you, but by power itself."

I had to admit that whatever Clara was doing certainly worked. She had lovely skin that set off her green eyes and dark hair. I had always believed that her youthful appearance was the consequence of her Indian genes. I never suspected that she deliberately cultivated it by means of specific movements.

"Whenever energy gathers, as in the case of these sorcery passes, we call it power," Clara continued. "Remember this, Taisha, power is when energy gathers, either by itself or under someone's command. You're going to hear much more about power, not just from me but from the others, too. They're expected back any time now."

Although Clara constantly referred to her relatives, I had by now given up all hope of ever meeting them. Her reference to power was another matter. I had never understood what she meant by power.

"I'm going to show you some sorcery passes that you must perform every day of your life from now on," she announced.

I let out a sigh of complaint. There were so many things that she told me to do every day of my life; the breathing, the recapitulation, the kung fu exercises, the long walks. If I lined up back to back everything she told me to do, there wouldn't be enough hours in the day for even half of them.

"For heaven's sake, don't take me so literally," Clara said, seeing my pained expression. "I'm cramming all I can into your peewee brain because I want you to know about all these things. Knowledge gathers energy, therefore knowledge is power. To make sorcery work, we must know what we're doing when we intend the result—not the purpose, mind you, but the result of the sorcery act. If we intended the purpose of our sorcery actions, we would be creating sorcery, and you and I don't have that much power."

"I don't think I'm following you, Clara," I said, moving my chair closer. "For what don't we have enough power?"

"I mean that even between the two of us, we can't gather the overwhelming energy it would take to create a new purpose. But individually, we can certainly gather enough energy to intend the result of these sorcery passes: no wrinkles for us. This is all we can do, since their purpose—to keep us young and youthful looking—is already set."

"Is it like the recapitulation whose end result had been intended beforehand by the ancient sorcerers?" I asked.

"Exactly," Clara said. "The intent of all sorcery acts has already been set. All we have to do is hook our awareness to it."

She moved her chair across from me so that our knees were barely touching. Then she vigorously rubbed each thumb on the palm of the opposite hand and placed them on the bridge of her nose. She moved them outward with light, even strokes over her eyebrows to the temples.

"This pass will keep furrows from developing between your eyebrows," she explained.

After quickly rubbing together her index fingers, like two sticks starting a fire, she brought them vertically to each side of her nose and gently moved them sideways over her cheeks several times.

"That's to clear the sinus cavities," she said, deliberately constricting her nasal passages. "Instead of picking your nose, do this movement."

I didn't appreciate her reference to my picking my nose, but I tried the movement and it did clear my sinuses as she had said.

"The next one is to keep the cheeks from sagging," she said.

She briskly rubbed her palms together, and with long, firm strokes, she slid them up each cheek to her temples. She repeated this movement six or seven times, always using slow, even, upward strokes.

I noticed her face was flushed, but she didn't stop yet. She placed the inner edge of her hand, with her thumb folded over her palm, above her upper lip and rubbed back and forth with a vigorous sawlike motion.

She explained that the spot where the nose and upper lip join, when briskly rubbed, stimulates energy to flow in mild, even bursts. But if greater bursts of energy were needed, they could be obtained by pricking the point at the center of the upper gum, underneath the upper lip and below the nose septum.

"If you get drowsy in the cave while recapitulating, rub this point briskly and it will temporarily revive you," she said.

I rubbed my upper lip and felt my nose and ears clear. I also experienced a slight numbing sensation on the roof of my palate. It lasted for a few seconds but took my breath away. It left me with the sensation that I was just about to uncover something that was veiled.

Next, Clara moved her index fingers sideways under her chin, again using a quick back-and-forth sawlike motion. She explained that stimulating the point under the chin produces a calm alertness. She added that we can also activate this point by resting the chin on a low table while sitting on the floor.

Following her suggestion, I moved my cushion to the floor and sat on it, and rested my chin on a wooden crate that was just level with my face. By leaning forward, I put a slight pressure on that chin point Clara had indicated. After a few moments, I felt my body settle down; a prickling sensation rose up my back, entered my head and my breathing became deeper and more rhythmic.

"Another way to awake the center under the chin," Clara continued, "is by lying on the stomach with the hands in fists, one on top of the other, under the chin."

She recommended that when doing the exercise with the fists, we should tense them to create pressure under the chin and then relax them to release the pressure. Tensing and relaxing the fists, she said, produces a pulsating movement that sends small bursts of energy to a vital center directly connected with the base of the tongue. She stressed that this exercise should be done cautiously, otherwise one might develop a sore throat.

I went to sit in the rattan chair again.

"This group of sorcery passes I've shown you," Clara continued, "must be practiced daily until they cease to be massagelike movements and become what they really are: sorcery passes. Watch me!" she ordered.

I saw her repeat the movements she had shown me, except that this time she was making her fingers and hands dance. Her hands seemed to penetrate deeply into the skin of her face; at other times, they passed over it lightly as if gliding on the skin's surface, moving so rapidly that they seemed to disappear. Watching her exquisite movements kept me mesmerized.

"This way of stroking was never in your inventory," she laughed when she had finished. "This is sorcery. It requires an intent different from the intent of the daily world. With all the tension that rises to the face, we certainly need a different intent if we are going to relax the muscles and tone the centers located there."

Clara said that all our emotions leave traces on our face, more than on any other part of our body. Therefore we have to release accumulated stress using the sorcery passes and their accompanying intent.

She stared at me for a moment and remarked, "I see from the tension in your face that you've been pondering over your recapitulation. Be sure to do your passes before going to bed tonight to remove those creases in your forehead."

I admitted that I had been worrying about my recapitulation.

"The problem is that you are spending too much time in the cave," Clara said with a wink. "I don't want you turning into a bat-girl. By now I think you've gathered enough energy to start learning other things."

She jumped out of the chair as if released by a spring. It was so incongruous to see such a powerful woman jumping up so agilely that I had to laugh. I myself got up more slowly, as if I were twice her size.

She looked at me and shook her head. "You're too stiff," she noted. "You need to do some special physical exercise to open your vital centers."

We went to the rack where the coats and boots were kept, outside the back door of the house. She handed me a wide-rimmed straw hat and led me to a clearing a short distance from the kitchen annex.

The sun shone brightly; it was an unusually warm day. Clara told me to put on the hat. She pointed to an area surrounded by a wire fence where the ground had been dug in furrows and lined with small plants in neat parallel rows.

"Who cleared the ground and put in all the plants?" I asked, surprised, for I hadn't noticed Clara working there. "It looks like a huge project. Did you do it yourself?"

"No. Someone else came and did it for me."

"But when? I've been here every day and didn't see anyone."

"That's no mystery," Clara said. "The person who worked on this vegetable garden came when you were at the cave."

Her explanation didn't satisfy me. The garden was so well organized that it looked like it had taken more than one person to lay it out. Before I could probe her further, Clara announced, "From now on you'll take care of this garden. Consider it your new task."

I tried not to show my disappointment at being given yet another task that required daily attention. I had thought that by physical exercise Clara had meant that we were going to practice a new martial art form, preferably one using a classical Chinese weapon like the broadsword or long pole. Seeing my downcast look, Clara assured me that cultivating a garden would be good for me. It would give me the physical activity and exposure to the sun that I needed for health and well-being. She also pointed out that for more than six months I had been doing nothing but focusing on incidents of my life. Caring for something outside of myself would prevent me from becoming more self-centered. It shocked me to realize that half a year had passed. To me, it seemed like only yesterday that I had come to Clara's house and my life had changed so drastically that nothing remained the same.

"Most people only know how to care for themselves," Clara said, jolting me out of my train of thought. "Although not very well at that. Because of this overwhelming emphasis, the self becomes distorted, full of outrageous demands."

We walked to a wooden gate, the entrance to the garden.

"Working in this garden will give you a special kind of energy that you can't get from recapitulating or breathing or practicing kung fu," Clara said.

"What kind of energy is that?"

"The energy of the earth," she replied, her eyes as green as the new plants. "It complements the energy of the sun. Perhaps you'll feel it entering through your hands as you work the soil. Or it may start to flow into your legs as you squat on the ground."

I had never worked in a garden before and wasn't sure what to do. I asked her to outline my duties. She peered at me for a moment as if wondering if she had picked the right person for the task.

"The ground is still moist from yesterday's rain," she said, stooping down to touch the soil. "But when it's dry, you'll have to carry buckets of water from the stream. Or if you're very clever, you can devise an irrigation system."

"I might just do that," I said confidently. "I'll construct an electric water pump, like one I saw in a house in the country, and connect it to the dynamo. Then I wouldn't have to lug the buckets of water up the hill."

"It doesn't matter how you do it as long as the plants get watered. Also, you'll have to feed the plants every two weeks from that pile of compost at the end of the garden. And make sure that all the weeds are pulled. Around here they spread like wildfire. And keep the gate closed so no rabbits can get in."

"No problem," I assured her half-heartedly.

"Good. You can begin now."

She pointed to a bucket and told me to fill it with compost and mix it into the soil around each plant. When I returned with the bucket full of what I hoped wasn't night soil, she gave me a digging tool with which to loosen the earth. For a while she watched as I worked, cautioning me not to dig too closely to the tender plants.

As I concentrated on the task, I felt a sense of well-being and a strange peace surround me. The dirt was cool and soft in my fingers. For the first time since I had been in Clara's house, I felt truly at ease, safe and protected.

"The energy of the earth is nurturing," she remarked, as if noticing my change of mood. "You're empty enough from your recapitulation that some of it is already creeping into your body. You feel at ease because you know that the earth is the mother of all things." She swept her hands over the rows of plants. "Everything comes from the earth. The earth sustains and nourishes us; and when we die, our bodies return to it." She paused for a moment then added, "Unless of course, we succeed in the great crossing."

"You mean there's a chance that we won't die?" I asked. "Really, Clara, aren't you exaggerating?"

"We all have a chance for freedom," she said softly, "but it's up to each one of us to seize it and turn it into an actuality."

She explained that by storing energy, we can dissolve our preconceptions about the world and the body, thus making room in our warehouse for other possibilities. A chance not to die was one of these possibilities. She said that the best explanation of this extravagant alternative was offered by the sages of ancient China. They claimed that it is feasible for one's personal awareness, or *te*, to link up knowingly with the all-encompassing awareness or Tao. Then when death comes, one's individual awareness is not dispersed, as in ordinary dying, but expands and unites with the greater whole.

She added that the recapitulation in the setting of a cocoonlike cave had enabled me to gather and store energy. Now I needed to use that energy to strengthen my bond with the abstract force called the spirit.

"That's why you have to cultivate the garden and absorb its energy and also the energy of the sun," she said. "The sun bestows its energy on the earth and causes things to grow. If you allow the sun's light to enter your body, your energy, too, will flourish."

Clara told me to wash my hands in a bucket of water and to sit on a log by a clearing outside the fenced garden, for she was going to show me how to begin to direct my attention to the sun. She said that I should always wear a wide-rimmed hat in order to shield my head and face. She also warned me never to do any of the breathing passes she was about to show me for more than a few minutes at a time.

"Why are they called breathing passes?" I asked.

"Because the preset intent of these passes is to pass energy from the breath to the area where we place our attention. It could be an organ in our body or an energy channel or even a thought or a memory, as in the case of the recapitulation. What is important is that energy is transmitted, thus fulfilling the intent established beforehand; the result is sheer magic, because it appears as if it had sprung out of nowhere. That's why we call these movements and breaths sorcery passes."

Clara instructed me to face the sun with my eyes closed, then take a deep breath through my mouth and pull the sun's warmth and light into my stomach. I had to hold it there for as long as I could, then swallow and, finally, exhale any air that was left.

"Pretend you're a sunflower," she teased. "Always keep your face toward the sun when you breathe. The light of the sun charges the breath with power. So be sure to take big gulps of air and completely fill your lungs. Do this three times."

She explained that in this exercise, the energy of the sun automatically spreads throughout the entire body. But we could deliberately send the sun's healing rays to any area by touching the spot where we want the energy to go, or simply by using the mind to direct energy to it.

"Actually, when you have practiced this breath long enough, you don't need to use your hands anymore," she went on. "You can just visualize the sun's rays oozing directly into a specific part of your body."

She suggested that I do the same three breaths, but this time breathing through my nose and visualizing the light flowing down into my back, thus energizing the channels along my spine. That way, the sun's rays would flood my entire body.

"If you want to bypass breathing through the nose or mouth altogether," Clara said, "you can breathe directly with your stomach or your chest or your back. You can even bring the energy up the body through the soles of your feet."

She told me to concentrate on my lower abdomen, on the spot just below my navel, and breathe in a relaxed fashion until I could feel a bond forming between my body and the sun.

As I inhaled under her guidance, I could feel the inside of my stomach becoming warmer and filled with light. After a while, Clara told me to practice breathing with other areas. She touched the spot on my forehead between my eyes. When I concentrated my attention there, my head became flushed with a yellow glow. Clara recommended that I absorb as much of the sun's vitality as I could by holding my breath, then rolling my eyes in a clockwise direction before exhaling. I did as she instructed and the yellow glow intensified.

"Now stand up and try breathing with your back," she said, and helped me to take off my jacket.

I turned my back to the sun and tried to place my attention on the various centers she pointed out with a touch. One was between my shoulder blades, another was at the nape of my neck. As I breathed, visualizing the sun on my back, I felt a warmth move up and down my spine, then rush to my head. I became so dizzy that I nearly lost my balance.

"That's enough for today," Clara said, handing me my jacket.

I sat down feeling giddy, as if I were happily drunk.

"The light of the sun is pure power," Clara said. "After all, it's the most intensely gathered energy there is."

She said that an invisible line of energy flows out directly from the top of the head, upward to the realm of not-being. Or it can flow from the realm of not-being down into us via an opening at the very center of the top of the head.

"If you like, you can call it the life line that links us to a greater awareness," she said. "The sun, if used properly, charges this line and causes it to spring into action. That's why the crown of the head must always be protected."

Clara said that before we returned to the house, she was going to show me another powerful sorcery pass, one involving a series of body movements. She said that it had to be executed in one single motion, with strength, precision and grace, but without straining.

"I can't urge you enough to practice all the passes I've shown you," she said. "They are the indispensable companions of the recapitulation. This one did wonders for me. Watch me closely. See if you can see my double."

"Your what?" I said, panicking. I was afraid I would miss something crucial, or not know what to make of it even if I saw it.

"Watch my double," she repeated, enunciating the words carefully. "It's like a double exposure. You have enough energy to intend with me the result of this sorcery pass."

"But tell me again, Clara, what is the result?"

"The double. The ethereal body. The counterpart of the physical body, which by now you must know, or at least suspect, is not merely a projection of the mind."

She moved to an area of level ground and stood with her feet together and her arms at her sides.

"Clara, wait. I'm sure I don't have enough energy to see what you're referring to, because I can't even understand it conceptually."

"It doesn't matter if you understand it conceptually. Just watch closely, maybe I have enough power for both of us to intend my double."

In the most agile movement I had yet seen her perform, she brought her arms over her head, with her palms touching in a gesture of prayer. Then she arched backward, forming an elegant bow with her arms stretched out behind her, almost to the ground. She flipped her body laterally to the left so that instantly she ended up bending forward almost touching the ground. And before I could even open my mouth in surprise, she had flipped back and her body was gracefully arched backward.

She flipped back and forth two more times, as if to give me a chance to see her inconceivably fast and graceful movements, or perhaps a chance to see her double. At one point in her movement, I saw her as a hazy shape, just as if she were a life-size photograph that had been double exposed. For a fraction of an instant, there were two Claras moving, one a millisecond behind the other.

I was completely perplexed by what I saw, which when I thought about it, I could explain as being an optical illusion created by her speed. But at a bodily level, I knew that my eyes had seen something inconceivable; I had had enough energy to suspend my common sense expectations and allow another possibility to enter in.

Clara stopped her exquisite acrobatics and came and stood beside me, not even out of breath. She explained that this sorcery pass enables the body to unite with its double in the realm of not-being, whose entrance hovers above the head and slightly behind it.

"By bending backward with the arms outstretched, we create a bridge," Clara said. "And since the body and the double are like two ends of a rainbow, we can intend them to join."

"Is there any specific time when I should practice this pass?" I asked.

"This is a sorcery pass of the twilight," she said. "But you have to have lots of energy and be extremely calm in order to do it. The twilight helps you to become calm and gives you an added boost of energy. That's why the end of the day is the best time to practice it."

"Should I try it now?" I asked. When she looked at me doubtfully, I assured her that I had studied gymnastics as a child and was eager to try it.

"The question is not whether you have studied gymnastics as a child, but how calm you are now," Clara replied.

I said that I was as calm as I could be. Clara laughed in disbelief, but told me to go ahead and try it. She would watch over me to make sure I didn't break anything by twisting too forcefully.

I planted my feet on the ground, bent my knees and began slowly executing my best backbend. But when I got past a certain point, gravity took over and I fell clumsily to the ground.

"You're the farthest thing from being calm," Clara concluded amiably as she helped me up. "What's bothering you, Taisha?"

Rather than revealing to Clara what was on my mind, I asked if I could try the movement again. But the second time, I had more trouble than before. I was sure my mental and emotional concerns had made me lose my balance. I knew that the demands of the self, as Clara had said, were really outrageous; they took all my attention. I saw no solution except to confess to Clara what was on my mind. I told her what bothered me the most was that I seemed to have reached a standstill in my recapitulation.

"What is causing it?" Clara asked.

I admitted that it had to do with my family. "I know now without a doubt that they dislike me," I said sadly. "Not that I didn't suspect it all along, because I did, and I used to get into rages about it. But now that I've reviewed my past, I can't get angry the way I used to. So I don't know what to do."

Clara eyed me critically, moving her head backward to size me up. "What is there to do?" she asked. "You've done the work and found out that they disliked you. That's good! I don't see the problem."

Her cavalier tone annoyed me. I expected if not sympathy, at least understanding and an intelligent comment.

"The problem," I said emphatically, on the verge of tears, "is that I'm stuck. I know that I need to go deeper than I have, but I can't. All I can think is that they disliked me, whereas I loved them."

"Wait, wait. Didn't you tell me that you hated them? I distinctly remember . . ."

"Yes, I did say that, but at the time I said it I didn't know what I was saying. I really loved them, my brothers too. Later I learned to despise them, but that was much later. Not as a child. As a child I wanted them to pay attention to me and play with me."

"I think I see what you mean," Clara said, nodding. "Let's sit down and discuss this."

We sat down again on the log.

"As I see it, your problem stems from a promise you made as a child. You did make a promise as a child, didn't you, Taisha?" she asked, looking at me squarely in the eye.

"I don't recall making any promises," I said sincerely.

In a friendly tone, Clara suggested that perhaps I didn't recall because I had been very young when I made it, or because it was more of a feeling than a promise actually stated in so many words. Clara explained that as children, we often make vows and then become bound by those vows, even though we can no longer remember making them.

"Such impulsive pledges can cost us our freedom," Clara said. "Sometimes we are bound by preposterous childish devotion or pledges of undying, eternal love."

She said that there are moments in everyone's life, especially in early childhood, when we have wanted something so badly that we automatically fixed our total intent on it, which, once fixed, remains in place until we fulfill our desire. She elaborated by saying that vows, oaths and promises bind our intent, so that from then on, our actions, feelings and thoughts are consistently directed toward fulfilling or maintaining those commitments regardless of whether or not we remember having made them.

She advised me to review, during the recapitulation, all the promises I had ever made in my lifetime, especially the ones made in haste or ignorance or faulty judgement. For unless I deliberately retrieved my intent from them, it would never rise freely to be expressed in the present.

I tried to think about what she was saying, but my mind was a mass of confusion. Suddenly I remembered a scene from my very early childhood. I must have been six. I wanted to be cuddled by my mother but she pushed me away, saying that I was too old for cuddling, and told me to go clean up my room. Yet the youngest of my brothers, who was four years older than I and my mother's favorite, was always cuddled by her. I swore then that I would never love or get close to any of them ever again. And from that day on, I seemed to have kept my promise by always remaining estranged from them.

"If it's true that they didn't love you," Clara said, "it was your fate not to be loved by your family. Accept it! Besides, what possible difference could it make now whether they loved you or not?"

It still made a difference, but I didn't tell Clara that.

"I too had a problem very much like yours," Clara went on. "I had always been aware of being a friendless, fat, miserable girl, but through recapitulating I found out that my mother had deliberately fattened me up since the day I was born. She reasoned that a fat, homely girl would never leave home, and she wanted me there as her servant for life."

I was horrified. This was the first time Clara had revealed anything about her past to me.

"I went to my teacher, who was definitely the greatest teacher one can ever have, for advice about this problem," she went on. "And he said to me, 'Clara, I feel for you, but you are wasting your time because then was then: now is now. And now there is only time for freedom.'

"You see, I sincerely felt that my mother had ruined me for life; I was fat and couldn't stop eating. It took me a long time to get the meaning of, 'Then was then: now is now. And now there is only time for freedom.'"

Clara was silent for a moment as if to let the impact of her words settle on me.

"You have only time to fight for freedom, Taisha," she said, giving me a nudge. "Now is now."

11

It was growing dark and I was becoming more and more apprehensive about finishing my task. Clara had asked me to rake the leaves in the clearing behind the house, and also to carry some rocks from the stream and make a border on each side of the path leading from the vegetable garden to the back of the patio. I had raked the leaves and was hurriedly lining up the river rocks along the path when Clara came out of the house to check on my progress.

"You're setting the rocks any which way," she said glancing at the path. "And you haven't raked up the leaves yet. What have you been doing all afternoon, daydreaming again?"

To my dismay, an untimely gust of wind had scattered the neat piles I had made before I had had a chance to put the leaves in a basket.

"The path looks pretty good to me," I said, on the defensive. "As for the leaves, well, can I help it if the wind made a mess of them?"

"When aiming for the perfect form, 'pretty good' isn't good enough," Clara interrupted. "You ought to know by now that the outward form of anything we do is really an expression of our inner state."

I told her that I didn't see how arranging heavy rocks could be anything but hard work.

"That's because you do everything just to get by," she retorted. She walked over to the row of rocks I had lined up and shook her head. "These rocks look as if you've dropped them without considering their proper placement."

"It's getting dark and I was running out of time," I explained. I was in no mood for a lengthy discussion on aesthetics or composition. Besides, I felt I already knew more than Clara about the subject of composition from my art classes.

"Placing rocks is just like practicing kung fu," Clara said. "It's how we do things that matters, not how fast or how much we get done."

I shook my wrists to relax my cramped fingers. "Do you mean that carrying rocks is a part of martial arts training?" I asked, surprised.

"What do you think kung fu is?" she countered.

I suspected she was asking me a trick question, so I deliberated for a moment to find the right answer. "It's a set of martial arts fighting techniques," I said confidently.

Clara shook her head. "Leave it to Taisha to come up with a pragmatic reply," she said with a laugh.

She sat down on one of the wicker chairs at the edge of the patio, from where we had a good view of the path. I slumped into the chair next to her. When I had settled comfortably, propping my feet on the rim of a huge ceramic pot, Clara began to explain that the term "kung fu" is derived from the juxtaposition of two Chinese characters, one meaning "work done over a period of time," the other signifying "man." When these two characters are combined, the term refers to man's endeavor to perfect himself through constant effort. She contended that whether we practice formal exercises, arrange rocks or rake leaves, we always express our inner state through our actions.

"Therefore, to perfect our acts is to perfect ourselves," Clara said. "This is the true meaning of kung fu."

"But still, I don't see the connection between garden work and practicing kung fu," I said.

"Then let me spell it out for you," Clara replied with a tone of exaggerated patience. "I asked you to carry the rocks from the stream so that walking up the hilly trail with the added weight would develop your internal strength. We are not just interested in building muscles, but rather in cultivating internal energy. Also, all the breathing passes I have taught you thus far, and that you should be practicing daily, are designed to increase your internal strength."

She made me feel guilty. From the way she had looked at me when she said I should be practicing the breathing exercises daily, I knew that she was aware I wasn't doing them religiously.

"What you have been learning here with me might be referred to in China as internal kung fu, or *nei kung*," Clara continued. "Internal kung fu uses controlled breathing and the circulation of energy to strengthen the body and augment one's health; whereas external martial arts, like the karate forms you learned from your Japanese teachers and some of the forms I showed you, focus on building muscles and quick body responses in which energy is released and is directed away from us."

Clara said that internal kung fu was practiced by monks in China long before they developed the external or hard styles of fighting that are popularly known as kung fu today.

"But understand this," Clara continued. "Regardless of whether you are learning martial arts or the discipline I have been teaching you, the goal of your training is to perfect your inner being so that it can transcend its outer form in order to accomplish the abstract flight."

A feeling of dejection swept over me like a somber cloud. I felt my old mood of failure taking hold of me. Even if I did do the breathing passes as Clara recommended, I felt I would never be able to succeed in whatever it was that she wanted. I didn't even know what the great crossing meant, let alone conceive of it as a pragmatic possibility.

"You've been very patient all these months," Clara said, patting me on the back as if sensing my need for encouragement. "You've never really pressed me about my constant insinuations that I am teaching you sorcery as a formal discipline."

I saw the perfect opportunity to ask something that had been on my mind from the first time she used the word. "Why do you call this formal discipline sorcery?" I asked.

Clara peered at me. The expression on her face was seriousness itself. "It's hard to say. My reluctance to discuss it is because I don't want to misname it and scare you away," she replied. "I think now is the time to talk about it, though. But first let me tell you something more about the people of ancient Mexico."

Clara leaned toward me and in a low voice said that the people of pre–Hispanic Mexico were very similar in many respects to the ancient Chinese. Perhaps because they both may have had the same origins, they shared a similar world view. The ancient Indians of Mexico, however, had a slight advantage, she said, because the world in which they lived was in transition. This made them extremely eclectic and curious about every facet of existence. They wanted to understand the universe, life, death and the range of human possibilities in terms of awareness and perception. Their great drive to know led them to develop practices that enabled them to arrive at unimaginable levels of awareness. They made detailed descriptions of their practices and mapped the realms that those practices unveiled. This tradition they handed down from generation to generation, always shrouding it in secrecy.

Nearly out of breath with excitement or perhaps wonderment, Clara ended her discussion of those ancient Indians by saying that they were indeed sorcerers. She stared at me wide-eyed; in the twilight, her pupils were enormous. She confided that her foremost teacher, a Mexican Indian, possessed a complete knowledge of those ancient practices, and he had taught them to her.

"Are you teaching me those practices, Clara?" I asked, matching her excitement. "You said the crystals were used as weapons by the ancient sorcerers, and the sorcery passes were empowered with their intent, and the recapitulation also was devised in ancient times. Does that mean that I am learning sorcery?"

"That is partially true," Clara said. "But for the time being, it's better not to focus on the fact that these practices are sorcery."

"Why not?"

"Because we are interested in something beyond the aberrant, esoteric rituals and incantations of those sorcerers of ancient times. You see, we believe that their bizarre practices and obsessive search for power resulted only in a greater enhancement of the self. This is a dead-end road, for it never leads to total freedom. Which is what we ourselves are after. The danger is that one can easily become swayed by the mood of those sorcerers."

"I wouldn't become swayed," I assured her.

"I really can't tell you any more at the moment," she said, exasperated. "But you'll find out more as you go along."

I felt betrayed and protested vehemently. I accused her of deliberately toying with my mind and feelings by keeping me dangling with bits of information that piqued my curiosity, and with promises that all was going to be clarified at some unspecified future date.

Clara completely ignored my protests. It was as if I hadn't said a word. She stood up, walked over to the pile of rocks and picked one up as if it were made of Styrofoam. After deliberating for a moment as to which side to turn up, she set the rock down on the edge of the path. She then arranged two more rocks the size of footballs on either side of it. When she was satisfied with their placement, she stepped back to study the effect. I had to admit that the garden path, the smooth gray rocks she had set and the jagged green leaves of the plants made a most harmonious composition.

"It is the grace with which you manipulate things that matters," Clara reminded me as she picked up another rock. "Your inner state is reflected in the way you move, talk, eat or place rocks. It doesn't matter what you do, as long as you gather energy with your actions and transform it into power."

For a while, Clara gazed at the path as if considering where to place the next rock she held in her hands. When she found a suitable spot, she gently set it down and gave it an affectionate pat.

"As an artist you should know that the rocks have to be put where they are in balance," she said, "not where it is the easiest for you to drop them. Of course, if you were imbued with power, you could drop them any which way and the result would be beauty itself. To understand this is the real purpose of the exercise of placing rocks."

From the tone of her voice, and the ugly, erratic arrangement of my rocks, I realized I had failed again at my task. I felt acutely dejected.

"Clara, I'm not an artist," I confessed. "I'm merely a student. In fact, I'm an ex-student. I dropped out of art school a year ago. I like to make believe that I'm an artist, but that's about all. I'm really nothing."

"We are all nothing," Clara reminded me.

"I know, but you are a mysterious, powerful nothing, while I'm a meager, stupid, petty nothing. I can't even set down a bunch of dumb rocks. There's no . . ."

Clara clamped her hand over my mouth. "Don't say another word," she warned. "I'm telling you again. Be careful of what you say out loud in this house. Especially in the twilight!"

It was almost dark then and everything was absolutely still to the point of being eerie. The birds were silent. Everything had quieted down; even the wind, which had been so annoying earlier while I was trying to rake the leaves, had settled.

"It's the time of no shadows," Clara whispered. "Let's sit under this tree in the dark and find out if you can summon the shadows' world."

"Wait a moment, Clara," I said in a loud whisper that bordered on a screech. "What are you going to do to me?" Waves of nervousness were cramping my stomach, and in spite of the cold, my forehead was perspiring.

Clara asked me then outright if I had been practicing the breaths and the sorcery passes she had taught me. I wanted more than anything to tell her that I had, yet that would have been a lie. In truth, I had practiced them minimally, just so I wouldn't forget them, because recapitulating took all of my available energy and left me no time for anything else. At night I was too tired to do anything, so I just went to bed.

"You haven't been doing them regularly or you wouldn't be in this sorry state now," Clara said, leaning closer. "You're trembling like a leaf. There's one secret to the breathing and the passes I've taught you that makes them invaluable."

"What is that?" I stammered.

Clara tapped me on the head. "They have to be practiced every day or else they're worthless. You wouldn't think of going without eating or drinking water, would you? The exercises I've taught you are even more important than food and water."

She had made her point. I silently vowed that every night before going to bed I would do them, and again upon awakening in the morning before going to the cave.

"The human body has an extra energy system that comes into play when we are under stress," Clara explained. "And stress happens any time we do anything to excess. Like being overly concerned with yourself and your performance, as you are now. That's why one of the fundamental precepts of the art of freedom is to avoid excesses."

She said that the movements she was teaching me, whether she called them breaths or sorcery passes, were important because they operate directly on the reserve system, and that the reason they can be called indispensable passes is because they allow added energy to pass into and through our reserve pathways. Then when we are summoned to action, instead of becoming depleted from stress, we become stronger and have surplus energy for extraordinary tasks.

"Now, before we summon the shadows' world, I'll show you two more indispensable sorcery passes which combine breathing and movements," she went on. "Do them every day and you not only won't get tired or sick, but you'll have plenty of surplus energy for your intending."

"For my what?"

"Your intending," Clara repeated. "For intending the result of anything you do. Remember?"

She held my shoulders and twisted me around so that I was facing north.

"This movement is particularly important for you, Taisha, because your lungs are weakened from excessive weeping," she said. "A lifetime of feeling sorry for yourself certainly has taken its toll on your lungs."

Her statement jolted me to attention. I watched her bend her knees and ankles and assume a martial art posture called the "straight horse," because it simulates the sitting position of a rider mounted on a horse, with his legs a shoulders' width apart and slightly bowed. The index finger of her left hand was pointed down, while her other fingers were curled at the second joint. As she began to inhale, she gently but forcefully turned her head to the right as far as she could, and rotated her left arm at the shoulder joint over her head in a full circle all the way to the back, ending up with the heel of her left palm resting on her tailbone. Simultaneously she brought her right arm around her waist to her back and placed her right fist over the back of her left hand, wedging it against her bent left wrist.

Using her right fist, she pushed up her left arm along her spinal column, her left elbow bent akimbo, and finished her inhalation. She held her breath for a count of seven, then released the tension on her left arm, lowered it to her tailbone again and rotated it at the shoulder joint straight overhead to the front, ending up with the heel of her left palm resting on her pubis. Simultaneously she brought her right arm around her waist to the front and placed that fist on the back of her left hand, and pushed the left arm up her abdomen as she finished exhaling.

"Do this movement once with your left arm and again with your right one," she said. "That way you will balance your two sides."

To demonstrate, she repeated the same movements, alternating arms, and this time turning her head to the left.

"Now you try it, Taisha," she said, stepping aside to give me room to circle my arm backward.

I replicated her movements. As I swung my left arm back, I felt a painful tension along the underside of my extended arm, running all the way from my finger to my armpit.

"Relax and let the breath's energy flow through your arm and out of the tip of your index finger," she said. "Keep it extended and the other fingers curved. That way you'll release any blockage of energy along the pathways in your arm."

The pain grew even more acute as I pushed my bent arm upward along my back. Clara noticed my pinched expression.

"Don't push too hard," she warned, "or you'll strain your tendons. And round your shoulders a bit more as you push."

After performing the movement with my right arm, I felt a burning in my thigh muscles from standing with my knees and ankles bent. Even though I stood in the same position every day while practicing kung fu, my legs seemed to vibrate as if an electric current were running through them. Clara suggested I stand up and shake my legs a few times to release the tension.

Clara emphasized that in this sorcery pass, rotating and pushing the arms up in conjunction with breathing moves energy to the organs in the chest and vitalizes them. It massages deep, underlying centers that rarely are activated. Turning the head massages the glands in the neck and also opens energy passageways to the back of the head. She explained that if awakened and nourished by the energy from breathing, these centers could unravel mysteries beyond anything we can imagine.

"For the next sorcery pass," Clara said, "stand with your feet together and look straight ahead as if you were facing a door that you are going to open."

Clara told me to raise my hands to eye level and to curl my fingers as if I were placing them inside the recessed handles of sliding doors that open in the middle.

"What you are going to open is a crack in the energy lines of the world," she explained. "Imagine those lines as rigid vertical cords that make a screen in front of you. Now grab a bunch of the fibers and pull them apart with all your might. Pull them apart until the opening is big enough for you to step through."

She told me that once I had made that hole, I should step forward with my left leg and then quickly, using my left foot as a pivot, rotate one hundred and eighty degrees counterclockwise to face the direction from which I had come. By my turning in this manner, the energy lines I had pushed apart would wrap around me.

To return, she said, I had to open the lines again by pulling them apart the same way I had done before, then step out with the right foot and quickly turn one hundred and eighty degrees clockwise as soon as I had taken the step. In this fashion, I would have unwrapped myself and would again be facing the direction in which I had begun the sorcery pass.

"This is one of the most powerful and mysterious of all the sorcery passes," Clara cautioned. "With it we can open doors to different worlds, provided of course that we have stored a surplus of internal energy and are able to realize the intent of the pass."

Her serious tone and expression made me ill at ease. I didn't know what to expect if I succeeded in opening that invisible door. In a brusque tone, she then gave me some final instructions.

"When you step in," she said, "your body has to feel rooted, heavy, full of tension. But once you are inside and have turned around, you should feel light and airy, as if you were floating upward. Exhale sharply as you lunge forward through the opening, then inhale slowly and deeply, filling your lungs completely with the energy from behind that screen."

I practiced the pass several times as Clara looked on. But it was as if I were only going through the outward motions; I couldn't feel the energy fibers forming the screen that Clara was talking about.

"You're not pulling the door open hard enough," Clara corrected me. "Use your internal energy, not just your arm muscles. Expel the stale air and pull in your stomach as you lunge forward. Once inside, breathe as many times as you can, but be on the alert. Don't stay longer than you need to."

I mustered up all my strength and grabbed the air. Clara stood behind me, held my forearms and gave them a tremendous pull sideways. Instantly I felt as if some sliding doors had opened. Exhaling sharply, I lunged through it, or rather Clara had given me a shove from behind, pushing me forward. I remembered to turn around and breathe deeply, but for a moment I worried that I wouldn't know when to come out. Clara sensed this and told me when to stop breathing and when to step out.

"As you practice this sorcery pass by yourself," Clara said, "you'll learn to do it perfectly. But be careful. All sorts of things can happen once you go through that opening. Remember, you have to be cautious and at the same time bold."

"How will I know which is which?" I asked.

Clara shrugged. "For a while, you won't. Unfortunately, prudence comes to us only after we've gotten blasted."

She added that cautiousness without cowardice is hinged on our ability to control our internal energy and to divert it into the reserve channels, so that it is available to us when we need it for extraordinary actions.

"With enough internal energy, anything can be accomplished," Clara said, "but we need to store and refine it. So let's both practice some of the sorcery passes you've learned and see if you can be cautious without being cowardly and summon up the shadows' world."

I experienced a surge of energy that began as small circles in my stomach. At first I thought it was fear, but my body didn't feel frightened. It was as if an impersonal force, void of desires or sentiment, was stirring inside me, moving from the inside out. As it ascended, my upper back jerked involuntarily.

Clara moved to the center of the patio; I followed her. She began doing some of the sorcery passes, slowing herself down to allow me to follow her.

"Close your eyes," she whispered. "When your eyes are closed, it's easier to use energy lines that are already there to keep your balance."

I shut my eyes and started to move in unison with Clara. I had no trouble following her cues for changing positions, yet I had difficulty in keeping my balance. I knew it was because I was trying too hard to do the movements correctly. It was like the time I had tried walking with my eyes shut, and kept stumbling because I desperately wanted to succeed. But gradually my desire to excel diminished and my body became more limber and subtle. As we kept on moving, I became so relaxed that I felt I had no bones or joints. If I raised my arms overhead, it seemed I could stretch them all the way to the tops of the trees. If I bent my knees and lowered my weight, a surge of energy rushed downward through my feet. I felt I had grown roots. Lines were extending from the soles of my feet deep into the earth, giving me an unprecedented stability. Gradually the boundary between my body and its surroundings dissolved. With every pass I did, my body seemed to melt and merge with the darkness until it began to move and breathe all by itself.

I could hear Clara breathing beside me, performing the same passes. With my eyes closed, I sensed her shape and postures. At one point, the strangest thing yet happened. I felt a light turning on inside my forehead. But as I looked up, I became aware that the light wasn't really inside me at all. It came from the top of the trees, as if a huge panel of electric lights had been turned on at night, illuminating an outdoor stadium. I had no trouble seeing Clara and everything on the patio, and what was around it.

The light had the strangest hue; I couldn't decide if it was rose-tinted, pinkish or peach, or like pale terra-cotta. In places, it seemed to change its glare depending on where I looked.

"Don't move your head," Clara said, peering at me curiously. "And continue keeping your eyes closed. Just concentrate on your breathing."

I didn't know why she had said to continue keeping my eyes closed when she saw that my eyes were wide open. I was trying to determine the coloration of the light, for it seemed to change with every movement of my head. And its intensity fluctuated depending on how hard I stared at it. I became so involved with the glow around me that I lost the rhythm of the breaths. Then as suddenly as the light had turned on, it switched off again and I was left in total darkness.

"Let's go into the kitchen and heat up some stew," Clara said, nudging me.

I hesitated. I felt disoriented, out of place. My body was so heavy I thought I must be sitting down.

"You can open your eyes now," Clara said.

I never remembered having had such a difficult time opening my eyes as I did at that moment. It seemed to take me forever to do it, for just as I got them open, they would droop shut again. This opening and closing seemed to go on for a long time, until I felt Clara shaking my shoulders.

"Taisha, open your eyes!" she commanded. "Don't you dare pass out on me. Do you hear?"

I shook my head to clear it and my eyes popped open. They had been closed all the time. It was pitch black, but there was enough moonlight coming through the foliage to see Clara's silhouette. We were sitting under the tree on the two rattan armchairs in the patio.

"How did I get here?" I asked dazed.

"You walked over here and sat down," Clara said matter-of-factly.

"But what happened? A moment ago it was light. I could see everything clearly."

"What happened is that you entered into the shadows' world," Clara said with a congratulatory tone. "I could tell by the rhythm of your breathing that you had gone there. But I didn't want to frighten you then by asking you to look at your shadow. If you had looked, you would have known that . . ."

I instantly understood what Clara was intimating. "There were no shadows," I gasped. "There was light but nothing had a shadow."

Clara nodded. "Tonight you've found out something of real value, Taisha. In the worlds outside this one, there are no shadows!"

12

After more than eight months of faithfully practicing the recapitulation, I was able to do it all day long without fretting or becoming distracted. One day, while I was visualizing the buildings where I attended the last year of high school, the classrooms, the teachers I had, I became so involved in going down the aisles and seeing where my classmates sat, that I ended up talking to myself.

"If you talk to yourself, you can't breathe correctly," I heard a man's voice say.

I was so startled that I bumped my head against the cave wall. I opened my eyes. The image of the classroom faded as I turned to look at the cave's entrance. Outlined against the opening, I saw a man squatting. I immediately knew that he was the master sorcerer, the man I had once seen in the hills. He wore the same green windbreaker and trousers, but this time I could see his profile; he had a prominent nose and a mildly sloping forehead.

"Don't stare," I heard the master sorcerer say. His voice was low, and rumbled like a stream over gravel. "If you want to learn more about breathing, remain very quiet and regain your equilibrium."

I continued taking deep breaths until his presence no longer frightened me and I became, instead, relieved that I was finally making his acquaintance. He sat down cross-legged at the cave entrance, and leaned in the way Clara always did.

"Your movements are too jerky," he said in a low murmur. "Breathe like this."

He inhaled deeply as he gently turned his head to the left. Then he exhaled thoroughly as he smoothly turned his head to the right. Finally, he moved his head from his right shoulder to the left and back to the right again without breathing, then back to the center. I copied his movements inhaling and exhaling as completely as I could.

"That's more like it," he said. "When exhaling, throw out all the thoughts and feelings you are reviewing. And don't just turn your head with your neck muscles. Guide it with the invisible energy lines from your midsection. Enticing those lines to come out is one of the accomplishments of the recapitulation."

He explained that just below the navel was a key center of power, and that all body movements, including one's breathing, had to engage this point of energy. He suggested I synchronize the rhythm of my breathing with the turning of my head, so that together they would entice the invisible energy lines from my abdomen to extend outward into infinity.

"Are those lines a part of my body or am I to imagine them?" I asked.

He shifted his position on the ground before answering. "Those invisible lines are a part of your soft body, your double," he said. "The more energy you entice out by manipulating those lines, the stronger your double will become."

"What I wanted to know was, are they real or just imaginary?"

"When perception expands, nothing is real and nothing is imaginary," he said. "There is only perception. Close your eyes and find out for yourself."

I didn't want to shut my eyes; I wanted to see what he was doing in case he made any sudden moves. But my body grew limp and heavy and my eyes began to droop shut in spite of my efforts to keep them open.

"What is the double?" I managed to ask before I drifted off into a drowsy stupor.

"That's a good question," he said. "It means that a part of you is still alert and listening."

I sensed him take a deep breath and inflate his chest. "The physical body is a covering, a container, if you will," he said after slowly exhaling. "By concentrating on your breathing, you can make the solid body dissolve so that only the soft, ethereal part is left."

He corrected himself, saying that it is not that the physical body dissolves, but that by changing the fixation of our awareness we begin to realize that it was never solid in the first place. This realization is the exact reversal of what took place as we matured. As infants, we were totally aware of our double; as we grew up, we learned to put increasingly more emphasis on the physical side and less on our ethereal being. As adults we are completely unaware that our soft side exists.

"The soft body is a mass of energy," he explained. "We are aware only of its hard, outer casing. We become aware of our ethereal side by allowing our intent to shift back to it."

He stressed that our physical body is inseparably linked with its ethereal counterpart, but that link has been clouded over by our thoughts and feelings, which are focused exclusively on our physical body. In order to shift our awareness from our hard appearance to its fluid counterpart, we must first dissolve the barrier that separates the two aspects of our being.

I wanted to ask him how that could be done, but I found it impossible to voice my thoughts.

"The recapitulation helps to dissolve our preconceptions," he said, answering me, "but it takes skill and concentration to reach the double. Right now you are using your ethereal part to some extent. You are half asleep but some part of you is awake and alert. It can hear me and sense my presence."

He warned me that there is considerable danger involved in releasing the energy that is locked within us, because the double is vulnerable and can easily become injured in the process of shifting our awareness to it.

"You can inadvertently create an opening in the ethereal net and lose vast amounts of energy," he cautioned me, "precious energy that is necessary to maintain a certain level of clarity and control in your life."

"What is that ethereal net?" I mumbled, as if talking in my sleep.

"The ethereal net is the luminosity that surrounds the physical body," he explained. "This web of energy gets torn to shreds during daily living. Huge portions of it become lost or entwined in other people's bands of energy. If a person loses too much vital force, he becomes ill or dies."

His voice had lulled me so thoroughly that I was breathing from my stomach as if in a deep sleep. I had slumped against the side of the cave, but I didn't feel its hard walls.

"Breathing works on both the physical and ethereal levels," he explained, "it repairs any damage in the ethereal net and keeps it strong and pliant."

I wanted to ask something about my recapitulation, but I couldn't formulate the words; they seemed so far away. Without my asking, he again supplied the answer.

"This is what you've been doing for the past months with your recapitulation. You are retrieving filaments of your energy from your ethereal net that have become lost or entangled as a result of your daily living. By focusing on that interaction, you are pulling back all that you dispersed over twenty years and in thousands of places."

I wanted to ask him whether the double had a specific shape or color. I was thinking of auras. He didn't reply. After a long silence, I forced my eyes open and saw that I was alone in the cave. I strained to peer through the dark to the light at the opening where I had first seen him outlined against the entrance. I suspected that he had slipped away and was waiting nearby for me to crawl out. As I looked, a bright patch of light appeared, hovering about two feet from me. The illusion startled me, yet at the same time it enthralled me so that I couldn't turn my eyes away. I had the irrational certainty that the light was alive, conscious and aware that my attention was focused on it. Suddenly the glowing sphere expanded to twice its size and became encircled by an intense purple ring.

Frightened, I squeezed my eyes shut, hoping that the light would disappear so I could leave the cave without passing through it. My heart pounded loudly in my chest and I was perspiring. My throat was dry and constricted. With great effort, I slowed down my breathing. When I opened my eyes, the light had vanished. I was tempted to explain away the entire event as a dream, for I often dozed off during my recapitulation. But the memory of the master sorcerer and what he had said was so vivid that I was almost certain it all had been real.

Cautiously I crawled out of the cave, put on my shoes and took the shortcut to the house. Clara was standing by the living room door as if she were expecting me. Panting, I blurted out that I had either just spoken with the master sorcerer or I had had a most vivid dream about him. She smiled and pointed with a subtle movement of her chin to the armchair. My mouth fell open. There he was, the same man who had been with me in the cave only minutes before, except that he was wearing different clothes. Now he had on a gray cardigan sweater, a sports shirt and tailored trousers.

He was much older than I thought, but also much more vital. It was impossible for me to tell his age; he may have been forty or seventy. He appeared to be extremely strong, and neither lean nor corpulent. He was dark, and looked Indian. He had a prominent nose, a strong mouth, a square chin and sparkling black eyes, which had the same intense look I had seen in the cave. All of these features were accentuated by a thick, lustrous crop of white hair. The remarkable effect of his hair was that it didn't turn him into an old man, as white hair ordinarily does. I remembered how old my father looked when his hair turned silver and how he covered it with dyes and hats; all to no avail because old age was in his face, in his hands, in his whole body.

"Taisha, let me introduce you. This is Mr. John Michael Abelar," Clara said to me.

The man politely stood up and extended his hand. "Very glad to meet you, Taisha," he said in perfect English as he gave my hand a strong shake.

I wanted to ask him what he was doing here and how he had changed his clothes so fast and whether or not he had really been in the cave. A dozen other questions ran through my mind, but I was too shocked and intimidated to ask any of them. I pretended to be calm and not nearly as unsettled as I was. I commented on how well he spoke English, and how clearly he had expressed himself when he talked to me in the cave.

"It's nice of you to say so," he said, with a disarming smile. "But I ought to speak English well. I'm a Yaqui Indian. I was born in Arizona."

"Do you live in Mexico, Mr. Abelar?" I asked awkwardly.

"Yes. I live in this house," he replied. "I live here with Clara."

He looked at her in a way I could only describe as sheer affection. I didn't know what to say. I felt self-conscious, embarrassed for some unknown reason.

"We are not man and wife," Clara said, as if to put me at ease, and at that both of them broke out laughing.

Rather than lightening things up, their laughter made me feel even more self-conscious. Then to my dismay, I recognized the emotion I was feeling: it was pure jealousy. In an inexplicable possessive impulse, I felt that he belonged to me. I tried to conceal my embarrassment by quickly asking some trivial questions. "Have you lived in Mexico for a long time?"

"Yes, I have," he said.

"Are you planning to return to the United States?"

He fixed me with his fierce eyes, then smiled and said in a charming way, "Those details are unimportant, Taisha. Why don't you ask me about the topic we discussed in the cave? Was anything unclear?"

At Clara's suggestion, we sat down; Clara and I on the sofa, and Mr. Abelar on the winged chair. I asked him if he would tell me more about the double. The concept interested me enormously.

"Some persons are masters of the double," he began. "They can not only focus their awareness on it but also spur it into action. The majority of us, however, are scarcely aware that our ethereal side exists."

"What does the double do?" I asked.

"Anything we want it to do; it can jump over trees or fly through the air or become large or small or take the shape of an animal. Or it can become aware of people's thoughts or become a thought and hurl itself in an instant over vast distances."

"It can even act like the self," Clara interjected, looking straight at me. "If you know how to use it, you can appear in front of someone and talk to him as if you were really there."

Mr. Abelar nodded. "In the cave, you were able to perceive my presence with your double. And it was only when your reason woke up that you doubted that your experience had been real."

"I'm still doubting," I said. "Were you really there?"

"Of course," he replied with a wink, "as much as I'm really here."

For a moment I wondered if I was dreaming now. But my reason assured me I couldn't possibly be. Just to make certain, I touched the table; it felt solid.

"How did you do it?" I asked, leaning back on the sofa.

Mr. Abelar was silent for a moment as if choosing his words. "I let go of my physical body and allowed my double to take over," he said. "If our awareness is tied to the double, we are not affected by the laws of the physical world; rather, we are governed by ethereal forces. But as long as awareness is tied to the physical body, our movements are limited by gravity and other constraints."

I still didn't understand if that meant that he could be in two places at once. He seemed to sense my confusion.

"Clara tells me you are interested in martial arts," Mr. Abelar said. "The difference between the average person and an expert in kung fu is that the latter has learned to control his soft body."

"My karate teachers used to tell me the same," I said. "They insisted that martial arts trained the soft side of the body, but I could never understand what they meant."

"What they probably meant was that when an expert practitioner attacks, he strikes the vulnerable points of his enemy's soft body," he said. "It's not the power of the physical body that is destructive, but the opening he makes in his enemy's ethereal body. He can hurl into that opening a force that rips through the ethereal net to cause major damage. A person may receive what seems at the time only a gentle hit, but hours or perhaps days later, the person may die from that blow."

"That's right," Clara agreed. "Don't be fooled by the outward movements or by what you see. It's what you don't see that counts."

From my karate teachers, I had often heard similar tales. When I had asked them how those feats were performed, they couldn't give me a coherent explanation. I had thought at the time that it was because my teachers were Japanese and couldn't express such intricacies of thought in English. Now Mr. Abelar was explaining something similar, and although his command of English was perfect, I still couldn't understand what he meant by the soft body or the double, and how to tap its mysterious powers.

I wondered if Mr. Abelar was a martial artist, but before I could ask him, he continued. "True martial artists, as Clara has described them to me from her training in China, are interested in mastering the control of their soft body," he said. "And the double is controlled not by our intellect but by our intent. There is no way to think about it or to understand it rationally. It has to be felt, for it is linked to some luminous lines of energy crisscrossing the universe." He touched his head and pointed upward. "For instance, a line of energy that extends up from the top of the head gives the double its purpose and direction. That line suspends and pulls the double whichever way it wants to go. If it wants to go up, all it has to do is to intend up. If it wants to sink into the ground, it just intends down. It's that simple."

At that point Clara asked me whether I remembered what she had told me in the garden the day we were doing the sun breathing exercises: how the crown of the head always needed to be protected. I told her I remembered very clearly—ever since then, I was afraid to leave the house without a hat. She then asked me if I was able to follow what Mr. Abelar was saying. I assured her that I was having no trouble understanding him even though I didn't comprehend the concepts. Paradoxically, I found what he was saying incomprehensible, yet also familiar and believable. Clara nodded and said that was so because he was directly addressing a part of me that was not quite rational and had the ability to grasp things directly, especially if a sorcerer spoke to it directly.

What Clara said was true. There was something about Mr. Abelar that put me even more at ease than Clara did. It wasn't his polite and soft-spoken manner, but something in the intensity of his eyes that forced me to listen and follow his explanations, despite the fact that rationally they seemed nonsensical. I heard myself asking questions as if I knew what I was talking about.

"Would I be able to reach my soft body some day?" I asked Mr. Abelar.

"The question is, Taisha, do you want to reach it?"

For a moment I hesitated. From my recapitulation, I had found out that I'm complacent and cowardly, and that my first reaction is to avoid anything that is too troublesome or frightening. But I also had an intense curiosity to experience things out of the ordinary, and as Clara had once told me, I possessed a certain reckless daring.

"I'm very curious about the double," I said, "so I definitely do want to get to it."

"At any price?"

"Anything short of selling my body," I said lamely.

At that they both burst out laughing so hard I thought they were going to convulse right there on the floor. I hadn't meant to be facetious either, for in truth, I wasn't certain what secret plans they had for me. As if sensing my train of thought, Mr. Abelar said that it was time to acquaint me with certain premises of their world. He straightened up and assumed a serious demeanor.

"The involvements of men and women are no longer our concern," he said. "That means we are not interested in man's morality, immorality or even amorality. All our energy is poured into exploring new paths."

"Can you give me an example of a new path, Mr. Abelar?" I asked.

"Certainly. How about the task you are engaged in, the recapitulation? The reason I'm talking to you now is because by means of it you have stored enough energy to break certain physical boundaries. You have perceived, if only for an instant, inconceivable things that are not part of your normal inventory, to use Clara's terminology."

"My normal inventory is pretty weird," I warned him. "I'm beginning to see from recapitulating the past that I was crazy. In fact, I still am crazy. The proof of it is that I'm here and I can't tell if I'm awake or dreaming."

At that they both burst out laughing again, as if they were watching a comedy program and the comedian had just dropped his punchline.

"I know very well how crazy you are," Mr. Abelar said with a note of finality. "But not because you're here with us. More than crazy, you're indulgent. Nevertheless, since the day you came here, contrary to what you might think, you haven't indulged as much as you had in the past. So in all fairness, I'd say that some of the things

Clara tells me you did, like entering what we call the shadows' world, wasn't indulging or being crazy. It was a new path; something unnamed and unimaginable from the point of view of the normal world."

A long silence followed that made me fidget uneasily. I wanted to say something to break the spell, but I couldn't think of anything. What made it worse was that Mr. Abelar kept giving me sideward glances. Then he whispered something to Clara and they both laughed softly, which irritated me no end because there was no doubt in my mind they were laughing at me.

"Maybe I'd better go to my room," I said, getting up.

"Sit down, we're not through yet," Clara said.

"You have no idea how much we appreciate your being here with us," Mr. Abelar said all of a sudden. "We find you humorous because you are so eccentric. Soon you will meet another member of our party, someone who is as eccentric as you are, but much older. Seeing you reminds us of her when she was young. That's why we laugh. Please forgive us."

I hated being laughed at, but his apology was so genuine that I accepted it. Mr. Abelar resumed talking about the double as if nothing else had been said.

"As we let go of our ideas of the physical body, little by little or all at once," he said, "awareness begins to shift to our soft side. In order to facilitate this shift, our physical side must remain absolutely still, suspended as if it were in deep sleep. The difficulty lies in convincing our physical body to cooperate, for it rarely wants to give up its control."

"How do I let go of my physical body, then?" I asked.

"You fool it," he said. "You let your body feel as if it were sound asleep; you deliberately quiet it by removing your awareness from it. When your body and mind are at rest, your double wakes up and takes over."

"I don't think I follow you," I said.

"Don't play the devil's advocate with us, Taisha," Clara snapped. "You must have done this in the cave. In order for you to have perceived the *nagual*, you must have used your double. You were asleep and yet aware at the same time."

What caught my attention in Clara's statement was the way she had spoken of Mr. Abelar. She had called him "the nagual." I asked her what that word meant.

"John Michael Abelar is the nagual," she said proudly. "He is my guide; the source of my life and well-being. He is not my man by any stretch of the imagination and yet he's the love of my life. When he is all that for you, he'll then be the nagual for you also. In the meantime, he's Mr. Abelar, or even John Michael."

Mr. Abelar laughed, as if Clara had said those things only in jest, but Clara held my gaze long enough to let me know that she had meant every word of it.

The silence that followed was finally broken by Mr. Abelar. "In order to activate the soft body, you have to first open certain body centers that function like gates," he continued. "When all the gates are open, your double can emerge from its protective covering. Otherwise, it will forever remain encased within its outer shell."

He asked Clara to get a mat out of the closet. He spread it on the floor and told me to lie face up with my arms at my sides.

"What are you going to do to me?" I asked suspiciously.

"Not what you think," he snapped.

Clara giggled. "Taisha is really wary of men," she explained to Mr. Abelar.

"It hasn't done her any good," he replied, making me feel utterly self-conscious. Then, facing me, he explained he was going to show me a simple method for shifting awareness from my physical body to the ethereal net that surrounds it.

"Lie down and close your eyes, but don't fall asleep," he ordered.

Embarrassed, I did as he asked, feeling strangely vulnerable lying down in front of them. He knelt down beside me and spoke in a soft voice. "Imagine lines extending out from the sides of your body, beginning at your feet," he said.

"What if I can't imagine them?"

"If you want to, you certainly can," he said. "Use all your strength to intend the lines into existence."

He elaborated that it was not really imagining those lines that was involved, but rather a mysterious act of pulling them out from the side of the body, beginning at the toes and continuing all the way up to the top of the head. He said that I should also feel lines emanating from the soles of my feet going downward and wrapping around the length of my body to the back of my head; and also other lines that radiated from my forehead upward and downward, along the front of my body to my feet, thus forming a net or a cocoon of luminous energy.

"Practice this until you can let go of your physical body and can place your attention at will on your luminous net," he said. "Eventually, you'll be able to cast and sustain that net with a single thought."

I tried to relax. I found his voice soothing. It had a mesmerizing quality; at times it seemed to come from very close, and at other times from far away. He cautioned me that if there was a place in my body where the net felt tight or where it was difficult to stretch the lines out or where the lines recoiled, that was the place where my body was weak or injured.

"You can heal those parts by allowing the double to spread out the ethereal net," he said.

"How do I do that?"

"By intending it, but not with your thoughts," he said. "Intend it with your intent, which is the layer beneath your thoughts. Listen carefully, look for it beneath the thoughts, away from them. Intent is so far away from thoughts that we can't talk about it; we can't even feel it. But we can certainly use it."

I couldn't even conceive how to intend with my intent. Mr. Abelar said that I shouldn't have too much difficulty casting my net, because for the past few months, unknowingly, I had been projecting such ethereal lines during my recapitulation. He suggested that I begin by concentrating on my breathing. After what seemed to be hours, during which time I must have dozed off once or twice, I could eventually feel an intense tingling heat in my feet and head. The heat expanded to form a ring encircling my body lengthwise.

In a soft voice, Mr. Abelar reminded me that I should focus my attention on the heat outside my body and try to stretch it out, pushing it out from within and allowing it to expand.

I focused on my breathing until all the tension in me vanished. As I relaxed even more, I let the tingling heat find its own course; it didn't move outward or expand; it contracted instead, until I felt

I was lying on a gigantic balloon, floating in space. I experienced a moment of panic; my breathing stopped and for an instant I was suffocating. Then something outside of myself took over and began to breathe for me. Waves of lulling energy surrounded me, expanding and contracting until everything went black and I could no longer focus my awareness on anything.

13

I awoke hearing Clara tell me to sit up. It took me a long time to respond, first, because I was totally disoriented, and second, because my legs were numb. Seeing my difficulty, Clara held me under the arms and pulled me forward, then propped some pillows behind my back so I could sit without her help. I was in my bed and I had my nightgown on. From the light, I could tell it was late afternoon.

"What happened?" I muttered. "Did I sleep all night?"

"You did," Clara replied. "I was concerned about you. You went off the deep end into a perceptual limbo. No one could get through to you. So we decided to let you sleep it off."

I leaned over and rubbed my legs until the prickling sensation stopped. I still felt groggy and strangely enervated.

"You've got to talk to me until you're yourself again," Clara said in her most authoritative tone. "This is one of those occasions when talking is good for you."

"I don't feel like talking," I said, plopping back onto the pillows. I had broken out in a cold sweat and my limbs felt limp and rubbery. "Did Mr. Abelar do something to me?"

"Not while I was looking," Clara replied, and laughed jovially at her own joke. She took my hands in hers and rubbed the backs of them, attempting to revive me.

I wasn't in the mood for levity. "What really happened, Clara?" I demanded. "I don't remember a thing."

She made herself comfortable on the edge of the bed. "Your first encounter with the nagual was too much for you," Clara said. "You're too weak; that's what happened. But I don't want you to focus on that because you become discouraged so easily. Also, I don't want you to read between the lines, as you're apt to do, and come up with the wrong conclusions."

"Since I don't know what's going on, how I am going to read between the lines?" I said, my teeth chattering.

"I'm sure you'd find a way," Clara sighed. "You're exceptionally adept at jumping to conclusions. Unfortunately, the wrong ones. And it doesn't matter that you don't know what's going on. You always assume that you do."

I had to admit I hated ambiguous situations. They always put me at a disadvantage. I wanted to know what was going on so I could deal with the contingencies.

"Your mother taught you to be a perfect woman," Clara said. "By observing the surroundings, perfect women infer everything they need to know, especially when a male is involved. They can anticipate his subtlest wishes. They're always aware of changes in his moods because they believe that these changes are caused by something they themselves said or did. Consequently, they feel it's up to them to appease their man."

Having seen myself, by means of my recapitulation, acting in such a fashion again and again, I had to admit, to my chagrin, that Clara was correct. I was well trained. I only needed a look or a sigh or tone of voice from my father and I would know exactly what he was thinking or feeling. The same was true of my brothers. They had me jumping at the most subtle cues. What's worse, I only had to imagine that a man didn't like me and I would bend over backward to please him.

Clara nudged my side gently as if to get my attention. "If you and I had been alone last night, you wouldn't have passed out so dramatically," she said, with a most annoying smile.

"What are you insinuating, Clara? That I find Mr. Abelar appealing?"

"Precisely. When a man is around, you undergo an instant transformation. You become the woman that will do anything for a man's attention, including passing out."

"I beg to differ with you," I said. "I really wasn't trying to play up to Mr. Abelar."

"Think about it! Don't just defend yourself," Clara said. "I'm not attacking you. I'm merely pointing out to you what I used to feel and do myself."

Deep down I knew what Clara was talking about. Mr. Abelar had such a charismatic charm that, in spite of his age, I found him utterly attractive. Yet I chose not to acknowledge this, neither to myself nor to Clara. To my relief, Clara didn't pursue the subject.

"I understand you perfectly because I too had my John Michael Abelar," she said. "He was the nagual Julian Grau, the most handsome and debonair being that ever lived. He was charming, impish and funny; he was truly unforgettable. Everyone adored him, including John Michael and the rest of my family. We all kissed the ground he walked on."

It occurred to me, listening to Clara rave about her teacher, that she had spent too much time in the Orient. I had always been disturbed by the obscene adoration that students in the karate world felt for their teacher, or *sensei*. They too literally kissed the ground their teacher walked on, bringing their heads to the floor in obeisance whenever the master entered the room. I didn't say this to Clara, but I felt that she was lowering herself by revering her teacher so much.

"The nagual Julian taught us everything we know," she went on, oblivious to my judgements. "He dedicated his life to leading us to freedom. He gave special instruction to the nagual John Michael Abelar, instruction that made him qualified to become the new nagual."

"Do you mean, Clara, that naguals are like kings?" I asked, wanting her to see the danger and fallacy of too much veneration.

"No. Not at all. Naguals have no self-importance whatsoever," she said. "And it is precisely for this reason that we can adore them."

"What I meant, Clara, was, do they inherit their post?" I corrected myself quickly.

"Oh, yes! They certainly inherit their post; but not like kings. Kings are sons of kings. A nagual, on the other hand, has to be singled out by the spirit. For unless the spirit chooses him, he cannot set himself up as a leader. A nagual, to begin with, is a person with extraordinary energy. But it is not until he is taught the rule of the naguals that he actually becomes a nagual himself."

I followed Clara's explanation, but I felt inexplicably ill at ease with it. Upon deliberation, I realized that the part that bothered me was that the spirit has to make the selection.

"How does the spirit decide whom to pick?" I asked.

Clara shook her head. "That, my dear Taisha, is a mystery beyond mysteries," she said softly. "All a nagual can do is fulfill the spirit's biddings, or fail miserably."

I thought of Mr. Abelar and wondered what bidding the spirit had in mind for him. I remembered also that Clara had said that he might one day be a nagual to me.

"By the way, where is Mr. Abelar?" I asked trying to sound casual.

"He left last night when he realized that you were out for the count."

"Will he be back?"

"Certainly. He lives here."

"Where, Clara? In the left side of the house?"

"Yes. At the moment, he is there. Not at this precise moment," she corrected herself, "but nowadays. At other times, he lives with me on the right side of the house. I take care of him."

I felt a pang of jealousy so potent that it charged me with a surge of energy. "You said he wasn't your husband, didn't you, Clara?" I asked, with a most disturbing twitch in the side of my mouth.

Clara laughed so hard that she rolled backward onto the bed out of breath.

"The nagual John Michael Abelar has transcended all aspects of being a male," she assured me, sitting up again.

"What do you mean, Clara?"

"I mean, he's not a human being any longer. But I can't explain all this to you because I lack the finesse and you lack the facility to understand me. The way I see it, my inability to explain things to you is the reason why the nagual gave you those crystals."

"What inability, Clara? You speak perfectly well."

"Then it's you who don't understand perfectly well."

"That's idiotic, Clara."

"Then how come I can't convey to you what we are and what we have in mind for you?"

I took several deep breaths to settle my nervous stomach. "What do you have in mind for me, Clara?" I asked, falling prey once more to panic.

"It's very hard for me to explain," she began. "You and I definitely belong to the same tradition. You are an integral part of what we are. Therefore we are compelled to teach you."

"Whom do you mean when you say 'we'? Do you mean you and Mr. Abelar?"

Clara took a moment as if giving herself time to answer correctly. "As I've told you already, we are more than two," she said. "In fact, I'm not really your teacher. And neither is the nagual John Michael. Someone else is."

"Wait, wait, Clara. You're confusing me again. Who is this other person you're referring to?"

"Another woman like yourself, but older and infinitely more powerful. I'm merely your usher. I'm in charge of preparing you, of getting you to store enough energy through your recapitulation so you can meet this other person. And believe me, her presence is much more devastating than the nagual's."

"I don't understand what you're trying to say, Clara. Do you mean she's dangerous and will harm me?"

"That's the problem when I try to answer your questions," Clara said. "You get confused because you and I have only a superficial connection. You ask me a question, expecting a clear-cut answer that would satisfy you, and I give you an answer that satisfies me and throws you into confusion. I recommend that you either don't ask questions or take my answers without getting into a dither."

I wanted to know more about Mr. Abelar and this other woman's plans for me, so with the hope of getting Clara to tell all, I promised that from then on, I would weigh all her answers with due consideration, but with no panic or agitation on my part.

"All right. Let's see how you take this," Clara said tentatively. "I'm going to tell you what the nagual told you last night before you passed out on him. But since I'm not a male, you no doubt are going to react differently to me than you did when the nagual talked to you. You might even listen to me."

"But I don't remember him telling me anything after I fell asleep on the mat," I protested.

She paused and searched my face, I suppose for some spark of recognition. She shook her head to denote she found none, although I tried to appear as calm and attentive as possible and even smiled to reassure her.

"He told you about all the beings that live in this house," Clara began. "He told you that they are all sorcerers, including Manfred."

At the mention of Manfred's name, something inside me clicked.

"I knew it," I blurted out without thinking. I found the idea that Manfred was a sorcerer perfectly believable, yet I hadn't the vaguest notion of why it should be so. I told Clara that at one point I must have already entertained that thought, although I still didn't know exactly what a sorcerer is.

"Of course you do," Clara assured me with a broad smile.

"But I tell you, I don't."

Clara looked at me bewildered. "You're sure you don't remember the nagual explaining this to you?"

"No. I really don't."

"A sorcerer, to us, is someone who, through discipline and perseverance, can break the limits of natural perception," Clara said with an air of formality.

"Well, that doesn't make things any clearer," I said. "How can Manfred do all that?"

She seemed to appreciate my confusion. "I think we're having a misunderstanding again, Taisha. I'm not just talking about Manfred. It hasn't sunk in yet that all of us in this house are sorcerers. Not just the nagual, Manfred and myself, but the fourteen others you haven't yet met. We are all sorcerers, all abstract beings. If you want to think of sorcery as something concrete, involving rituals and magic potions, all I can tell you is that there are sorcerers who are as concrete as that, but you won't find them in this house."

Obviously we were on different trains of thought. I was talking about Manfred and she was talking about people I hadn't even laid eyes on. It was only then, after she had told me so directly, that it finally struck me that Clara, Mr. Abelar and the elusive others to whom they kept alluding were all sorcerers. Rather than ask any more questions, I remembered her advice and thought it best to remain silent.

She went on to elaborate that abstract sorcerers seek freedom through enhancing their capacity to perceive; while concrete sorcerers, like the traditional ones who lived in ancient Mexico, seek personal power and gratification through increasing their self-importance.

"What's wrong with seeking personal gratification?" I asked, taking a sip of water from a glass on the bedside table.

"Leave it to Taisha to side up with the concrete sorcerers," she said with a look of concern. "No wonder the nagual gave you those crystal darts."

In spite of my promise to stay calm, at the mention of the crystals, waves of nervousness ran through me. My stomach began to cramp with such intensity that I was certain I was coming down with an intestinal flu.

"It's nearly impossible for me to explain to you what we do, and even harder to convey why we do it," Clara said. "You must ask those questions of your teacher."

"My teacher?"

"You're not listening to me, Taisha. I've already told you that you have a teacher. You haven't met her yet because you don't have the necessary energy. Meeting her requires ten times more energy than meeting the nagual, and you still haven't recovered from that encounter. You look green and pasty."

"I think I have a case of the flu," I said, feeling dizzy again.

Clara shook her head. "You have a bad case of indulging," she interjected before continuing. "The nagual can also explain anything you ask him. The only problem is that you think he's a male, and if he talks to you for more than a few minutes, rest assured, you're going to fall into your female mold. That's why your teacher has to be a woman."

"Aren't you making too much of this male–female thing?" I said, trying to get out of bed.

I felt weak and my legs were trembling. The room began to spin and I nearly fainted. Clara caught me by the arm in the nick of time.

"We'll soon find out if I'm making too much of it," she said. "Let's go outside and sit in the shade of a tree. Maybe the fresh air will help revive you."

She helped me put on a long jacket and some pants, and led me like an invalid out of the room to the back patio.

We sat on some straw mats under the enormous zapote tree that shaded nearly the entire patio. Once, I had asked Clara if I could eat the fruit. She had hushed me and said, "Just eat, but don't talk about it." I did what she told me, but I felt guilty ever since, as if I had insulted the tree.

We sat in silence listening to the wind rustling the leaves. It was cool and peaceful there and I felt relaxed and at ease again. After a while, Manfred sauntered over from around the side of the house where he had a room with a large swinging panel cut into the door so he could come and go as he pleased. He came up to me and began licking my hand. I looked into his soulful eyes and I knew we were the best of friends. As if by an unstated invitation, he eased himself across my lap, making himself comfortable. I stroked his soft silky coat and felt the most profound affection for him. Gripped by an inexplicable compassion, I leaned forward and embraced him. The next thing I knew I was weeping, for I felt so sorry for him.

"Where are your crystals?" Clara demanded. Her harsh tone brought me back to reality.

"In my room," I said, letting go of Manfred to wipe my eyes on the sleeve of my jacket.

He took one look at Clara's disapproving stare, jumped off my lap and moved across the walk to sit under a nearby tree.

"You should have them with you at all times," she snapped. "As you already know, weapons like those crystals have nothing to do with war or peace. You can be as peace-loving as you wish and yet still need weapons. In fact, you need them at this moment, to fight your enemies."

"I don't have any enemies, Clara," I sniffled. "No one even knows I'm alive."

Clara leaned toward me. "The nagual gave you those crystals to help you to destroy your enemies," she said softly. "If you had them with you at this moment, you could make your sorcery passes with them and that would help dissipate your nagging self-pity."

"I wasn't feeling sorry for myself, Clara," I said, on the defensive. "I was feeling sorry for poor Manfred."

Clara laughed and shook her head. "There's no way to feel sorry for poor Manfred. No matter what form he's in, he's a warrior. Self-pity, on the other hand, is inside you, and expresses itself in different ways. Right now you're calling it 'feeling sorry for Manfred.' "

My eyes began to tear once more because, together with my insecurity, I did have a bottomless pool of pity, centered totally on myself. I had done enough recapitulating to realize that I had learned this reaction from my mother, who felt sorry for herself every day of her life, or at least every day of my life with her. Since I never knew any other personal expression in her, that was what I had learned to feel myself.

"You should hold the crystal weapons in your fingers and make your sorcery passes at the heart of your elusive enemies, such as self-importance, that come to you disguised as self-pity, moral indignation or righteous sadness," Clara went on.

I could only stare at her in dismay. She went on to accuse me of being weak, of falling apart the moment a little pressure is put on me. But what hurt me the most was when she told me that my months of recapitulating were meaningless; they were nothing but shallow reveries, for all I had done was to reminisce nostalgically about my marvelous self or wallow in pity remembering my not-so-marvelous moments.

I couldn't understand why she was attacking me so viciously. My ears were buzzing as I experienced a surge of fury. I began to weep uncontrollably, hating myself for having allowed Clara the opportunity to devastate me emotionally. I heard her words as if they were coming from far away; she was saying, ". . . self-importance, lack of purpose, unchecked ambition, unexamined sensuality, cowardice; the list of enemies that try to stop your flight to freedom is endless and you must be relentless in your fight against them."

She told me to calm down. She said she had just been trying to illustrate to me that our attitudes and feelings were our real enemies and that they were just as damaging and dangerous as any bandit armed to the teeth that we might encounter on the road.

"The nagual gave you those crystals to round up your energy," she said. "They are extraordinary for gathering our attention and fixing it. It's a quality of quartz crystals in general, and the specific intent of these crystals in particular. To accomplish this, all you have to do is perform your sorcery passes with them."

I wished I had the crystals with me then; instead I looked at Manfred's sympathetic, shiny eyes. The thought occurred to me that they were reflecting light just as the quartz crystals had done. For a moment, his eyes held my gaze and as I stared at them an irrational certainty popped into my mind. I knew Manfred was a sorcerer of the ancient tradition, a sorcerer's spirit that had somehow gotten trapped in a dog's body. The moment I thought that, Manfred let out a sharp yelp as if in affirmation.

I wondered, too, if it wasn't Manfred who had found the crystals for me in a cave, or rather had led the nagual to them, the same way he had led me to my favorite lookout point in the hills overlooking the house and grounds.

"You asked me once how it was possible that I knew so much about crystals," Clara said, interrupting my speculations. "I couldn't tell you then, because you hadn't yet met the nagual. But now that you've been introduced to him, I can tell you that . . ." She took a deep breath and leaned toward me, "We are sorcerers from the same tradition as those of ancient times. We have inherited all their esoteric rituals and incantations, but although we know how to use them, we aren't interested in making them work."

"Manfred is an ancient sorcerer!" I exclaimed in sincere amazement, but forgetting that I hadn't mentioned to her my mental speculations.

Clara looked at me as if questioning my sanity and then laughed so hard that conversation stopped. I heard Manfred barking as if he too were laughing. And the eerie part was that I could have sworn that either Clara's laughter had an echo or that someone hiding behind the corner of the house was also laughing.

I felt like a complete imbecile. Clara didn't want to hear the details about light being reflected in Manfred's eyes.

"I've told you that you are slow and not that intelligent, but you didn't believe me," she chided. "But don't worry, none of us is that intelligent either. We are all arrogant, dumb, thick-headed apes."

She gave me a rap on my head to bring the point home. I didn't like being called a thick-headed ape, but I was still so excited about my discovery that I let the remark pass.

"The nagual has many other reasons for giving you those crystals," Clara continued, "but he'll have to explain them to you himself. The one thing I know for certain is that you will have to make a pouch for them."

"What kind of pouch?"

"A sheath made with whatever material you feel is right. You can use suede, felt or quilt or even wood if that is what you want to use."

"What kind of pouch did you make for yours, Clara?"

"I didn't get any crystals myself," she said, "but I handled them at one time, in my youth."

"You speak of yourself as if you were old. The more I see you, the younger you look."

"That's because I do plenty of sorcery passes to create that illusion," she replied, laughing with childlike abandon. "Sorcerers create illusions. Just look at Manfred."

At the mention of his name, Manfred stuck his head out from behind the tree and stared at us. I had the uncanny sensation that he knew we were talking about him and he didn't want to miss a single word.

"What about Manfred?" I asked, automatically lowering my voice.

"One would swear that he's a dog," Clara said in a whisper. "But that's his power to create an illusion." She nudged me and gave me a conspiratorial wink. "You see, you are absolutely right, Taisha. Manfred is not a dog at all."

I couldn't tell whether she was coaxing me to agree with her for Manfred's sake, for now he was sitting up, definitely listening to every word we were saying, or whether she really meant what she said, that Manfred was not a dog. Before I could find out which, a shrill noise from inside the house made both Clara and Manfred jump up and rush in that direction. I began to follow, but Clara turned to me and said gruffly, "You stay where you are. I'll be back in a moment."

She ran into the house with Manfred close on her heels.

14

Weeks went by, then months. I didn't really pay attention to dates and time. Clara, Manfred and I lived in perfect harmony. Clara had ceased to insult me, or perhaps it was that I had ceased to feel insulted. I spent all my time recapitulating and practicing kung fu with Clara and with Manfred, who, at one hundred pounds of bone and muscle, was a mighty dangerous opponent. I was certain that to be rammed with his head was equivalent to being punched by a prize fighter.

The one thing that worried me was a contradiction I found difficult to resolve. While Clara maintained that my energy was unmistakably on the rise because I could now have conversations with Manfred, I believed the opposite was true: I was slowly going over the deep end.

Whenever Manfred and I were alone, a bond of indescribable affection would possess me. I actually adored him. And it was this blind feeling of love that created a bridge between us so he could, at times, transmit his thoughts and moods to me. I knew Manfred's feelings were simple and direct like a child's. He experienced happiness, discomfort, pride in any accomplishment and fear of everything, which was instantly turned to wrath. But the traits that I found most admirable in him were his courage and his capacity for compassion. I sensed that he actually felt sorry for Clara for looking like a toad. With respect to courage, Manfred was unique. His was the courage of an evolved consciousness aware of his imprisonment. To me, Manfred was alone beyond comprehension. And no one can face that imposed solitude the way he did without possessing peerless courage.

One afternoon, upon returning from the cave, I sat down to rest under the shade of the zapote tree. Manfred came to me and lay across my legs and fell instantly asleep. Listening to his snoring and feeling his warm weight in my lap made me drowsy. I must have fallen asleep, because I suddenly woke up from a dream in which I was arguing with my mother over the advantages of not putting the silverware away after washing them. Mr. Abelar was staring at me with fierce, cold eyes. His gaze, the posture of his body, his extremely defined features and his concentration gave me the total impression that he was an eagle. He imbued me with awe and fear.

"What happened?" I asked. The temperature and the light had changed. It was almost dark; twilight shadows had fallen over the patio.

"What happened is that Manfred's got hold of you and is using your energy like a fiend," he said with a broad smile. "He did the same with me. There seems to be a genuine rapport between you two. Try calling him *sapito* and let's see if he gets angry."

"No. I can't do that," I said, running my fingers on Manfred's head. "He's beautiful and solitary and in no way does he resemble a t-o-a-d."

I found it absurd that I had actually spelled the word, but something in me didn't want to risk offending Manfred.

"Toads are also beautiful and solitary," Mr. Abelar said with a glint.

Spurred by a sudden curiosity, I leaned over to Manfred and whispered in his ear, "*Sapito*," having only the best of feelings. Manfred yawned, as if bored with my empathy.

Mr. Abelar laughed. "Let's go into the house," he said, "before Manfred saps all your energy. Besides, it's warmer there."

I pushed Manfred off my lap and followed Mr. Abelar inside the house. I sat down very formally in the living room, acutely self-conscious at being alone with a man in a dark, empty house. He lit the gasoline lantern, then sat on the sofa a respectable distance away and said, "I understand you wanted to ask me some questions. Now is a good time, so go ahead and ask them."

For an instant my mind went blank. Being confronted so directly with his intense stare made me lose my composure. Finally, I asked, "What happened to me the night I met you, Mr. Abelar? Clara felt she couldn't explain it to me adequately, and I don't remember much about it."

"Your double took over," he said matter-of-factly. "And you lost control of your everyday self."

"What do you mean, I lost control?" I asked, worried. "Did I do anything I shouldn't have?"

"Nothing that you couldn't tell your mother about," he chuckled. His eyes sparkled, full of mischief. "Seriously, Taisha, all you did was to cast your luminous net as far as you were able to. You learned how to rest on that invisible hammock that is actually a part of you. Someday, as you become more adept, you may begin to use its lines to move and alter things."

"Is the double inside or outside the physical body?" I asked. "That night, it seemed to me that, for a moment, something clearly outside of myself had taken over."

"It's both," Mr. Abelar said. "It is inside and outside the physical body at the same time. How can I put it? In order to command it, the part of it that is outside floating freely has to be linked to the energy that is housed inside the physical body. The external force is beckoned and held by an unwavering concentration, while the internal energy is released by opening some mysterious gates in and around the body. When the two sides merge, the force that is produced allows one to perform inconceivable feats."

"Where are those mysterious gates you're talking about?" I asked, incapable of meeting his gaze directly.

"Some are close to the skin, others are deep inside the body," Mr. Abelar replied. "There are seven main gates. When they are closed, our inner energy remains locked within the physical body. The presence of the double inside us is so subtle that we can go through our entire lives without ever knowing that it is there. However, if one is going to release it, the gates must be opened and this is done through the recapitulation and the breathing exercises Clara showed you."

Mr. Abelar promised that he himself would guide me to deliberately open the first gate after I had successfully accomplished the abstract flight. He emphasized that in order to open the gates, a complete change of attitude is necessary because our preconceived notion that we are solid is what keeps the double imprisoned, rather than any physical structure of the body itself.

"Couldn't you describe to me where the gates are so I can open them myself?"

He looked at me and shook his head. "To tamper haphazardly with the power behind the gates is foolish and dangerous," he warned. "The double must be released gradually, harmoniously. A prerequisite, however, is that one remains celibate."

"Why is celibacy important?" I asked.

"Didn't Clara tell you about the luminous worms a man leaves inside a woman's body?"

"Yes," I said, ill at ease and embarrassed. "But I must confess I didn't really believe her."

"That was a mistake," he said, annoyed. "For without a thorough recapitulation first, you would literally be opening a can of worms. And to have sex would only be adding more fuel to the fire."

He laughed heartily making me feel ridiculous.

"Seriously, though, storing sexual energy is the first step in the journey toward the ethereal body, the journey into awareness and total freedom."

Just then, Clara entered the living room wearing a white flowing kaftan that made her look like a huge toad. I began to snicker for thinking such a disrespectful thought, and immediately glanced over at Mr. Abelar, who I could have sworn was thinking the same thing. Clara sat down on the armchair and smiled at both of us sitting awkwardly on the couch.

"Have you gotten to the subject of the gates yet?" she asked Mr. Abelar curiously. "Is that why Taisha is pressing her legs together so tightly?"

Mr. Abelar nodded in utter seriousness. "I was just about to tell her that an enormous gate is in the sexual organs. But I don't think she will understand what I'm talking about. She still has quite a few misconceptions in that department."

"She certainly does," Clara agreed with a wink in my direction.

Simultaneously, they both broke out in such peals of laughter that I felt utterly disconnected. I resented being laughed at and talked about as if I weren't in the room. I was about to tell them that they didn't understand me at all, when Clara spoke again, this time addressing me.

"Do you understand why we are recommending that you remain celibate?" she asked.

"To journey to freedom," I said, repeating Mr. Abelar.

I boldly asked Clara if she and Mr. Abelar were celibate, or if they were just recommending behavior they were not prepared to practice themselves.

"I told you we are not man and wife," Clara replied, not the least bit perturbed. "We are sorcerers interested in power, in gathering energy, not losing it."

I turned to Mr. Abelar and asked him if he really was a sorcerer and what that entailed. He didn't answer me but looked at Clara as if he were asking her permission to divulge something. Clara nodded her almost imperceptible assent.

"I don't feel at ease with the word 'sorcerer,'" he said, "because it connotes beliefs and actions that are not part of what we do."

"What exactly do you do?" I asked. "Clara said only you could tell me."

Mr. Abelar straightened his back and gave me a frightening look that jolted me to attention. "We are a group consisting of sixteen people, myself included, and one being: Manfred," he began formally. "Ten of the people are women. All of us do the same thing: we have dedicated our lives to developing our double. We use our ethereal bodies and defy many of the natural laws of the physical world. Now, if that's being a sorcerer, then all of us are sorcerers. If not, then we're not. Does that make things any clearer?"

"Since you are teaching me about the double, am I going to be a sorceress too?" I asked.

"I don't know," he replied, scanning me curiously. "It'll all depend on you. It is always up to us individually to fulfill or to flub our fate."

"But Clara said everyone in this house has a purpose for being here. Why was I selected?" I asked. "Why me in particular?"

"That's a very difficult question to answer," Mr. Abelar said, smiling. "Let's say that we are compelled to include you. Do you remember that night, about five years ago, when you were caught in a compromising situation with a young man?"

I immediately began to sneeze, my usual reaction when I felt threatened. During my recapitulating I had remembered time and again being in compromising situations. Since I was fourteen, I had been obsessed with boys and had aggressively run after them, as I had run after my brothers as a child. I wanted desperately to be loved by anyone because I knew my family didn't like me. But I always ended up scaring off my would-be suitors before they could get too close. My aggressiveness made everyone think I was a loose woman, capable of anything. Consequently, I had the worst reputation imaginable in spite of the fact that I hadn't done even half of the things my friends and family attributed to me.

"You were caught on the food counter where you worked in the concession stand of a drive-in theater in California. Remember?" I heard Mr. Abelar say.

How could I possibly not remember? That was by far one of the worst experiences of my life. And because it was so sensitive, I had put off recapitulating it deeply, always skirting its fringes. At that time, I had a high school summer job selling hot dogs and soft drinks in a drive-in theater. Near the end of the summer, Kenny, the young man who managed the concession stand, told me that he loved me. Up to that moment, I had been indifferent to him because I had my eye on the boss, who was handsome and rich. Unfortunately, he was interested in Rita, my red-headed nemesis, who was nineteen and gorgeous. Every night soon after the movie began, she would slip into the boss's office and lock the door. When she emerged just before intermission, her pink and white checkered uniform was wrinkled and her hair was limp and tangled. I acutely envied Rita for all the attention she was getting. What made it even worse was her promotion to running the cash register, while I had to continue passing out popcorn and serving soft drinks at the counter.

When Kenny told me that I was beautiful and desirable, I began to think of him in a different light. I overlooked the fact that he had severe acne, drank beer by the gallon, listened to country music, wore boots and spoke with a heavy Texan drawl. All of a sudden I found him manly and affectionate, and all I cared to know about him was that his parents were Catholic and didn't know that he smoked marijuana. I was beginning to fall in love with him and didn't want personal details to stand in the way.

When I told him that I had to quit working at the end of the week because my family was leaving for a holiday in Germany and I had to go with them, Kenny became incensed. He accused my parents of deliberately trying to separate us. He took my hand and swore that he couldn't live without me. He proposed marriage, but I was not quite sixteen so I told him that we would have to wait. He embraced me passionately and said that the least we could do was to have sex. I didn't know if he meant sometime before I left for Germany or right then, but I thoroughly agreed with him and opted for right then. We had about twenty minutes until the show broke, so I moved the rest of the buns from the worktable and began taking off my clothes.

He was frightened. He shook like a little boy, although he was twenty-two. We hugged and kissed, but before anything else could happen, we were interrupted by an old man who burst into the room. Upon seeing us in such a compromising situation, he grabbed a broom, hit me on the back with the straw side and chased me half-naked into the foyer, in full view of the people who had lined up at the snack shop. They laughed and jeered at me. The worst part was that I recognized two of my teachers from school. They were as shocked to see me as I was to see them. One of my teachers reported the incident to the principal, who in turn informed my parents. By the time everyone finished gossiping, I was the laughingstock of the school. For years afterward, I hated that horrid old man who took it upon himself to be my moral judge. I thought he had actually ruined my life, for I was never allowed to see Kenny again.

"I was that man," Mr. Abelar said, as if he had been following my thoughts.

At that moment, the full impact of remembering my public humiliation struck me. And to have the person responsible for it in front of me was more than I could bear. I began to weep out of sheer frustration. The worst part was that Mr. Abelar didn't seem at all sorry for what he had done.

"I've been looking for you ever since that night," Mr. Abelar said, grinning slyly.

I read all kinds of kinky sexual nuances into his look and words. My heart was about to explode out of wrath and fear. I knew then that Clara had brought me to Mexico for sinister reasons, centering on some secret scheme the two of them had been hatching from the start that included plenty of aberrant sex. I didn't believe their claim of celibacy, not for an instant.

"What do you intend to do to me?" I asked, my voice cracking with fear.

Clara looked at me puzzled then began to laugh as if she had understood all that had been going through my mind. Mr. Abelar imitated my cracked voice as he asked Clara the same question, "What do you intend to do to me?" Then his booming laughter joined Clara's to reverberate throughout the house. I heard Manfred's howls from his room; it sounded like he too was laughing. I was more than miserable; I was devastated. I got up to leave, but Mr. Abelar pushed me back onto the couch.

"Shame and self-importance make terrible companions," he said seriously. "You haven't recapitulated that incident or you wouldn't be in such a state now." Then softening his fierce stare to an almost kind look, he added, "There's nothing Clara and I want to do to you. You've done more than enough yourself. That night, I was looking for the rest room and opened a door for employees only. Since a nagual never makes such a careless mistake because he is always aware of what he does, I had to assume that I was fated to find you, and that you had a special significance for me. Seeing you there half naked, about to give yourself to a weak man who might have destroyed your life, I acted in a very specific manner and hit you with the broom."

"What you did was to make me the laughingstock of my family and friends," I yelled.

"Perhaps. But I also grabbed your ethereal body and tied an energy line around it," he said. "From that day on, I've always known where you were, yet it has taken me five years to get you in a position where you would listen to what I have to say."

For the first time, what he was saying registered. I stared at him incredulously.

"You mean you've known where I was all the time?" I asked.

"I've been tracking your every move," he said definitely.

"You mean you've been spying on me." The implications of what he was saying were slowly rising to the surface.

"Yes, in a manner of speaking," he admitted.

"Did Clara also know I lived in Arizona?"

"Naturally. We all knew where you were."

"Then, it was not by accident that Clara found me in the desert that day," I gasped. I turned to Clara, furious. "You knew I would be there, didn't you?"

Clara nodded. "I admit it. You went there so regularly it wasn't hard to follow you."

"But you told me that you just happened to be there," I shouted. "You lied to me; you tricked me into coming to Mexico with you. And you've been lying to me ever since, laughing behind my back for God only knows what reason." All my doubts and suspicions that hadn't had expression for months finally surfaced and exploded. "This has been nothing but a joke to you," I yelled, "to see how stupid and gullible I am."

Mr. Abelar gave me a ferocious look, but that didn't stop me from staring right back at him. He tapped me on the top of my head to quiet me.

"You're deadly wrong, young lady," he said sternly. "All this has not been a joke to us. It's true we laugh a great deal at your idiocies, but none of our actions are lies or tricks. They are utterly serious; in fact, they are a matter of life or death to us."

He was so earnest and looked so commanding that the bulk of my anger dissipated, leaving in its place a hopeless bewilderment.

"What did Clara want with me?" I asked, looking at Mr. Abelar.

"I entrusted Clara with a most delicate mission: that of bringing you home," he explained. "And she succeeded. You followed her, obeying your own inner drive. It's extremely difficult to get you to accept an invitation from anyone, but from a total stranger, it's nearly impossible. But she did it. Hers was a masterful stroke! I have only praise and admiration for a job well done."

Clara jumped up to her feet and took a graceful bow. "Leaving all joking aside," she said, assuming a solemn expression as she sat down again, "the nagual is right; it was the most difficult thing I've ever done in my life. For a while there, I thought you were going to let your suspicious nature get the better of you and tell me to get lost. I even had to lie and tell you that I have a secret Buddhist name."

"You don't have one?"

"No, I don't. My desire for freedom has burned every secret in me."

"But I'm still not clear as to how Clara knew where to find me," I said, looking at Mr. Abelar. "How did she know I was in Arizona at that particular time?"

"By means of your double," Mr. Abelar replied, as if it were the most obvious thing.

The instant he said that, my mind cleared and I understood exactly what he meant. In fact, I knew it was the only possible way they could have kept track of me.

"I tied an energy line to your ethereal body the night I burst in on you," he explained. "Since the double is composed of pure energy, it isn't that difficult to mark it. I felt that, given the circumstances of our meeting, it was the least I could do for you. As a form of protection."

Mr. Abelar looked at me, waiting for me to ask a question. But my mind was too busy trying to remember more details of what had happened that night when he had run into the room.

"Aren't you going to ask me how I marked you?" he said, gazing at me intently.

My ears popped, the room became energized and everything fell into place. I didn't have to ask Mr. Abelar how he had done it, I already knew it.

"You marked me when you hit me with the broom!" I exclaimed. It was perfectly clear, but when I thought about it, it made no sense whatsoever, for it didn't explain anything.

Mr. Abelar nodded, pleased that I had arrived at that realization myself.

"That's right. I marked you when I struck your upper back with the broom as I chased you out the door. I left a particular energy inside you. And this energy has been lodged in you ever since that night."

Clara came over and scrutinized me. "Haven't you noticed, Taisha, that your left shoulder is higher than the right?"

I had been aware that one of my shoulder blades protruded more than the other, causing my neck and shoulders to be tense.

"I thought I was born that way," I said.

"Nobody is born with the nagual's mark," Clara laughed. "The nagual's energy is lodged behind your left shoulder blade. Think about it; your shoulders got out of alignment after the nagual struck you with the broom."

I had to admit that it had been around the time I had had my summer job in the drive-in theater that my mother first noticed that there was something wrong with my upper back. She was fitting a sundress she was sewing for me and saw that it didn't fit properly. She was shocked to find that the flaw was not in the dress but in my shoulder blades; one was definitely higher than the other. The next day she had the family doctor examine my back; he concluded that my spine was slightly curved to one side. He diagnosed my condition as congenital scoliosis, but assured my mother that the curvature was so slight that we shouldn't concern ourselves with it.

"It's a good thing the nagual didn't leave too much energy in you," Clara teased, "otherwise you'd be a hunchback."

I turned to face Mr. Abelar. I felt the muscles in my back tense, the way they usually did when I was nervous. "Now that you have me reeled in, what are your intentions?" I asked.

Mr. Abelar took a step closer. He fixed me with his cold stare. "All I've wanted, since the day I found you, was to do the same thing I did for you that night," he replied solemnly, "to open the door and chase you out. This time, I want to open the door of the daily world and chase you out to freedom."

His words and mood unleashed a wealth of feelings. For as long as I can remember, I had been always searching, looking out of windows, peering down streets as if something or someone was around the corner waiting for me. I've always had premonitions, dreams of escaping, although I didn't know from what. It was this feeling that had compelled me to follow Clara to an unknown destination. And it was also what prevented me from leaving in spite of the impossibility of my tasks. As I held Mr. Abelar's gaze, an indescribable wave of well-being enveloped me. I knew that I had at last found what I had been looking for. Following an impulse of the purest affection, I leaned over and kissed his hand. And out of the unsuspected depth of me, I muttered something that had no rational but only an emotional significance. "You are the nagual to me, too," I said.

His eyes were shining, happy we had finally come to an understanding. He ruffled my hair in an affectionate way, and all my pent-up fears and frustrations exploded in a deluge of anguished tears.

Clara got up and handed me a handkerchief. "The way to get you out of this sad mood is to make you angry or to make you think," she said. "I'm going to do both by telling you this. Not only did I know where to find you in the desert, but do you remember that hot, stuffy little apartment you asked me to move your things out of? Well, the building is owned by my cousin."

I looked at Clara shocked, unable to utter a single word. Clara's and Mr. Abelar's laughter was like a giant explosion reverberating inside my head. I couldn't have been more surprised at anything they might have said or sprung on me. As my initial numbness subsided, instead of becoming angry for being manipulated, I was filled with awe at the incredible precision of their maneuvering and at the immensity of their control, which I finally realized was not control over me, but over themselves.

15

One day, several months after I had met Mr. Abelar, instead of sending me to the cave to recapitulate, Clara asked me to keep her company while she worked in the yard. Near the vegetable garden, beyond the back patio of her house, I watched Clara meticulously rake leaves into a pile. On top of the heap, she carefully arranged some crisp brown leaves into an elliptical pattern.

"What are you doing?" I asked, moving closer to take a better look.

I was feeling tense and somber for I had spent the entire morning in the cave recapitulating memories of my father. I had always thought he was a bombastic and arrogant ogre. To realize he was actually a sad, defeated man, broken by the war and his thwarted ambitions, left me emotionally drained.

"I'm making a nest for you to sit on," Clara replied. "You are to brood like a hen hatching eggs. I want you to be rested because we may have a visitor this afternoon."

"And who might that be?" I asked casually.

For months Clara had promised to introduce me to the other members of the nagual's group—her mysterious relatives that had finally returned from India—but she never had. Every time I had expressed my desire to meet them, she always said I needed to cleanse myself first with a more thorough recapitulation because in my present state

I wasn't fit to meet anyone. I believed her. The more I examined memories of my past, the more I felt in need of cleansing.

"You haven't answered my question, Clara," I said testily. "Who's coming?"

"Never mind who," she said, handing me a bunch of dry, copper-colored leaves. "Put these over your navel and tie them with your recapitulation sash."

"I left my sash in the cave," I said.

"I hope you're using it properly," she commented. "The sash supports us while we recapitulate. You're to wrap your stomach with it and tie one end of it to the stake I planted in the ground inside the cave. That way, you won't fall over and bang your head if you doze off or in case your double decides to wake up."

"Should I go and get it?"

She clicked her tongue, exasperated. "No, we don't have time. Our visitor might be here any minute and I want you to be relaxed and at your best. You can use my sash."

Clara hurried inside the house and momentarily returned with a strip of saffron cloth. It was truly beautiful. It had an almost imperceptible pattern woven in it. In the sunlight the strip of silk shimmered, changing its hue from a dark gold to a mellow amber.

"If any part of your body is injured or in pain, wrap this sash around it," Clara explained. "It will help you recover. It has a bit of power, for I've done years of recapitulating wearing it. Someday you'll be able to say the same about your sash."

"Why can't you tell me who's coming to visit?" I pressed. "You know I hate surprises. Is it the nagual?"

"No, it's someone else," she said, "but equally powerful, if not more so. When you meet her, you have to be quiet and empty of thoughts, or you won't benefit from her presence."

With exaggerated solemnity, Clara said that today, as a matter of principle, I had to use all the sorcery passes she had taught me— not because anyone was going to test me to make sure I knew them, but because I had come to a crossroad and I had to begin moving in a new direction.

"Wait, Clara, don't frighten me with talk of changing," I pleaded. "I'm terrified of new directions."

"To frighten you is the farthest thing from my mind," she assured me. "It's just that I'm a bit worried myself. Do you have your crystals with you?"

I unbuttoned my vest and showed her the leather double-shoulder holster I had fashioned, with her help, to hold the two quartz crystals. They were secured one under each arm, like two knives in their own sheath, complete with an overlapping flap and fastened with a snap.

"Take them out and have them ready," she said. "And use them to rally your energy. Don't wait for her to tell you to do so. Do it at your own discretion whenever you feel you need an extra boost of energy."

From Clara's statements, it was easy to deduce two things: that this was going to be a serious encounter, and that our mystery guest would be a woman.

"Is she one of your relatives?" I asked.

"Yes, she is," Clara replied with a cold smile. "This person is my relative, a member of our party. Now relax and don't ask any more questions."

I wanted to know where her relatives were staying. It was impossible that they were staying in the house because I would have run across them or at least seen signs of their presence. The fact that I hadn't seen anybody had turned my curiosity into an obsession. I imagined that Clara's relatives were deliberately hiding from me and even spying on me. This made me angry and at the same time even more determined to catch a glimpse of them. The origin of my turmoil was the unmistakable feeling that I was constantly being watched.

I deliberately tried to entrap whoever it was by leaving one of my drawing pencils lying around to see if anyone picked it up, or by placing a magazine open at a certain page and checking it later to see if that page had been changed. In the kitchen, I carefully examined the dishes for signs of use. I even went as far as smoothing out the packed dirt on the path by the back door, then coming back later and searching the ground for footprints or unfamiliar tracks. In spite of all my efforts at sleuthing, the only prints I ever saw were those of Clara, Manfred and myself. If a person was hiding from me, I was convinced I would have noticed it. But as it was, there seemed to be no one else in the house in spite of my being certain that other people were present.

"Forgive me, Clara, but I have to ask you," I finally blurted out, "because it's driving me nuts. Where are your relatives staying?"

Clara looked at me surprised. "This is their house. They are staying here, of course."

"But where exactly?" I demanded. I was on the verge of confessing how I had laid traps to no avail, but decided against it.

"Oh! I see what you mean," she said. "You haven't found any signs of them, in spite of your efforts at playing detective. But that's no mystery. You never see them because they're staying in the left side of the house."

"Don't they ever come out?"

"They do, but they avoid the right side because you're staying here and they don't want to disturb you. They know how much you value your privacy."

"But not to show themselves ever? Isn't that carrying the idea of privacy a bit too far?"

"Not at all," Clara said. "You need absolute solitude to concentrate on your recapitulation. When I said that you're going to have a visitor today, I meant that one of my relatives is going to come from the left side of the house to where we are and meet you. She's been looking forward to talking to you, but had to wait until you had cleansed yourself minimally. I told you that to meet her is even more taxing than to meet the nagual. You need to have stored enough power or else you'll go off the deep end as you did with him."

Clara helped me put the leaves on my stomach and tie them with the cloth.

"These leaves and this sash will buffer you from the woman's onslaughts," Clara said, then looking at me added softly, "and from other blows too. So whatever you do, don't take it off."

"What's going to happen to me?" I asked, nervously packing in more leaves.

Clara shrugged. "That'll depend on your power," she said and gave the knot in the cloth a firm tug. "But from the looks of you, God only knows."

With trembling fingers I rebuttoned my shirt and tucked it into my baggy pants. I looked bloated with the wide saffron band around my middle. The leaves were like a brittle, scratchy pillow covering my abdomen. But gradually my jittery stomach stopped shivering; it became warm and my entire body felt relaxed.

"Now sit on the pile of leaves and do what hens do," Clara ordered.
I must have given her a surprised look because she asked me,
"What do you think hens do when they brood?"

"I really couldn't say, Clara."

"A hen remains still and listens to her eggs underneath her, directing all her attention to them. She listens and never lets her concentration waver. In this unbending manner she intends the chicks to hatch. It's a quiet listening that animals do naturally, but which human beings have forgotten, and therefore must cultivate."

Clara sat down on a large, pale gray rock and faced me. The rock had a natural depression in it and looked like an armchair.

"Now, doze like a hen does and listen with your inner ear while I talk. Concentrate on the warmth in your womb and don't let your attention wander. Be aware of the sounds around you, but don't allow your mind to follow them."

"Do I really have to sit here like this, Clara? I mean, wouldn't it be better if I just took a refreshing nap?"

"I'm afraid not. As I've said, our visitor's presence is terribly taxing. If you fail to gather energy, you'll sink pitifully. Believe me, she's not soft like me. She's more like the nagual, pitiless and hard."

"Why is she so taxing?"

"She can't help it. She's so far removed from human beings and their concerns that her energy might completely disrupt you. By now, there's no difference between her physical body and her ethereal double. What I mean to say is that she is a master sorceress."

Clara gave me a searching look and commented on the dark circles under my eyes. "You've been reading at night by the light of the lantern, haven't you?" she scolded. "Why do you think we don't have electricity in the bedrooms?"

I told her I hadn't read a single page since the day I arrived at her house, because the recapitulation and all the other things she had asked me to do gave me no time for anything else. "I'm not particularly fond of reading though," I admitted. "But I do browse from time to time through your bookshelves in the halls." I didn't tell her that what I really meant to say was that I went there snooping to see if any of the books had been removed by her relatives.

She laughed and said, "Some of the members of my family are avid readers. I'm not one of them."

"But don't you read for pleasure, Clara?"

"Not me. I read for information. But some of the others do read for pleasure."

"So how come I never see any of the books missing?" I asked, trying to sound casual.

Clara giggled. "They have their own library on the left side of the house," she said, then asked me, "You don't read for pleasure, Taisha?"

"Unfortunately, I also only read for information," I said.

I told Clara that for me the joy of reading was nipped in the bud when I was in grade school. One of my father's friends, who owned a book distribution firm, had the habit of giving him boxes of books that were out of print. My father used to screen them and give me the literary books, which he said I had to read in addition to my regular homework. I always took it for granted that he meant I had to read every word. What's more, I thought I had to finish one book before beginning the next one. It came as a complete surprise to me when I found out later that some people start several books simultaneously and switch back and forth, reading according to their mood.

Clara looked at me and shook her head as if I were a lost cause. "Children do strange things under pressure," she said. "Now I know why you've turned out to be so compulsive. I bet if you try to remember those stories now, you'll be shocked at what you find. As children, we can never question what's presented to us, just as you didn't question that you had to read a book from cover to cover. All the members of my family have serious contentions about what's done to children."

"I've become obsessed with meeting your family, Clara."

"That's only natural. I've talked about them so often."

"It's not just that, Clara," I said. "It's more of a physical sensation. I don't know why, but I can't stop thinking about them. I even dream about them."

The minute I voiced that, something arranged itself in my mind. I bluntly confronted Clara with a query. Since she knew who I was, and her cousin, being my landlord knew me, it suddenly occurred to me to ask whether I knew her other relatives too.

"Naturally all of them know you," Clara said, as if it were the most obvious thing, but she didn't answer my question.

I couldn't possibly imagine who they might be. "Now let me bluntly ask you this, Clara. Do I know them?" I insisted.

"These are all impossible questions, Taisha. I think it's best that you don't ask them."

I became sulky. I got up from my seat of leaves but Clara gently pushed me down again. "All right, all right, Little Miss Snoop," she said. "If it will make you stay put, I'll tell you. You know them all, but you certainly don't remember having met them. Even if any one of my relatives were standing right in front of you, my guess is that you still wouldn't have even the slightest twitch of recognition. But at the same time, something in you will get extremely agitated. Now are you satisfied?"

Her reply didn't satisfy me in the least. In fact, it convinced me that she was deliberately mystifying me, leading me on, playing with words.

"You must enjoy tormenting me, Clara," I said, disgusted.

Clara laughed out loud. "I'm not playing with you," she assured me. "To explain what we are and what we do is the most trying thing in the world. I wish I could make it clearer, but I can't. So it's pointless to keep on insisting on explanations when there are none."

I shifted uncomfortably on the ground. My legs had fallen asleep. Clara suggested that I lie on my stomach and rest my head on my right arm, bending it at the elbow. I did that and found the position comfortable. The ground and the leaves seemed to keep me rooted while my mind was still but alert. Clara leaned over and caressed my head affectionately. Then she fixed me with her gaze in such an odd way that I grabbed her hand for a moment and held it. "I've got to go now, Taisha," she said softly, loosening my grip, "but rest assured I'll see you again." Her green eyes had specks of light amber in them. And their glow was the last thing I saw.

I woke up when someone was poking my back with a stick. A strange woman was standing over me. She was tall, slender and incredibly striking. Her features were exquisitely chiseled; small mouth, even teeth, perfectly defined nose; oval face; delicate, almost transparent white Nordic complexion; lustrous, curly gray hair. When she smiled, I thought she was an adolescent girl, full of daring and sensuality. When she looked serene, she seemed to be a continental European woman, fashionable and mature. There was elegance in her stylish dress, especially in her sensible shoes, something I had never seen in the United States, where well-dressed women wearing comfortable shoes always appeared matronly.

The woman was at once older and younger than Clara; she was definitely older in age, but years younger in appearance. And she possessed something I could only call inner vitality. By contrast, Clara seemed to be still in a formative stage, while this being was the finished product. I knew that someone incredibly different, perhaps as different as a member of another species, was examining me with genuine curiosity.

I sat up and quickly introduced myself. She reciprocated warmly.

"I am Nelida Abelar," she said in English. "I live here with the rest of my companions. You already know two of them, Clara and the nagual, John Michael. You will meet the rest of us soon."

She spoke with a slight inflection. Her voice was appealing and so utterly familiar that I couldn't help staring at her. She laughed, I think at the fact that due to my surprise, my face muscles were locked in a frozen smile. The sound of her raspy laughter was also remotely familiar; I had the sensation that I had heard that laughter before. The thought crossed my mind that I had seen this woman on another occasion, although I could not fathom where. The more I stared at her, the more convinced I became that I knew her at one time but had forgotten when.

"What's the matter, dear?" she asked in a solicitous tone. "Do you have the feeling we've met before?"

"Yes, yes," I said excitedly, for I felt that I was about to remember where I had seen her.

"You'll remember sooner or later," she said in a soothing tone that led me to understand that there was no hurry. "The cleansing breath you do while recapitulating will eventually allow you to remember everything you have ever done, including your dreams. Then you'll know where and when we've met."

I felt embarrassed for staring at her and for being caught so completely off guard. I stood up and faced her, not challengingly, but with awe.

"Who are you?" I asked, in a daze.

"I already told you who I am," she said, smiling. "Now, if you want to know if I am a sort of personage, you'll be disappointed. I'm not anyone important. I'm only one of a group of people who seek freedom. Since you've met the nagual, the next step for you was to meet me. That's because I am responsible for you."

Upon hearing that she was responsible for me, I experienced a pang of fear. All my life I had fought to gain my independence; and I had struggled for it as fiercely as I was capable of.

"I don't want anyone to be responsible for me," I said. "I've fought too hard to be independent to fall under anyone's thumb now."

I thought she would take offense, but she laughed and patted me on the shoulder. "I never meant it like that," she said. "No one wants to keep you down. The nagual has an explanation about your unruly personality. He really believes that you have a fighting spirit. In fact, he thinks you're undeniably crazy, but in a positive sense."

She said that the nagual's explanation of my craziness was that I was conceived under unusual and desperate conditions. Nelida then related to me facts about my parents' history that no one except my parents knew. She disclosed that before I was conceived, while my parents lived and worked in South Africa, my father was incarcerated for reasons he never revealed. I had always fantasized that he was not really in a prison but in a political detention camp. Nelida said that my father had saved a guard's life. Later, that guard helped my father to escape by turning his back at a crucial moment.

"With his pursuers on his trail," Nelida continued, "he went to see his wife, to be with her for the last time on earth. He was certain he would be caught and killed. During that passionate life-death embrace, your mother became pregnant with you. The intense fear and passion for life that your father was feeling then was transmitted to you. Consequently, you were born restless and unruly and with a passion for freedom."

I could barely hear her words. I was so stunned by what she was revealing to me that my ears were buzzing and my knees went weak.

I had to lean against a tree trunk to keep from falling down. Before I could speak, she continued.

"The reason your mother was so unhappy and secretly despised your father was because he used up all of her family inheritance to pay for his mistakes, whatever they might have been. The money ran out and they had to leave South Africa before you were born."

"How can you know things about my parents that not even I am clear about?" I asked.

Nelida smiled. "I know those things because I am responsible for you," she replied.

Again I felt a jolt of fear run through me, making me shiver. I was afraid that if she knew my parents' secrets, she must also know things about me. I had always felt safe, hidden in my impregnable subjective fortress. I was lulled into a false security, certain that what I felt and thought and did didn't matter as long as I kept it hidden, as long as no one else knew about it. But now it was obvious that this woman had access to my inner self. I desperately needed to reaffirm my position.

"If I'm anything," I said defiantly, "I'm my own person. No one is responsible for me. And no one is going to dominate me."

Nelida laughed at my outburst. She tousled my hair the way the nagual had done, a gesture both soothing and utterly familiar. "Nobody is trying to dominate you, Taishika," she said in a friendly tone. Her gentleness served to dissipate my anger. "I've said all those things to you because I need to prepare you for a very specific maneuver."

I listened to her intently because I sensed from her tone that she was about to reveal something awesome to me.

"Clara has brought you to your present level in a most artistic and effective way. You will forever be indebted to her. Now that she's finished her task, she has gone. And the sad part is that you didn't even thank her for her care and her kindness."

Some horrible, unnamed feeling loomed over me. "Wait a minute," I muttered. "Did Clara leave?"

"Yes, she did."

"But she'll be coming back, won't she?" I asked.

Nelida shook her head. "No. As I told you, her job is done."

At that moment, I had the only true feeling I had ever had in my entire life. Compared to it, nothing of what I had felt before was real; not my anger, not my fits of rage, not my outbursts of affection, not even my self-pity was true when compared with the searing pain I felt at that moment. It was so intense, it numbed me. I wanted to weep, but I couldn't. I knew then that real pain brings no tears.

"And Manfred? Is he gone too?" I asked.

"Yes. His job of guarding you is finished too."

"And what about the nagual? Will I see him again?"

"In the sorcerers' world anything is possible," Nelida said, touching my hand. "But one thing is for certain: it is not a world to be taken for granted. In it, we must voice our thanks now, because there is no tomorrow."

I stared at her blankly, totally stunned. She gazed back at me and whispered, "The future doesn't exist. It's time you realized this. And when you have finished recapitulating and have completely erased the past, all that will be left is the present. And then you will know that the present is but an instant, nothing more."

Nelida gently rubbed my back and told me to breathe. I was so grief-stricken that my breathing had stopped. "Will I ever be different? Is there a chance for me?" I asked pleadingly.

Without answering, Nelida turned around and walked toward the house. When she reached the back door, she signaled me with a beckoning crook of the index finger to follow her inside.

I wanted to run after her but I couldn't move. I began to whimper, then the oddest whine came out of me, a sound that was not quite human. I knew then why Clara had tied her protective sash around my stomach—it was to shield me from this blow. I lay face down on the pile of leaves and released into them the animal cry that was choking me. It didn't relieve my anguish. I took out my crystals, placed them in my fingers and turned my arms in counterclockwise circles that became smaller and smaller. I pointed the crystals at my indolence, at my cowardice and at my useless self-pity.

16

Nelida was patiently waiting for me at the back door. It had taken me hours to calm down. It was late afternoon. I followed her inside the house. In the hall, just outside the living room, she stopped so abruptly that I nearly collided with her.

"As Clara told you, I live in the left side of the house," she said, turning to face me. "And I'm going to take you there. But first, let's go in the living room and sit down for a while so you can catch your breath."

I was panting and my heart was beating disturbingly fast.

"I'm in good physical condition," I assured her. "I practiced kung fu with Clara every day. But right now I'm not feeling very well."

"Don't worry about being out of breath," Nelida said reassuringly. "The energy of my body is pressing on you. That extra pressure is what's making your heart beat faster. When you get used to my energy, it will no longer bother you."

She took my hand and guided me to sit on a cushion on the floor with my back propped against the front of the sofa.

"When you are agitated as you are now, prop your lower back against a piece of furniture. Or bend your arms backward, pressing your hands against the top of your kidneys."

To sit on the floor with my back propped in that fashion had a definite relaxing effect on me. In a few moments, I was breathing normally and my stomach was no longer tied in knots.

I watched Nelida pace back and forth in front of me.

"Now, let's understand something once and for all," she said, continuing her relaxed, easy stride. "When I say that I'm responsible for you, I mean that I am in charge of your ultimate freedom. So don't give me any more nonsense about your struggle for independence. I'm not interested in your capricious fight against your family. Even though you've been at odds with them all your life, your fight has had no purpose or direction. It's time to give your natural strength and compulsive drive a worthy cause."

Her pacing, I noticed, was not nervous at all. It seemed to be rather a way of trapping my attention, for it had put me completely at ease yet kept me attentive.

I asked her once more if I would ever see Clara and Manfred. Nelida looked at me with a pitiless gaze that sent chills through me.

"No, you won't see them," she said. "At least not in this world. Both of them have done their impeccable best to prepare you for the great flight. Only if you are successful in awakening the double and crossing over into the abstract will you meet again. If not, they will become memories that you will talk about with others for a while, or keep to yourself, then gradually forget."

I swore to her that I would never forget Clara or Manfred; that they would be a part of me always, even if I never saw them again. And although something in me knew that that would be so, I couldn't bear such a final separation. I wanted to weep as I had done so easily all my life, but somehow my sorcery pass with the crystals had worked; weeping had fallen off me. Now when I really needed to cry, I couldn't. I was hollow inside. I was what I've always been: cold. Except that now I had no more pretenses. I remember what Clara had told me, that coldness is not cruelty or heartlessness but an unbending detachment. At last I knew what it meant to be without pity.

"Don't focus on your loss," Nelida said, sensing my mood. "At least not for the time being. Let's deal rather with helpful ways to gather energy to attempt the inevitable: the abstract flight. You know now that you belong to us, to me in particular. You must try today to come to my side of the house."

Nelida took off her shoes and sat down in an armchair across from me. In one graceful movement, she raised her knees to her chest and planted her feet on the seat. Her full skirt was pulled over her calves so that only her ankles and feet showed.

"Now, try not to be bashful, judgy or kinky," she said.

Then before I could respond, she lifted her skirt and spread her legs apart. "Look at my vagina," she ordered. "The hole between the legs of a woman is the energetic opening of the womb, an organ that is at the same time powerful and resourceful."

To my horror, Nelida had no underwear on. I could see right into her crotch. I wanted to look away but I was mesmerized. I could only stare with my mouth half open. She was hairless and her abdomen and legs were hard and smooth with absolutely no wrinkles or fat.

"Since I'm not in the world as a female, my womb has acquired a different mood than the mood of an average, undisciplined woman," Nelida said, without a hint of embarrassment. "So you simply shouldn't see me in a derogatory light."

She was indeed beautiful and I felt a jolt of sheer envy. I was at least one third her age and I couldn't possibly have looked that good in a similar position. In fact, I wouldn't dream of letting anyone see me naked. I always wore long bathrobes, as if I had something to hide. Remembering my own shyness, I politely looked away, but not before I got an eyeful of what I can only call sheer energy—the area around her vagina seemed to radiate a force that if I stared at it made me dizzy.

I shut my eyes and didn't care what she thought of me. Nelida's laughter was like an endless cascade of water, soft and bubbly.

"You are perfectly relaxed now," she said. "Look at me again and take a few deep breaths to charge yourself."

"Wait just a moment, Nelida," I said, struck by sudden fear, not of looking at her vagina, but of what I had just realized. Showing me her nakedness had done something inconceivable to me: it had soothed my anguish and made me abandon all my prudishness. In one instant, I had become extraordinarily familiar with Nelida. Stammering pitifully, I told her what I had just realized.

"That's exactly what the energy from the womb is supposed to do," Nelida said cheerfully. "Now really, you must look at me and breathe deeply. After that, you can analyze things to your heart's content."

I did as she said, and felt no shyness at all. Breathing in her energy made me feel strangely invigorated, as if a bond had formed between us that needed no words.

"You can accomplish wonders by controlling and circulating the energy from the womb," Nelida said, pulling her skirt over her calves again.

Nelida explained that the womb's primary function is reproduction in order to perpetuate our species. But unbeknownst to women, the womb also has subtle and sophisticated secondary functions. And it was these, she said, that she and I were interested in developing.

I was so pleased when Nelida had included me in her statement that I actually experienced a tickling sensation inside my stomach. I listened attentively as she explained that the most important secondary function of the womb is to serve as a guiding unit for the double. Whereas males have to rely on a mixture of reason and intent to guide their doubles, females have at their disposal their womb, a powerful source of energy with an abundance of mysterious attributes and functions all designed to protect and nurture the double.

"All this is possible, of course, if you have rid yourself of all the encumbering energy men have left inside you," she said. "A thorough recapitulation of all your sexual activity will take care of that."

She emphasized that using the womb is an extremely powerful and direct method of reaching the double. She reminded me of the sorcery pass I had learned in which one breathes directly with the opening of the vagina.

"The womb is the way female animals sense things and regulate their bodies," she said. "Through the womb, women can generate and store power in their doubles to build or destroy or to become one with everything around them."

Again I felt a tingle in my abdomen, a mild vibration that spread this time to my genitals and inner thighs.

"Another way of reaching the double, also called the other, besides using the energy of the womb, is through movement," Nelida continued. "This is the reason why Clara taught you the sorcery passes. There are two passes that you must use today to prepare yourself adequately for what is to come."

She walked to the closet, pulled out a straw mat, unrolled it on the floor and told me to lie on it. When I was flat on my back, she asked me to bend my knees a bit, fold my arms across my chest and roll once to my right side, then once to my left. She made me repeat this movement seven times. As I rolled, I was to slowly curl my spine at the shoulders.

She told me then to sit cross-legged once more on the floor leaning my back against the couch, while she took her seat on the armchair. Slowly and softly, she inhaled through her nose. Then she gracefully wiggled her left arm and hand out and upward as if she were boring a hole in the air with her hand. Then she reached in, grasped something and pulled her arm back, giving me the total impression of a long rope being retrieved from a hole in the air. She then did the same movements with her right arm and hand.

As she performed her sorcery pass, I recognized it to be a movement of the same nature as the ones Clara had shown me, but it was different too, lighter, smoother, more energetically charged. Clara's sorcery passes were like martial art movements; they were graceful and filled with internal strength. Nelida's passes were ominous, threatening and yet at the same time a pleasure to watch; they radiated a nervous energy but they were not agitated.

While she executed her pass, Nelida's face was like a beautiful mask. Her features were symmetrical, perfect. Watching her exquisite movements done with utter aloofness and detachment, I remembered what Clara had said about Nelida having no pity.

"This pass is for gathering energy from the vastness that lies just behind all that we see," she said. "Try making a hole and reach behind the façade of visible forms and grasp the energy that sustains us. Do it now."

I tried to replicate her swift, graceful movements but felt stiff and clumsy in comparison. I couldn't feel I was reaching through a hole and grasping energy, not by any stretch of the imagination. Nevertheless, after I had finished the pass, I felt strong and bursting with energy.

"It doesn't really take much to communicate or reach the ethereal body," Nelida went on. "Besides using the womb and movement, sound is a powerful way of attracting its attention."

She explained that by systematically directing words to our source of awareness—the double—one can receive a manifestation of that source.

"Provided, of course, that we have enough energy," she added. "If we do, it may take only a few selected words or a sustained sound to open something unthinkable in front of us."

"How exactly can we direct those words to the double?" I asked.

Nelida extended her arms in a sweeping gesture. "The double is nearly infinite," she said. "For just as the physical body is in communication with other physical bodies, the double is in communication with the universal life force."

Abruptly Nelida stood up. "We've done our sorcery passes and also plenty of talking," she said. "Now let's see if we can act. I want you to stand in front of the door leading to the left side of the house. I want you to remain very quiet but acutely aware of everything around you."

I followed her down the hall to the door that had always been closed. Clara had explained to me that it was kept closed even when all of the family members were present in the house. Since she had made me promise that I would never under any circumstances try to open it, no matter how curious I became, I never paid much attention to the door.

As I looked at it now, I could see nothing unusual; it was just a common wooden door much like all the others in the house. Nelida carefully opened it. There was a hallway, just like the right-side hallway that led to the other side of the house.

"I want you to repeat one word," Nelida said, standing close behind me. "The word is 'intent.' I want you to say 'intent' three or four times or even more, but bring it out from the depths of you."

"From the depths of me?"

"Allow the word to burst out from your midsection loud and clear. In fact, you should shout the word 'intent' with all your strength."

I hesitated. I hated to shout and I disliked it when people raised their voices at me. As a child, I learned it was impolite to shout and I dreaded to hear my parents arguing in loud voices.

"Don't be bashful," Nelida said. "Shout as loud and as many times as it's needed."

"How will I know when to stop?"

"You stop when something happens or when I tell you to stop because nothing has happened. Do it! Now!"

I said the word "intent"; my voice sounded hesitant, feeble, unsure. Even to my ear, it lacked conviction. But I kept on repeating it, each time with more vigor. My voice became not deep but shrill and loud, until I shocked myself into a near faint with a hair-raising scream that wasn't my own. And yet I had heard it before. It was the same shrill noise I had heard the day Clara and Manfred had dashed into the house, leaving me under the tree. I began to shiver and became so dizzy that I slumped down on the spot and leaned against the doorframe.

"Don't move!" Nelida ordered, but it was too late. I was already limp on the floor.

"Too bad you moved when you should have stayed put," Nelida said sternly, but added a smile when she saw I was about to pass out. She squatted next to me and rubbed my hands and neck to revive me.

"What did you make me shout for?" I muttered, straightening up against the wall.

"We were trying to catch the attention of your double," Nelida said. "Seemingly there are two levels to the universal awareness: the level of the visible, of order, of everything that can be thought or named; and the unmanifested level of energy that creates and sustains all things.

"Because we rely on language and reason," Nelida continued, "it is the level of the visible that we regard as reality. It appears to have an order, and is stable and predictable. Yet in actuality, it is elusive, temporary and ever changing. What we judge as permanent reality is only the surface appearance of an unfathomable force."

I felt so drowsy, I could barely follow her words. I yawned several times to take in more air. Nelida laughed when I opened my eyes wide in an exaggerated manner to give her the impression I was paying full attention.

"What you and I want to do with all this shouting," she went on, "is to catch the attention not of the visible reality, but rather the attention of the unseen, the force that is the source of your existence, a force that we hope will carry you across the chasm."

I wanted to listen to what she was saying, but a strange thought kept distracting me. Just before I had slumped to the floor, I had caught a glimpse of a rare sight. I had noticed that the air in the hall behind that door was bubbling, just like it had in the darkness of my room the first night I had slept in the house.

As Nelida continued speaking, I turned to look into the hallway again, but she moved in front of me and blocked my view. She bent over and picked up a leaf that, while I was shouting, must have fallen out of the protective bundle Clara had tied around my midsection.

"Perhaps this leaf will help clarify things," she said, holding it up for me to see. She talked fast, as if she knew my attention was waning and she wanted to get as much in as she could before my mind wandered off again. "Its texture is dry and brittle; its shape is flat and round, its color is brown with a touch of crimson. We can recognize it as a leaf because of our senses, our instruments of perception, and our thought that gives things names. Without them, the leaf is abstract, pure, undifferentiated energy. The same unreal, ethereal energy that flows through this leaf flows through and sustains everything. We, like everything else, are real on the one hand, and only appearances on the other."

She carefully put the leaf back on the floor as if it were so fragile that it would shatter at the slightest touch.

Nelida paused for a moment as if to wait for my mind to assimilate what she had said, but my attention was again drawn through the open door to the hallway where I saw filaments of light streaming through a large window at the end of the hall. I caught a fleeting glimpse of men and women; that is, three or four people for an instant had stuck their heads out of doors opening onto the hallway. They all seemed to have been awakened at once by my shouts and had poked their heads out of their bedrooms to see what all the commotion was about.

"You're certainly undisciplined," Nelida barked at me. "Your attention span is much too short."

I tried to tell Nelida what I had seen, but she subdued me with one look. I felt a chill going up my spine into my neck and I ended up shivering involuntarily. It was then, as I sat there confused and defenseless, that the strangest thought thus far occurred to me: Nelida seemed familiar to me because I had seen her in a dream. In fact, I had seen her not in one dream but in a series of recurring dreams, and the people in the hall . . .

"Don't let your mind go beyond this point!" Nelida shouted at me. "Don't you dare, do you hear me? Don't you dare to wander away! I want your undivided attention here with me."

She pulled me to my feet and told me to gather my wits. I did my best to gather them because I was definitely intimidated by her. I had always taken pride in believing that no one could dominate me, yet one look from this woman could stop my thoughts and fill me with awe and dread at the same time.

Nelida gave me a firm knock on the top of my head with a knuckle. It sobered me up as easily as her shouts had unsettled me.

"I've been talking my head off because Clara assured me that talking is the best way to relax you and pique your interest," she said. "I want you ready to go through this door at any cost."

I told her that I had the certainty that I had seen her in my dreams. But that was not all; I had the feeling that the people that had poked their heads into the hall were also known to me.

When I mentioned the people, Nelida stepped back and scrutinized me as if looking for markings on my body. She was silent for a moment, perhaps considering whether or not to divulge something.

"We are a group of sorcerers, as the nagual and Clara have already told you. We are a lineage, but not a family lineage. In this house there are two branches of that lineage, each has eight members. The members of Clara's branch are the Graus and the members of my branch are the Abelars. Our origin is lost in time. We count ourselves by generations. I am a member of the generation in power, and that means I can teach what my group knows to someone who is like me. In this case, you. You are an Abelar."

She stood behind me and turned me in the direction of the hallway. "Now, no more talking. Face the hallway and shout again the word 'intent.' I think you are ready to meet all of us in person."

I shouted "intent" three times. This time my voice didn't screech, but resonated loudly beyond the walls of the house. On the third shout, the air in the hall began to fizzle. Billions of tiny bubbles sparkled and glowed as if they had all lit up at the same instant. I heard a soft hum that reminded me of the sound of a muffled generator. Its mesmeric purr drew me inside, past the threshold where Nelida and I had been standing. My ears were plugged and I had to swallow repeatedly to unplug them. Then the humming stopped and I found myself in the middle of a hallway that was the exact mirror image of the hallway in the right side of the house where my room was. Only this hallway was full of people. They all had come out of their rooms and were staring at me as if I had dropped in from another planet, materializing right in front of their very eyes.

Among them, at the far end of the hallway, I saw Clara. She had a beaming smile and opened her arms inviting me to come and embrace her. Then I saw Manfred, pawing the floor. He was as happy to see me as Clara was. I ran toward them, but instead of feeling my steps on the wooden floor, I felt that I had been catapulted in the air. To my agony, I flew past Clara and Manfred and all the other people in the hallway. I had no control over my movements; all I could do was shout Clara's and Manfred's names in anguish as I flew past them, beyond the hall, the house, beyond the trees and the hills into a blinding glare, and finally into an absolutely black stillness.

17

I was dreaming that I was digging the ground in the garden when a sharp pain in my neck awoke me. Without opening my eyes, I groped for the pillows in order to ease my neck into their soft comfortable folds. But my hands searched in vain. I couldn't find the pillows; I couldn't even feel the mattress. I began swaying as if I had eaten or drunk too much the night before and was feeling the unsettling effects of indigestion. Gradually I opened my eyes. Instead of seeing the ceiling or walls, I saw branches and green leaves. When I tried to rise up, everything around me began moving. I realized that I was not in my bed; I was suspended in midair in some sort of leather harness and it was I who was swaying, not the world around me. I knew beyond a doubt that this was not a dream. As my senses tried to make order out of chaos, I saw that I was hoisted with pulleys into the highest branch of a tree.

The sensation of unexpectedly waking up restrained, coupled with the realization that there was nothing beneath me, created in one instant a physical terror of heights. I had never been up in a tree in my life. I began to scream for help. No one came to my rescue so I continued screaming until I lost my voice. Exhausted, I hung there like a limp carcass. Being physically terrified had made me lose control of my excretory functions. I was a mess. But screaming had drained me of my fears. I looked around and slowly began to assess my situation.

I noticed that my arms and hands were free, and when I turned my head downward, I saw what was suspending me. Thick brown leather belts were buckled around my waist, chest and legs. Around the trunk of the tree was another belt, which I could reach if I stretched my arms. That belt had the end of a rope and a pulley attached to it. I saw then that all I had to do to free myself was to release the rope and let myself down. It took an excruciating effort to reach the rope and then lower myself because my arms and hands were trembling. But once I was lying on the ground, I was able to painstakingly unbuckle the straps from around my body and slip out of the harness.

I ran into the house calling for Clara. I had a vague recollection that I wouldn't be able to find her, but it was more of a feeling than a conscious certainty. Automatically, I began searching for her but Clara was nowhere to be found and neither was Manfred. I became aware then that somehow everything had changed, but I didn't know what or when or even why things were different from the way they used to be. All I knew was that something had been irreparably broken.

I lapsed into a long inner monologue. I said to myself how I wished that Clara hadn't gone off on one of her mysterious trips precisely when I needed her most. Then I reasoned that there might be other explanations for her absence. She might be deliberately avoiding me or visiting with her relatives in the left side of the house. Then I remembered meeting Nelida and I rushed to the door of the left side hallway and tried to open it, ignoring Clara's warning never to tamper with that door. I found it was locked. I called out to her through the door a few times, then kicked it in anger and went to my bedroom. To my dismay, that door was locked too. Frantically I tried opening the doors to the other bedrooms in the hallway. All of them were locked except one, which was a sort of storage room or den. I had never entered it, obeying Clara's specific instructions to keep out of it. But that door had always remained ajar, and every time I had passed by, I had peeked inside.

This time I went in, calling out for Clara and Nelida to show themselves. The room was dark but filled to capacity with the most bizarre collection of objects I had ever seen. In fact, it was so crammed with grotesque sculptures, boxes and trunks that there was hardly any room to move around. Some light came in from a beautiful stained-glass bay window along the back wall. It was a mellow glow that cast eerie shadows on all the objects in the room. It made me think that this was the way storage rooms of elegant but no longer in-service ocean liners that have cruised the world over must look like. The floor underneath me suddenly began to sway and creak and the objects around me also seemed to shift. I let out an involuntary shriek and rushed out of the room. My heart was pounding so fast and loud that it took several minutes and quite a few deep breaths to quiet it.

In the hallway, I noticed that the large walk-in closet opposite to that storage room was open and all my clothes were there, neatly placed on hangers or folded on shelves. Pinned to the sleeve of the jacket that Clara had given me the first day I came to the house was a note addressed to me. It read, "Taisha, the fact that you are reading this note tells me that you have let yourself down from the tree. Please follow my instructions to the letter. Do not go back to your old room, for it is locked. From now on, you will sleep in your harness or in the tree house. We have all gone on an extended trip. The whole house is in your care. Do your best!" It was signed "Nelida."

Stunned, I stared at the note for a long time, reading it again and again. What did Nelida mean that the house was in my care? What was I supposed to do there all alone? The thought of sleeping in that horrible harness, hung like a side of beef, gave me the eeriest feeling of all.

I wanted tears to flood my eyes. I wanted to feel sorry for myself because they had left me alone and angry with them for leaving without warning me first, but I couldn't do any of these. I stomped around trying to work up momentum for a tantrum. Again, I failed miserably. It was as if something inside me had been turned off, making me indifferent and incapable of expressing my familiar emotions. But I did feel abandoned. My body began to shiver as it always had just before I burst out weeping. But what gushed out next wasn't a deluge of tears but a stream of memories and dreamlike visions.

I was hanging in that harness, looking down. Below, people were standing at the foot of the tree laughing and clapping. They were shouting up at me trying to get my attention. Then all of them made a sound in unison like a lion's roar, and left. I knew it was a dream. But I knew meeting Nelida had definitely not been a dream. I had her note in my hand to prove it. What I wasn't certain of was why and how long I had been hanging from the tree. Judging from the state of my clothes and how famished I was, I might have been there for days. But how did I get up there?

I grabbed some of my clothes from the closet and went to the outhouse to wash and change. When I was clean again, it dawned on me that I hadn't looked in the kitchen. I had a persistent hope that maybe Clara was there eating and hadn't heard me calling. I pushed the door open, but the kitchen was deserted. I poked around for food. I found a pot of my favorite stew on the stove and wanted desperately to believe that Clara had left it for me. I tasted it and gasped with a tearless sob. The vegetables were finely sliced, not diced, and there was hardly any meat. I knew that Clara hadn't made it and that she was gone. At first I didn't want to eat the stew, but I was terribly hungry. I took my bowl from the shelf and filled it to the brim.

It was only after I had eaten and was assessing my present situation that it occurred to me there was one other place I had forgotten to look. I hurried to the cave with the vague hope of finding Clara or the nagual there. But I found no one; not even Manfred. The solitude of the cave and the hills gave me such a feeling of sadness that I would have given anything in the world to be able to weep. I crawled inside the cave feeling the despair of a mute that only yesterday knew how to talk. I wanted to die there on the spot, but instead I fell asleep.

When I woke up, I returned to the house. Now that everyone was gone, I thought, I may as well leave too. I walked to the place where my car was parked. Clara had driven it constantly and serviced it in a garage in the city. I started it to charge the battery, and to my relief, it worked perfectly. After stuffing some of my things into an overnight bag, I got as far as the back door when a strong pang of guilt stopped me. I reread Nelida's note. In it she had asked me to take care of the house. I couldn't just abandon it. She had said to do my best. I felt that they had entrusted me with a particular task and I had to stay, even if it was only to find out what that task was. I put my things back in the closet and lay down on the couch to take stock of myself.

All the screaming I had done had definitely irritated my vocal cords. My throat was terribly sore; but other than that, I seemed to be in good physical condition. Shock, fear and self-pity had passed, and all that was left was the certainty that something monumental had happened to me in that left hallway. But try as I could, I couldn't remember what happened after I had stepped over the threshold.

Aside from these fundamental concerns, I also had one serious immediate problem: I wasn't certain how to start the wood-burning stove. Clara had demonstrated over and over how to do it, but I just couldn't get the knack of it, perhaps because I never expected that I would have to start it myself. One solution that occurred to me was to keep the fire burning by feeding it all night.

I rushed to the kitchen to place more wood on the fire before it went out. I also boiled more water and washed my bowl with some of it. The rest of the water I poured into the limestone filter, which looked like a thick, inverted cone. The huge receptacle sat on a sturdy wrought-iron stand and, drop by drop, filtered the boiled water. From the receptacle where the water collected under the filter, I poured a couple of ladles into my mug. I drank my fill of the cool, delicious water, then decided to go back to the house. Perhaps Clara or Nelida had left me other notes telling me more specifically what I had to do.

I looked for keys to the bedroom doors. In a hall cabinet, I found a set that were marked with different names. I picked one out that had Nelida's name on it; I was surprised to find that the key fit my bedroom. Then I picked out Clara's key and tried it in different doors until I found the lock that it fit. I turned the key and the door opened, but when it came to going inside her room and snooping around, I couldn't do it. I felt that even if she was gone, she was still entitled to her privacy.

I closed the door again, locked it and put the keys back where I had found them. I returned to the living room and sat on the floor, leaning my back against the sofa the way Nelida had suggested I do when I was tense. It definitely helped to calm my nerves. I thought of getting in my car again and leaving. But I really had no desire to leave. I decided to accept the challenge and house-sit for as long as they were gone, even if it was forever.

Since I had nothing else in particular to do, it occurred to me that I could try reading. I had recapitulated my early negative experiences with books, and I thought I would test myself to see if my attitude toward them had changed. I went to browse through the book-shelves. I found that most of the books were in German, some were in English and a few were in Spanish. I made a quick survey and saw that the majority of the German books were on botany; there were also some on zoology, geology, geography and oceanography. On a different shelf, hidden from view, was a collection of astronomy books in English. The Spanish books, on a separate bookshelf, were literature, novels and poetry.

I decided that I would first read the books on astronomy, since the subject had always fascinated me. I picked out a thin book with plenty of pictures and began to leaf through it. But soon it put me to sleep.

When I woke up, it was pitch black in the house and I had to grope my way in total darkness to the back door. On my way to the shed where the generator was housed, I noticed light coming from the kitchen. I realized that someone must have already turned the generator on. Elated that perhaps Clara had come back, I rushed toward the kitchen. As I approached, I heard soft singing in Spanish. It wasn't Clara. It was a male voice, but not the nagual's. I continued with great trepidation. Before I reached the door, a man poked his head out and, upon seeing me, let out a loud scream. I screamed at the same time. Apparently I had frightened him as much as he had scared me. He came out the door, and for a moment, we just stood there staring at each other.

He was slim but not skinny; wiry yet muscular. He was my height or perhaps an inch taller than I, about five eight. He was wearing blue mechanic's coveralls, like those worn by gas station attendants. He had a light pinkish complexion. His hair was gray. He had a pointed nose and chin, prominent cheek bones and a small mouth.

His eyes were like those of a bird, dark and round yet shining and animated. I could hardly see the whites of his eyes. As I stared at him, I had the impression that I wasn't looking at an old man, but at a boy that had wrinkled due to an exotic disease. There was something about him that was at once old and young, winning yet unsettling. I managed to ask him in my best high school Spanish to please tell me who he was and to explain his presence in this house.

He stared at me curiously. "I speak English," he said, with hardly an accent, "I've lived for years in Arizona with Clara's relatives. My name is Emilito; I'm the caretaker. And you must be the tree dweller."

"I beg your pardon?"

"You are Taisha, aren't you?" he said, taking a few steps toward me. He moved with ease and agility.

"Yes, I am. But what was that you said about me being a tree dweller?"

"Nelida told me that you live in the big tree by the front door of the main house. Is that true?"

I nodded automatically, and it was only then that I became aware of something so obvious that only a thick-headed ape could have missed: the tree was on the forbidden front part of the house, the east; the part of the grounds that I could only see from my observation post in the hills. That revelation sent a surge of excitement through me for I realized, too, that I was now free to explore terrain that had always been denied me.

My delight was cut short when Emilito shook his head as if he felt sorry for me. "What did you do, you poor girl?" he asked, patting my shoulder gently.

"I didn't do anything," I said, taking a step back. The clear implication was that I had done something wrong for which I had been strung up in the tree as a form of punishment.

"Now, now, I didn't mean to pry," he said, smiling. "You don't have to fight with me. I'm nobody important. I'm merely the caretaker, a hired hand. I'm not one of them."

"I don't care who you are," I snapped. "I'm telling you, I didn't do anything."

"Well, if you don't want to talk about it, it's all right with me," he said, turning his back to reenter the kitchen.

"There's nothing to talk about," I yelled, wanting to get in the last word.

I had no problem in yelling at him, a thing I wouldn't have dared to do if he had been young and handsome. I surprised myself again by shouting, "Don't give me a hard time. I'm the boss. Nelida asked me to take care of this house. She said so in her note."

He jumped as if struck by lightning. "You are a weird one," he muttered. Then he cleared his throat and shouted at me, "Don't you dare to come any closer. I might be old, but I'm plenty tough. To work here doesn't include risking my neck or being insulted by idiots. I'll quit."

I didn't know what had come over me. "Wait a minute," I said apologetically. "I didn't mean to raise my voice, but I'm extremely nervous. Clara and Nelida left me here without any warning or explanation."

"Well, I didn't mean to shout either," he said, in the same apologetic tone I had used. "I was only trying to figure why they strung you up before they left. That's the reason I asked if you had done something wrong. I didn't mean to pry."

"But I assure you, sir, I didn't do anything, believe me."

"Why are you a tree dweller, then? These people are very serious. They wouldn't do this to you just for the hell of it. Besides, it's obvious that you are one of them. If Nelida leaves you notes saying to take care of the house, you have to be buddy-buddy with her. She doesn't give the time of the day to anyone."

"The truth is," I said, "that I don't know why they left me in the tree. I was with Nelida in the left side of the house, and then the next thing I knew, I woke up with my neck bent all out of shape and hanging from that tree. I was terrified."

Remembering my anguish upon finding myself alone, with everyone gone, I couldn't help becoming agitated again. I began to shake and sweat right in front of this strange man.

"You were in the left side of the house?" His eyes widened; the surprise on his face seemed genuine.

"For an instant I was there, but then everything went black," I said.

"And what did you see?"

"I saw people in the hallway. Lots of them."

"How many, would you say?"

"The hallway was full of people. Maybe twenty or thirty."

"That many, huh? How strange!"

"Why is that strange, sir?"

"Because there weren't that many people in the whole house. There were only ten people here at that time. I know, because I'm the caretaker."

"What does this all mean?"

"I'll be damned if I know! But to me, it seems that there is something very wrong with you."

My stomach knotted as a familiar cloud of doom settled over me. It was the exact sensation I had had as a child in the doctor's office when they found out I had mononucleosis. I had no idea what that was, but I knew I was done for; and from the grim looks on everyone's face, they seemed to know it too. When they were going to give me a shot of penicillin, I screamed so hard that I fainted.

"Now, now," the caretaker said gently. "There's no use in being so upset. I didn't mean to hurt your feelings. Let me tell you what I know about that harness. Maybe it'll make things clear for you. They use it when the person they are treating is . . . well . . . a bit off his or her rocker. If you know what I mean."

"What do you mean, sir?"

"Call me Emilito," he said, smiling. "But, please, don't call me 'sir.' Or you can refer to me as the caretaker, just as everyone refers to John Michael Abelar as the nagual. Now, let's go into the kitchen and sit at the table where we can talk more comfortably."

I followed him into the kitchen and sat down. He poured warm water he had heated on the stove into my mug and brought it to me.

"Now, about the harness," he began, sitting down on the bench opposite me. "It's supposed to cure mental maladies. And they usually put people in it after they've gone off the deep end."

"But I'm not crazy," I protested. "If you or anyone else is going to insinuate that I am, I'm leaving."

"But you must be crazy," he reasoned.

"That does it. I'm going back to the house." I stood up to leave.

The caretaker stopped me. "Wait, Taisha. I didn't mean to say that you're crazy. There may be another explanation," he said, in a conciliatory tone. "These people mean very well. They probably thought that you should reinforce your mental power while they are away, not cure you from a mental disease. That's why they put you in the harness. It's my fault for jumping to the wrong conclusion. Please accept my apologies."

I was more than willing to let bygones be bygones, and sat down at the table again. Besides, I needed to be on good terms with the caretaker because he obviously knew how to light the stove. Also, I didn't have the energy to continue feeling offended. And at this point, I felt he was right. I was crazy. I just didn't want the caretaker to know it.

"Do you live nearby, Emilito?" I asked, trying to sound at ease.

"No. I live here in the house. My room is across the hall from your closet."

"You mean you live in that storage room full of sculptures and things?" I gasped. "And how do you know where my closet is?"

"Clara told me," he replied with a grin.

"But if you live here, how come I've never seen you around?"

"Ah, that's because you and I obviously keep different hours. To tell you the truth, I've never seen you either."

"How is that possible, Emilito? I've been here for over a year."

"And I've been here for forty years, on and off."

We both laughed out loud at the absurdity of what we were saying. What I found unsettling was that at a very deep level, I knew that it was this person's presence I had so often sensed in the house.

"I know, Emilito, that you have been watching me," I said bluntly. "Don't deny it, and don't ask me how I know it. What's more, I also know that you knew who I was when you saw me outside the kitchen door. Isn't that so?"

Emilito sighed and nodded. "You're right, Taisha. I did recognize you. But you still gave me a genuine fright."

"But how did you recognize me?"

"I've been watching you from my room. But don't get angry. I never thought that you would feel me watching you. My humble apologies if I made you feel uncomfortable."

I wanted to ask him why he had been watching me. I hoped that he would say that he found me beautiful or at least interesting, but he cut our conversation short and said that since it was dark, he felt obliged to help me hoist myself up into the tree.

"Let me make a suggestion," he said. "Sleep in the tree house instead of the harness. It's a thrilling experience. I, too, once was an occupant of that tree house for an extended stay, although it was quite a long time ago."

Before we left, Emilito served me a bowl of delicious soup and a stack of flour tortillas. We ate in complete silence. I tried to talk to him, but he said that conversing while eating was bad for the digestion. I told him that Clara and I always chatted endlessly during our meals.

"Her body and mine aren't even remotely alike," he muttered. "She's made of iron, so she can do anything she wants to her body. I, on the other hand, can't take any chances with my puny little body. And neither can you."

I liked him for including me among the little bodies, although I had hoped what he meant was that I was frail rather than puny.

After dinner, he walked me very solicitously through the main house to the front door. I had never been in that section of the house, and I deliberately slowed my pace, trying to take in as much of it as I could. I saw an enormous dining room with a long banquet table and a china cabinet full of crystal goblets, champagne glasses and dishes. Next to the dining room was a study. As I passed, I got a glimpse of a massive mahogany desk and bookcases filled with books lining one wall. Another room had electric lights on but I couldn't see inside because its door was only slightly ajar. I heard muffled voices coming from inside.

"Who's in there, Emilito?" I asked excitedly.

"Nobody," he said. "That whispering you heard is the wind. It plays strange tricks on the ears as it blows through the shutters."

I gave him a who-are-you-kidding stare and he gallantly opened the door for me to look inside. He was right; the room was empty. It was just another living room, similar to the one on the right side of the house. However, when I looked closer I noticed something odd in the shadows cast on the floor. A shudder went through me, for I knew the shadows were wrong. I could have sworn that they were agitated, shimmering, dancing, but there was no wind or movement in the room.

In a whisper, I told Emilito what I noticed. He laughed and patted me on the back. "You sound exactly like Clara," he said. "But that's good. I'd be worried if you sounded like Nelida. Do you know that she has power in her pussy?"

The way he said that, his tone of voice and the curious birdlike wonder in his eyes struck me as so funny that I began to laugh, nearly to the point of tears. My laughter vanished as suddenly as it had begun, as if a switch inside me had been turned off. That worried me. And it worried Emilito too, for he looked at me warily as if questioning my mental stability.

He unlatched the main door and led me out front where the tree was. He helped me put on the harness and showed me how to use the pulleys to hoist myself up in a sitting position. He gave me a small flashlight and I pulled myself up. From the top branches, I could vaguely see a wooden tree house. It was close to the place where I had first awakened in the harness, but I hadn't seen it then because of my extreme fright, and because of all the foliage that surrounded it.

From the ground, the caretaker beamed his flashlight directly onto the structure and yelled up after me, "There's a maritime flashlight inside, Taisha, but don't use it too long. And in the morning, before you come down, be sure to disconnect its batteries."

He held his flashlight in place until I crawled onto a small landing in front of the tree house and finished unhooking the harness.

"Good night. I'm leaving now," he called up. "Pleasant dreams."

I thought I heard him chuckling as he moved his beam of light away and headed for the main house. I entered the tree house using my own weak flashlight and I searched for what he called the maritime flashlight. It was a huge light that was fixed to a shelf; on the floor there was a large square battery in a casing nailed to the boards. I connected it to the light and turned it on.

The tree house was one tiny room with a small raised platform that served as both a bed and a low table. It had a sleeping bag rolled up on top of it. The structure had windows all around, with hinged shutters that could be propped open by thick sticks that lay on the floor. In the corner of the room was a chamber pot that fit inside a basket that had a lid attached to one side. After this cursory examination of the room, I disconnected the big flashlight and crawled into the sleeping bag.

It was absolutely dark. I could hear the crickets and the hum of the stream in the distance. Nearby, the wind rustled the leaves and gently rocked the whole house. As I listened to the sounds, unknown fears began to enter my awareness and I fell prey to physical sensations I had never felt before. Total darkness distorted and masked the sounds and movements so thoroughly that I felt them as if they were coming from inside my body. Every time the house shook, the soles of my feet tingled. Whenever the house creaked, the inner part of my knees twitched, and the back of my neck popped whenever a branch snapped.

Then fear entered my body as a tremor in my toes. The vibration rose to my feet and then to my legs, until my entire lower body shook out of control. I became drowsy and disoriented. I didn't know where the door or the flashlight were. I began to feel the house tilting. It was barely perceptible at first, but it became more noticeable until it seemed that the floor was inclined at a forty-five degree angle. I let out a scream as I felt the platform tilt even more. The thought of having to hoist myself down petrified me. I was certain I would die by falling from the tree. On the other hand, the sensation of being tilted was so dramatic that I was sure I would slide off the platform and out the door. At one point the incline was so acute that I felt as if I were actually standing up instead of lying down.

I screamed at every sudden movement, holding on to one of the beams on the side to keep from sliding. The whole tree house seemed to be coming apart. I became nauseous from the motion. The swaying and creaking grew so intense that I knew this would be my last night on earth. Just when I had completely given up all hope of pulling through, something inconceivable came to my rescue. A light spilled out from within me. It poured out through all the openings of my body. The light was a heavy luminous fluid that fixed me to the platform by covering me like a shiny armor. It constricted my larynx and subdued my screams, but it also opened my chest area so I could breathe easier. It soothed my nervous stomach and stopped the shaking of my legs. The light illuminated the entire room so I could see the door a few feet in front of me. As I basked in its glow, I grew calm. All my fears and concerns vanished so that nothing mattered anymore. I lay perfectly still and tranquil until the dawn broke. Totally refreshed, I hoisted myself down and went to the kitchen to make breakfast.

18

I found a plate of tamales on the kitchen table. I knew that Emilito had prepared them, but he wasn't anywhere in sight. I poured some water into my mug and ate all the tamales, hoping that the caretaker had already had his breakfast.

After I washed the plate, I went to work in the vegetable garden, but I tired easily. I made myself a nest of leaves under a tree, the way Clara had showed me, and sat on it to rest. For a while, I watched the swaying branches of the tree across from me. And the motion of those branches brought me back to my childhood. I must have been four or five years old; I was grabbing onto a handful of willow branches. It wasn't that I was remembering it; I was actually there. My feet were dangling beneath me, barely touching the ground. I was swinging. I screamed with delight as my brothers took turns pushing me. Then they jumped up to grab higher branches; bringing their knees up, they swung back and forth, putting their feet down only to push off the ground to gain momentum for another ride.

As soon as it ended, I breathed in everything I was reliving; the joy, the laughter, the sounds, the feelings I had for my brothers. I swept the past away with a turning motion of my head. Gradually, my eyelids grew heavy. I slumped down on my nest of leaves and fell into a sound sleep.

I was awakened by a sharp poke in my ribs. The caretaker was nudging me with a walking stick.

"Wake up, it's already afternoon," he said. "Didn't you sleep well last night in the tree house?"

As I opened my eyes, a beam of light kindled the treetop with orange hues. The caretaker's face, too, was lit up by an eerie glow that made him look ominous. He had on the same blue coveralls he had worn the day before, and tied to his belt were three gourds. I sat up and watched as he carefully removed the stopper of the largest gourd, lifted it to his mouth and took a gulp. Then he smacked his lips with satisfaction.

"Didn't you sleep well last night?" he asked again, peering at me curiously.

"Are you kidding?" I moaned. "I can truthfully say it was one of the worst nights of my life."

A torrent of whining complaints began pouring out of me. I stopped, horrified, when I realized that I sounded just like my mother. Whenever I would ask her how she had slept, she would give me a similar discourse of discontent. I had hated her for that, and to think I was doing the same thing!

"Please, Emilito, forgive me for my petty outburst," I said. "It's true that I didn't sleep a wink, but I'm fine."

"I heard you screaming like a banshee," he ventured. "I thought you were either having nightmares or falling out of the tree."

"I thought I was falling out of the tree," I said, wanting sympathy. "I nearly died of fright. But then a strange thing happened and I got through the night."

"What strange thing happened?" he asked, curious, sitting down on the ground a safe distance from me.

I saw no reason not to tell him, so I described in as much detail as I could the events of the night, culminating with the light that came to save me. Emilito listened with genuine interest, nodding at the appropriate times as if he understood the feelings I was describing.

"I'm very glad to hear that you are so resourceful," he said. "I really didn't expect you to make it through the night. I thought you would faint. And what this all boils down to is that you're not as bad off as they said you were."

"Who said I was bad off?"

"Nelida and the nagual. They left me specific instructions not to interfere with your healing. That's why I didn't come to help you last night, even though I was greatly tempted—if for no other reason than to get some peace and quiet."

He took another gulp from his gourd. "Do you want to take a swig?" he offered, holding it out for me to take.

"What's in the gourd?" I asked, wondering if it was liquor. In which case, I wouldn't have minded having a sip.

He hesitated for a moment, then he turned the gourd upside down and gave it a few strong shakes.

"It's empty," I scoffed. "You were trying to trick me."

He shook his head. "It only seems empty," he retorted. "But it's filled to the brim with the strangest drink of all. Now, do you or don't you want to drink from it?"

"I don't know," I said. For an instant, I wondered if he was toying with me. Seeing him in his neatly ironed blue coveralls with gourds tied to his belt, I had the impression that he was an escapee from a mental institution.

He shrugged and stared at me, wide-eyed. I watched as he re-corked the gourd and securely tied it to his belt with a thin leather thong.

"All right, let me have a sip," I said, driven by curiosity and a sudden urge to find out what his game was.

He uncorked the gourd again and handed it to me. I shook it and peered inside. It was indeed empty. But when I put it to my lips, I had a most unfamiliar oral sensation. Whatever flowed into my mouth was somehow liquid, but it wasn't anything like water. It was more like a dry, almost bitter pressure that suffocated me for an instant and then filled my throat and my entire body with a cool warmth.

It occurred to me that the gourd had a fine powder that had gotten into my mouth. To find out if that was true, I shook it onto the palm of my hand, but nothing came out.

"There is nothing in the gourd that the eyes can see," the caretaker said, noting my surprise.

I took another imaginary sip and was jolted nearly out of my shoes. Something electric flowed through me and made my toes tingle. The tingling went up my legs to my spine like a lightning bolt, and when it entered my head I nearly passed out.

I saw the caretaker jumping up and down laughing like a prankster. I grabbed onto the ground to steady myself with my hands. When I had somewhat regained my equilibrium, I confronted him angrily. "What the hell is in this gourd?" I demanded.

"What's in it is called 'intent,' " he said in a serious tone. "Clara told you a little about it. It's now up to me to tell you a bit more."

"What do you mean that it's now up to you, Emilito?"

"I mean that I'm your new usher. Clara did part of that work and I must do the rest."

My first reaction was simply not to believe him. He himself had said that he was merely a hired hand and not part of the group. It was obvious that this was a prank, and I wasn't going to fall for any more of his tricks.

"You're just pulling my leg, Emilito," I said, forcing a laugh.

"I am now," he said, and leaped over and actually gave my leg a yank.

Before I could get up, he celebrated his own joke by tugging my leg again. He was so animated that he hopped around in a squatting position like a rabbit, laughing playfully.

"You don't like your teacher to pull your leg?" he giggled.

I didn't like him to touch me, period. And definitely not my leg. But I didn't like Clara to touch me either. I began to toy with the idea of why I didn't like to be touched. Despite my having recapitulated all my encounters with people, my feeling regarding physical contact was as strong as ever. I filed this problem away for future examination, because the caretaker had settled down and was beginning to explain something that needed all my attention.

"I'm your teacher," I heard him say. "Besides Clara, Nelida and the nagual, you have me to guide you."

"You're a mass of misinformation, that's what you are," I snapped. "You yourself told me that you're merely a hired caretaker. So what's this business that you're my teacher?"

"It's true. I really am your other teacher," he said seriously.

"What could you possibly have to teach me?" I shouted, disliking the prospect immensely.

"What I have to teach you is called 'stalking with the double,' " he said, blinking like a bird.

"Where are Clara and Nelida?" I demanded.

"They are gone. Nelida said that in her note, didn't she?"

"I know they are gone, but where exactly did they go?"

"Oh, they went to India," he said with a grin that looked like an uncomfortable desire to burst out laughing.

"Then they won't be back for months," I said, feeling vicious.

"Right. You and I are alone. Not even the dog is here. You have, therefore, two options open to you. You can either pack your junk and leave or you can remain here with me and settle down to work. I don't advise you to do the former, because you don't have any place to go."

"I don't have any intention of leaving," I informed him. "Nelida left me in charge to take care of the house and that's what I'm going to do."

"Good, I'm glad you've decided to follow the sorcerers' intent," he said.

Since it must have been obvious to him that I hadn't understood, he explained that the intent of sorcerers differs from that of average people in that sorcerers have learned to focus their attention with infinitely more force and precision.

"If you're my teacher, can you give me a concrete example to illustrate what you mean?" I asked, staring at him.

He thought for a moment as he looked around. His face lit up and he pointed at the house. "This house is a good example," he said. "It is the result of the intent of countless sorcerers who amassed energy and pooled it over many generations. By now, this house is no longer just a physical structure, but a fantastic field of energy. The house itself could be destroyed ten times over, which it has been, but the essence of the sorcerers' intent is still intact, for it is indestructible."

"What happens when the sorcerers want to leave?" I asked. "Is their power trapped here forever?"

"If the spirit tells them to leave," Emilito said, "they are capable of lifting off the intent from the present spot where the house stands and placing it somewhere else."

"I have to agree that the house is really spooky," I said and told him how it had resisted my detailed measurements and calculations.

"What makes this house spooky is not the disposition of the rooms or walls or patios," the caretaker remarked, "but the intent that generations of sorcerers poured into it. In other words, the mystery of this house is the history of the countless sorcerers whose intent went into building it. You see, they not only intended it, but constructed it themselves, brick by brick, stone by stone. Even you have already contributed your intent and your work to it."

"What could my contribution be?" I asked, sincerely taken aback by Emilito's statement. "You can't possibly mean that crooked garden path I laid."

"No one in his right mind could call that a contribution," he said, laughing. "No, you've made a few others."

He remarked that on the mundane level of bricks and structures, he considered my contribution to be the careful electric wiring, the pipe fitting and the cement casing for the water pump I had installed to pump water from the stream up the hill to the vegetable garden.

"On the more ethereal level of energy flow," he went on, "I can tell you in all sincerity that one of your contributions is that never before have we witnessed in this house anyone merging her intent with Manfred."

At that moment something popped into my mind. "Are you the one who can call him 'toad' to his face?" I asked. "Clara once told me that someone could do it."

The caretaker's face beamed as he nodded. "Yes, I'm the one. I found Manfred when he was a puppy. He had been either abandoned or he had run away, perhaps from a motor home in the area. When I found him he was almost dead."

"Where did you find him?" I asked.

"On Highway 8, about sixty miles from Gila Bend, Arizona. I had stopped on the side of the road to go to the bushes and I actually pissed on him. He was lying there almost dead from dehydration. What impressed me the most was that he hadn't run onto the highway, as he could have done so easily. And, of course, that he was lying right where I went to piss."

"Then what happened?" I asked. I was so overtaken with sympathy for poor Manfred's plight that I forgot all my anger at the caretaker.

"I took Manfred home and put him in water but didn't let him drink," the caretaker said. "And then I offered him to the sorcerers' intent."

Emilito said that it was up to the sorcerers' intent to decide not only whether Manfred lived or died, but whether Manfred would be a dog or something else. And he lived and became something more than a dog.

"The same thing happened to you," he continued. "Maybe that's why the two of you got along so well. The nagual found you spiritually dehydrated, ready to make a shambles of your life. Since he was in the drive-in movie with Nelida, it was up to them to offer you to the sorcerers' intent, which they did."

"How did they offer me to the sorcerers' intent?" I asked.

"Didn't they already tell you?" he asked, surprised.

I considered for a moment before replying, "I don't think so."

"The nagual and Nelida called intent out loud, no doubt right there by the concession stand, and announced that they were putting their lives on the line for you without hesitation or regrets, without holding anything back. And both of them knew at once that they couldn't take you with them at that time, but would have to follow you around wherever you went.

"So you can say now that the sorcerers' intent took you in. The nagual's and Nelida's invocation worked. Look where you are! Talking to yours truly."

He looked at me to see if I was following his argument. I stared back with a silent plea for a more precise elucidation of the sorcerers' intent. He shifted to a more personal level and said that if he would take all the things I had said to Clara about myself as an example of intending, he would conclude that my intent is one of total defeat. I had, in a sustained fashion, always intended to be a crazy, desperate loser.

"Clara told me everything you told her about yourself," he said, clicking his tongue. "For instance, I would say that you jumped into that arena in Japan not to demonstrate your martial arts skills, but to prove to the world that your intent is to lose."

He pounced on me, saying that everything I did was tainted by defeat. Therefore the most important thing I had to do now was to set up a new intent. He explained that this new intent was called sorcerers' intent because it isn't just the intent of doing something new, but the intent of joining something already established: an intent that reaches out to us through thousands of years of human toil.

He said that in that sorcerers' intent there wasn't room for defeat, for sorcerers have only one path open to them: to succeed in whatever they do. But in order to have such a powerful and clear view, sorcerers have to reset their total being, and that takes both understanding and power. Understanding comes from recapitulating their lives, and power gathers from their impeccable acts.

Emilito looked at me and tapped his gourd. He explained that in his gourd he had stored his impeccable feelings, and that he had given me that sorcerers' intent to drink in order to counteract my defeatist attitude and prepare me for his instruction. He said something else, but I couldn't pay attention to him; his voice began to make me feel drowsy. My body got heavy all of a sudden. As I focused on his face, I saw only a whitish haze, like fog in the twilight. I heard him tell me to lie down and cast out my ethereal net by gradually relaxing my muscles.

I knew what he wanted me to do and automatically followed his instructions. I lay down and began moving my awareness from my feet upward to my ankles, calves, knees, thighs, abdomen and back. Then I relaxed my arms, shoulders, neck and head. As I moved my awareness to the various parts of my body, I felt myself become more and more drowsy and heavy.

Then the caretaker ordered me to make small counterclockwise circles with my eyes allowing them to roll back and up into my head. I continued relaxing until my breathing became slow and rhythmic, expanding and contracting by itself. I was concentrating on the lulling waves of my breathing, when he whispered that I should move my awareness out of my forehead to a place as far above me as I could, and there make a small opening.

"What kind of opening?" I muttered.

"Just an opening. A hole."

"A hole into what?"

"A hole into the nothingness your net is suspended on," he replied. "If you can move your awareness outside your body, you'll realize that there is blackness all around you. Try to pierce that blackness; make a hole in it."

"I don't think I can," I said, tensing up.

"Of course you can," he assured me. "Remember, sorcerers are never defeated, they can only succeed."

He leaned toward me and in a whisper said that after I had made the opening, I should roll my body up like a scroll and allow myself to be catapulted along a line extending from the crown of my head into the blackness.

"But I'm lying down," I protested feebly. "The crown of my head is nearly against the ground. Shouldn't I be standing up?"

"The blackness is all around us," he said. "Even if we are standing on our heads, it is still there."

He changed his tone to a hard command and ordered me to place my concentration on the hole I had just made and to let my thoughts and feelings flow through that opening. Again my muscles tightened because I hadn't made any hole. The caretaker urged me to relax, to let go and act and feel as if I had made that hole.

"Throw out everything that's inside you," he said. "Allow your thoughts, feelings and memories to flow out."

As I relaxed and released the tension from my body, I felt a surge of energy push through me. I was being turned inside out; everything was being pulled out from the top of my head, rushing along a line like an inverted cascading waterfall. At the end of that line, I sensed an opening.

"Let yourself go even deeper," he whispered in my ear. "Offer your whole being to nothingness."

I did my best to follow his suggestions. Whatever thoughts arose in my mind instantly joined the cascade at the top of my head. I vaguely heard the caretaker say that if I wanted to move, I only needed to give myself the directive and the line would pull me wherever I wanted to go. Before I could give myself the command, I felt a gentle but persistent tugging on my left side. I relaxed and allowed this sensation to continue. At first, only my head seemed to be pulled to the left, then the rest of my body slowly rolled to the left. I felt as if I were falling sideways, yet I sensed that my body had not moved at all. I heard a dull sound behind my neck, and saw the opening grow larger. I wanted to crawl inside, to squeeze through it and disappear. I experienced a deep stirring inside me; my awareness began moving along the line at the crown of my head and slipped through the opening.

I felt as if I were inside a gigantic cavern. Its velvety walls enveloped me; it was dark. My attention was caught by a luminescent dot. It flickered on and off like a beacon, appearing and disappearing whenever I focused on it. Then the area in front of me became illuminated by an intense light. Then gradually everything became dark again. My breathing seemed to cease altogether and no thoughts or images disturbed the blackness. I no longer felt my body. My last thought was that I had dissolved.

I felt a hollow popping sound. My thoughts returned to me all at once, tumbling down on me like a mountain of debris, and with them came the awareness of the hardness of the ground, the stiffness of my body, and some insect biting my ankle. I opened my eyes and looked around; the caretaker had taken my shoes and socks off and was poking the soles of my feet with a stick to revive me. I wanted to tell him what had happened, but he shook his head.

"Don't talk or move until you're solid again," he warned. He told me to close my eyes and breathe with my abdomen.

I lay on the ground until I felt I had regained my strength, then I sat up and leaned my back against a tree trunk.

"You opened a crack in the blackness and your double slid to the left and then went through it," the caretaker said, before I had asked him anything.

"I definitely felt a force pulling me," I admitted. "And I saw an intense light."

"That force was your double coming out," he said, as if he knew exactly what I was referring to. "And the light was the eye of the double. Since you've been recapitulating for over a year, you've also been, at the same time, casting your energy lines and now they're beginning to move by themselves. But because you're still involved in talking and thinking, those energy lines don't move as easily and completely as they are going to someday."

I had no idea what he meant when he said that I had been casting my energy lines as I recapitulated. I asked him to explain.

"What's there to explain?" he said. "It's a matter of energy; the more of it you call back through recapitulating, the easier it is for that recovered energy to nourish your double. To send energy to the double is what we call casting your energy lines. Someone who sees energy will see it as lines coming out of the physical body."

"But what does that mean to someone like me who doesn't see?"

"The greater your energy," he explained, "the greater your capacity to perceive extraordinary things."

"I think what has happened to me is that the greater my energy becomes, the crazier I get," I said, without trying to be facetious.

"Don't run yourself down in such a casual manner," he remarked. "Perception is the ultimate mystery because it's totally unexplainable. Sorcerers as human beings are perceiving creatures, but what they perceive is neither good nor evil; everything is just perception. If human beings, through discipline, can perceive more than is normally permitted, more power to them. Do you see what I mean?"

He refused to say one more word about it. Instead, he took me through the house then out the front door to my tree. He pointed to the top branches and said that because this particular tree had living quarters in it, it was equipped with a lightning rod.

"In this area, lightning is sudden and dangerous," he said. "There are lightning storms even without a drop of rain. So when it does rain or when there are too many cumulonimbus clouds in the sky, go to the tree house."

"When there are too many what in the sky?" I asked.

Emilito laughed and gently patted me on the back. "When the nagual Julian put me in a tree house, he told me the same thing, but at that time I didn't dare to ask him what he meant. And he didn't tell me either. I found out much later that he meant thunderclouds."

He laughed at my look of dismay. "Is there any danger of lightning striking the tree?" I asked.

"Well, there is, but your tree is safe," he replied. "Now get up there while it's still light."

Before I hoisted myself up, he gave me a sack of walnuts that were cracked but not shelled. He said that if I had to be a tree dweller,

I had to eat like a squirrel, little bits at a time and nothing at night.

That was fine with me, I told him, because I never really liked to eat anyway.

"Do you like to shit?" he asked, chuckling. "I hope not, for the worst part about living in a tree house is when you have to evacuate your bowels. Human excrement is difficult to deal with. My philosophy is that the less you have of it, the better off you are."

He found his statements so utterly funny that he doubled over laughing. Still chuckling, he turned around and left me to ponder over his philosophy.

19

That night it rained, and there was thunder and lightning. But there is no way on earth for me to explain what it was like to be in a tree house while bolt after bolt of lightning ripped through the sky and fell on the trees around me. My fear was indescribable. I screamed even harder than I had the first night when I felt my platform bed tilting. It was an animal fright, and it paralyzed me. The only thought that occurred to me was that I am a natural coward and when tension is too great I always pass out.

I didn't regain consciousness until around noon the next day. When I let myself down, I found Emilito waiting for me, sitting on a low branch with his feet nearly touching the ground.

"You look like a bat from hell," he commented. "What happened to you last night?"

"I nearly died of fright," I said. I wasn't going to pretend toughness or play at being in control. I felt like I must have looked—like a living rag.

I said to him that for the first time in my life, I had commiserated with soldiers in battle; I had felt the same fear they must experience when bombs explode all around them.

"I disagree," he said. "Your fear last night was even more intense. Whatever was shooting at you wasn't human. So at the level of the double, it was a gigantic fear."

"Please, Emilito, explain to me what you mean by that."

"Your double is about to become aware, so under conditions of stress, like last night, it becomes partially aware but also totally frightened. It's not used to perceiving the world. Your body and your mind are accustomed to it, but your double isn't."

I was certain that if I had been prepared for the storm, I would have relaxed, and if my fear and my thoughts about it hadn't interfered, some force inside me would have come completely out of my body and perhaps might have even stood up, moved around or come down from the tree. What frightened me most was the sensation of being cooped up, trapped inside my body.

"When we enter into absolute darkness, where there are no distractions," the caretaker said, "the double takes over. It stretches its ethereal limbs, opens its luminous eye and looks around. Sometimes experiencing it can be even more frightening than what you felt last night."

"The double won't be that frightening," I assured him. "I'm ready for it."

"You aren't ready for anything yet," he retorted. "I'm sure your screams last night could have been heard all the way to Tucson."

His comment annoyed me. There was something about him I didn't like, but I couldn't pinpoint what it was. Perhaps it was because he looked so odd. He wasn't manly; he seemed to be the mere shadow of a man and yet he was deceptively strong. But what really bothered me was that he didn't let me push him around, and that irritated my competitive side no end.

In a surge of anger I asked him belligerently, "How dare you run me down every time I say something you don't like!"

The moment I said that I regretted it and apologized profusely for my aggressiveness. "I don't know why I get so irritated with you," I ended up confessing.

"Don't feel bad," he said. "It's because you sense something about me that you can't explain. As you yourself put it, I'm not manly."

"I didn't say that," I protested.

From his look, he obviously didn't believe me. "Of course you did," he insisted. "You said it to my double just a moment ago. My double never ever makes mistakes or misinterprets things."

My nervousness and embarrassment reached their peak. I didn't know what to say. My face was red and my body trembled. I couldn't understand what had caused my exaggerated reaction. The caretaker's voice broke into my thoughts.

"You are reacting like that because your double is perceiving my double," he said. "Your physical body is frightened because its gates are opening and new perceptions are flowing in. If you think you feel bad now, imagine how much worse it'll be when all your gates are open."

He spoke so convincingly that I wondered if he was right.

"Animals and infants," he continued, "have no problem perceiving the double and they are often disturbed by it."

I mentioned that animals didn't particularly like me and that, except for Manfred, the feeling was mutual.

"Animals don't like you," he clarified, "because some of your body gates have never been completely closed and your double is struggling to come out. Be prepared. For now that you're deliberately intending it, they're going to fling open. One of these days your double is going to awake all at once and you might find yourself across the patio without having walked over."

I had to laugh, mostly out of nervousness and at the absurdity of what he was suggesting.

"And what about children, especially infants?" he asked. "Don't they holler when you pick them up?"

They usually did, but I didn't tell the caretaker.

"Babies like me," I lied, knowing too well that the few times I had been around infants, they had begun to cry as soon as I came near them. I had always told myself that it was because I lacked a maternal instinct.

The caretaker shook his head in disbelief. I challenged him to explain how animals and infants could sense the double when I didn't know it existed myself. In fact, until Clara and the nagual told me about it, I had never heard of such a thing. Nor had I ever met anyone who knew about it. He rebuffed me, saying that what animals and infants sense has nothing to do with knowing, but with the fact that they have the equipment to sense it: their open gates. He added that those gates are permanently receptive in animals, but that human beings close theirs as soon as they begin to talk and think and their rational side takes over.

Thus far, I had given the caretaker my full attention because Clara had told me that no matter who might be talking to me and no matter what he might be saying, the exercise is to listen. But the more I listened to Emilito, the more annoyed I became, until I found myself in the throes of a bona-fide rage.

"I don't believe any of this," I said. "Why do you say that you're my teacher, anyway? You still haven't made that clear."

The caretaker laughed. "I certainly didn't volunteer for the post," he said.

"Then who appointed you?"

After a thoughtful pause, he said, "It's a long chain of circumstances. The first link of this chain was set when the nagual found you naked with your legs up in the air." He burst out laughing with a shrill birdlike sound.

I resented immensely his insulting sense of humor. "Get to the point, Emilito, and tell me what's going on," I yelled.

"I'm sorry, I thought you'd enjoy an account of your doings, but I see I was wrong. We, on the other hand, have enjoyed ourselves immensely with your antics. For years we have laughed at the tribulations and hardships John Michael Abelar inherited because he walked into the wrong room and found a naked girl, when all he wanted to do was to piss." He doubled up laughing.

I didn't see the humor of it. My fury was so gigantic that I wanted to lash out at him with a few punches and well-placed kicks. He looked at me and moved back, undoubtedly sensing I was about to explode.

"Don't you find it hilarious that John Michael had to go through hell with the problem he inherited, just because he wanted to piss? The nagual and I have that in common: whereas I only found a half-dead puppy, he found a completely crazed girl. And we both are responsible for them for the rest of our lives. Seeing what happened to us, the members of our party got so scared that they vowed never to take another leak again before they checked and rechecked the place." He burst out laughing so hard he had to pace back and forth to keep from choking.

Seeing that I wasn't even smiling, he quieted down. "Well . . . let's continue then," he said, composing himself. "Once the first link was cast, when he found you with your legs up, it was the nagual's duty to mark you, which he promptly did. Then he had to keep track of you. He used Clara and Nelida to help him. The first time he and Nelida came to visit you was the summer you had graduated from high school and worked as a camp counselor in a mountain resort."

"Is it true that he found me through an energy channel?" I asked, trying not to sound patronizing.

"Absolutely. He had marked your double with some of his energy so he could follow your movements," he said.

"I don't remember ever seeing them," I said.

"That's because you always believed you were having recurring dreams. But the two of them actually came to see you in the flesh. They continued to visit you many times over the years, especially Nelida. Then, when you came to live in Arizona, following her suggestions, all of us had a chance to visit you."

"Wait a minute, this is getting too bizarre. How could I follow her suggestion when I don't even remember meeting her?"

"Believe me, she kept telling you to live in Arizona, and you did, but of course you thought you were deciding it yourself."

As the caretaker talked, my mind flashed back to that period of my life. I remembered thinking that Arizona was the place where I should be. I did the southern horizon gazing technique to decide where to get a job and received the strongest feeling that I should head for Tucson. I even had a dream in which someone was telling me I should work in a bookstore. I wasn't fond of books and it was odd that I should be working with them, but when I got to Tucson, I went directly to a bookstore with a "Help Wanted" sign. I took the job, typing up order forms, working the cash register and shelving books.

"Whoever came to see you," Emilito went on, "always pulled your double, so you have only a vague dreamlike memory of us, with the exception of Nelida. You know her as you know the back of your hand."

So many people came into that bookstore, but I vaguely remembered an elegantly dressed, beautiful woman who came in once and talked to me in a friendly way. It was so unusual because no one else paid any attention to me. She might very well have been Nelida.

At a deep level, everything Emilito had said made sense. But to my rational mind, it seemed so far-fetched that I'd have to be crazy to believe him.

"What you're saying is pure horse manure," I said, more defensively than I had intended.

My harsh reaction didn't perturb him in the least. He stretched his arms above his head and rotated them in circles. "If what I said is really just a pile of manure, I dare you to explain what's happening to you," he challenged with a grin. "And don't try to be a little girl with me and get all weepy and flustered."

I heard my cracking voice yell, "You're full of shit, you God damn—" And my burning fury ended right then.

I couldn't believe I was shouting profanities. Immediately I began to apologize, saying that I was not accustomed to shouting or using foul language. I assured him that I had been reared in a most civil way, by a well-mannered mother who wouldn't dream of raising her voice.

The caretaker laughed and lifted a hand to stop me. "Enough apologizing," he said. "It's your double that's talking. It's always direct and to the point and since you have never allowed it expression, it is full of hatred and bitterness."

He explained that at that moment my double was extremely unstable due to being bombarded by thunder and lightning, but especially due to the events of five days ago, when Nelida pushed me into the left hallway so I could begin the sorcerers' crossing.

"Five days ago!" I gasped. "You mean I was hanging in the tree for two days and two nights?"

"You were there exactly two days and three nights," he said with a malevolent smirk. "We took turns hoisting ourselves up there to see if you were all right. You were out but doing fine, so we left you alone."

"But why was I strapped that way?"

"You failed miserably trying to accomplish a maneuver we call the abstract flight or the sorcerers' crossing," he said. "The attempt depleted your energy reserves."

He clarified that it wasn't actually a failure on my part, but rather a premature attempt that had ended in complete disaster.

"What would have happened if I had succeeded?" I asked.

He assured me that success would not have put me in a more advantageous position, but that it would have served as a point of departure, a sort of lure or a beacon that would have accurately marked the way for a future time when I would have to make the final flight all by myself.

"You are now using the energy of all of us," he went on. "We are all compelled to help you. In fact, you're using the energy of all the sorcerers that have preceded us and once lived in this house. You're living off their magic. It is exactly as if you were lying on a magic carpet that takes you to incredible places, places that exist only in the magical carpet's path."

"But I still don't understand why I am here," I said. "Is it just because the nagual John Michael Abelar made a mistake and found me?"

"No, it's not quite that simple," he said, looking at me squarely. "In fact, John Michael isn't really your nagual. There is a new nagual and a new era. You are a member of the new nagual's party."

"What are you saying, Emilito? What new party? Who decides that?"

"Power, the spirit, that boundless force out there decides all that. For us, the proof that you belong to the new era is your total similarity with Nelida. She was, in her youth, just like you are now; to the point that she, too, used up all her reserve energy when she first attempted the abstract flight. And just like you, she nearly died."

"You mean I could have actually died attempting it, Emilito?"

"Certainly. Not because the sorcerers' flight is so dangerous, but because you are so unstable. Someone else doing the same thing would have merely gotten a bellyache. But not you. You, like Nelida, have to exaggerate everything, so you nearly died.

"After that, the only way to restore you was by leaving you up in the tree, off the ground for whatever time it took for you to come to your senses. There was nothing else we could have done."

Incredible as it sounded, what had happened gradually began making sense to me. Something had gone dreadfully wrong during my encounter with Nelida. Something in me had been out of control.

"I let you drink from my intent gourd yesterday to find out if your double is still unstable," Emilito explained. "It is! The only way to buttress it is with activity. And like it or not, I'm the only one who can guide your double in this activity. This is the reason I'm your teacher. Or rather, I am the teacher of your double."

"What do you think happened to me with Nelida?" I asked, still uncertain as to what exactly went wrong.

"You mean what didn't happen," he corrected me. "You were supposed to cross the chasm gently and harmoniously and wake up your double to full awareness in the left hallway." He went into a convoluted explanation of what they had hoped would happen.

Under Nelida's direction I was supposed to shift my awareness back and forth between my body and my double. This shifting was to have erased all the natural barriers developed through life, barriers that separate the physical body from the double. The sorcerers' plan, he said, was to allow me to get acquainted with all of them in person, since my double already knew them. But because of my craziness, I didn't cross gently and harmoniously. In other words, the awareness my double acquired had nothing to do with the daily awareness of my body. This resulted in a sensation that I was flying and couldn't stop. All my reserve energy drained out of me without any restraint and my double went berserk.

"I regret to tell you this, Emilito, but I don't understand what you're talking about," I said.

"The sorcerers' crossing consists of shifting the awareness of daily life, which the physical body possesses, to the double," he replied. "Listen carefully. The awareness of daily life is what we want to shift from the body to the double. The awareness of daily life!"

"But what does that mean, Emilito?"

"It means that we are after sobriety, measure, control. We are not interested in craziness and helter-skelter results."

"But what does it mean in my case?" I insisted.

"You indulged in your excesses and didn't shift your awareness of daily life to your double."

"What did I do?"

"You imbued your double with an unknown, uncontrollable awareness."

"Regardless of what you say, Emilito, it's impossible for me to believe all this," I said. "In fact, it's really inconceivable."

"Naturally, it's inconceivable," he agreed. "But if you're after something conceivable, you don't have to sit here holding on to your doubts, shouting at me. Something conceivable for you is to be naked and with your legs up."

He flashed a lecherous smile that gave me the chills. But before I could defend myself, he changed his expression to one of utter seriousness.

"To draw out the double gently and harmoniously and shift to it our awareness of daily life is something without parallel," he said softly. "To do that is something inconceivable.

"Now let's do something thoroughly conceivable. Let's go and eat breakfast."

20

My third night in the tree house was like camping out. I simply slipped into the sleeping bag, fell into a sound sleep and woke up at dawn. Lowering myself down was easier too. I had gotten the knack of moving the ropes and pulleys without straining my back and shoulders.

"This is the last day of your transition phase," Emilito announced after we had eaten breakfast. "You have much work to do. But you're fairly industrious, so it won't be too difficult."

"What do you mean by a transition phase?"

"Yours is a six-day transition from the last time you talked to Clara till now. Don't forget, you have spent six nights in the tree, three of which you were unconscious, the other three, you were aware. Sorcerers always count events in sets of threes."

"Do I also have to do things in sets of threes?" I asked.

"Certainly. You're Nelida's heir, aren't you? You're the continuation of her line." He gave me a sly grin and added. "But for now you have to do whatever I do. Remember, for however long it takes, I'm your guide."

Hearing Emilito say that made me swallow hard. Whereas I had felt a twitch of pride whenever Nelida included me with her in any of her statements, I didn't like it one bit when the caretaker joined me with him.

Noticing my discomfort, he assured me that forces beyond any-one's control had placed us together to fulfill a specific task. There-fore, we had to abide by the rule, for that was the way things were done in his sorcery tradition.

"Clara prepared your physical side by teaching you to recapitulate, and loosened your gates with the sorcery passes," he explained. "My job is to help solidify your double and then teach it 'stalking.' "

He assured me that no one else could teach me how to stalk with the double except himself.

"Can you explain what stalking with the double is?" I asked.

"Of course I can. But it wouldn't be wise to talk about it because stalking means doing, not talking about doing. Besides, you already know what it means, since you've done it."

"Where and when have I done it?"

"The first night you slept in the tree house," Emilito said, "when you were about to die of fright. On that occasion your reason was at a loss as to how to handle the situation, so circumstances forced you to depend on your double. It was your double that came to your rescue. It flowed out of the gates that your fear had thrown wide open. I call that stalking with the double.

"The nagual and Nelida are the masters of the double and they'll give you the finishing touches," he went on, "provided I do the rough work. So it's up to me to get you ready for them, just like it was up to Clara to get you ready for me. And unless I get you ready, they won't be able to do anything at all with you."

"Why couldn't Clara continue being my teacher?" I asked, taking a sip of water.

He peered at me, then he blinked like a bird. "It's the rule to have two ushers," Emilito said. "Every one of us had two ushers, including myself. But my final teacher was a nagual; that is also the rule."

Emilito explained that the nagual Julian Grau was not only his teacher, but the teacher of each of the sixteen members of the house-hold. The nagual Julian, together with his own teacher, another nagual by the name of Elías Abelar, had found each of them one by one and helped them on their way to freedom.

"Why is it that the names Grau and Abelar keep on recurring?"

"Those are power names," Emilio explained. "Every generation of sorcerers uses them. And every nagual's name follows an alternate-generation rule. That means that John Michael Abelar inherited the name from Elías Abelar, but the new nagual, the one that will come after John Michael Abelar, will inherit the name Grau from Julian Grau. That's the rule for the naguals."

"Why did Nelida say that I am an Abelar?"

"Because you are just like her. And the rule says that you will inherit her last name or her first name or, if you wish, you can inherit both names. She herself inherited both names from her predecessor."

"Who decided on that rule and why have it in the first place?" I asked.

"The rule is a code by which sorcerers live to keep from becoming arbitrary or whimsical. They have to adhere to the precepts set up for them because they were made by the spirit itself. This is what I was told and I have no reason to doubt it."

Emilito said that his other teacher was a woman named Talía. He described her as the most exquisite woman anyone could ever imagine existing on this earth.

"I think Nelida is the most exquisite being," I blurted out, but stopped myself from saying more. Otherwise I would have sounded just like Emilito, totally overcome with absolute devotion.

Emilito leaned across the kitchen table and with the air of a conspirator about to reveal a secret said, "I agree with you. But wait until Nelida really gets hold of you; then you'll love her as if there's no tomorrow."

His words didn't surprise me for he had correctly assessed something I already felt; I loved Nelida as if I had known her forever. As if she were the mother I never really had. I told him that she was to me the kindest, most beautiful and impeccable being I had ever encountered, in spite of the fact that until a few days ago I didn't even know she existed.

"But of course you knew her," Emilito protested. "Every one of us came to see you and Nelida saw you more often than anyone. When you came with Clara, Nelida had taught you endless things already."

"What do you think she's taught me?" I asked uneasily.

He scratched the top of his head for a moment. "She taught you, for example, to call your double for advice," he said.

"You say that I did that my first night in the tree house. But I don't know what I did."

"Of course you do. You've always done it. What about your technique of relaxing and looking at the southern horizon to ask for advice?"

The moment he said this, something cleared in my mind. I had completely forgotten about some dreams I had had over the years in which a beautiful, mysterious lady used to talk to me and leave gifts for me on my bedside table. Once I dreamt that she left an opal ring and another time a gold bracelet with a tiny heart charm. Sometimes she would sit on the edge of my bed and tell me things that upon awakening I would begin to do, like gazing at the southern horizon or wearing certain colors or even styling my hair a certain way that was more becoming.

When I felt sad or alone, she would soothe and comfort me and whisper sweet nothings in my ear. The thing I remember most vividly was that she told me that she loved me for what I was. She used those exact words, "I love you for what you are." Then she would rub my back where I was tense or stroke my head and tousle my hair. I realized that it was because of her that I didn't want my mother to touch me. I didn't want anyone to touch me except that lady. When I woke up after any of these dreams, my feeling was that nothing in the world mattered as long as that lady held me in her heart.

I always thought that those were my fantasy dreams. Having gone to Catholic schools, I even thought perhaps she was the Blessed Virgin or one of the saints that kept on appearing to me. I had been taught that all good things come from them. At one time, I even thought she was my fairy godmother, but never in my wildest imagination did I think that such a being really existed.

"That was not the Virgin or a saint, you idiot," Emilito laughed. "That was our Nelida. And she really did give you those jewels. You'll find them in the box under the platform in the tree house. They were given to her by her predecessor; now she passes them on to you."

"You mean that opal ring really exists?" I gasped.

Emilito nodded. "Go see for yourself. Nelida told me to tell you—"

Before he could finish his statement, I ran out of the kitchen to the front of the house. With record speed, I hoisted myself up to the tree house. There, in a silk box hidden under the platform, were exquisite jewels. I recognized the opal ring that had red fire in it and the gold charm bracelet, and there were other rings and a gold watch and a diamond necklace. I took out the gold bracelet with the heart and put it on, and for the first time since Clara left, I found my eyes filled with tears. But they were not tears of self-pity or sadness, but of sheer joy and elation. For now I knew beyond a doubt that the beautiful lady had not been merely a dream.

I called out Nelida's name and thanked her at the top of my voice for all her favors. I promised to change, to be different and do whatever Emilito told me, anything, as long as I could see and talk to her again.

When I let myself down I found Emilito standing by the door in the kitchen. I showed him the bracelet and rings and asked him how it was possible for me to have seen the same jewels years ago in my dreams.

"Sorcerers are extremely mysterious beings," Emilito said, "because most of the time they act from the energy of their double. Nelida is a great stalker. She stalks in dreams. Her power is so unique that she can not only transport herself but bring things with her. That's how she could visit you. And that's why her name is Abelar. Abelar to us means stalker. And Grau means dreamer. All the sorcerers in this house are either dreamers or stalkers."

"What's the difference, Emilito?"

"Stalkers plan and act out their plans; they connive and invent and change things whether they are awake or in dreams. Dreamers move onward without any plan or thought; they jump into the reality of the world or into the reality of dreams."

"All this is incomprehensible to me, Emilito," I said, examining the opal ring in the light.

"I'm guiding you so it will become comprehensible," Emilito replied. "And to help me guide you, you must do what I tell you: Everything I will say, do or recommend that you do, is either the exact replica of what my two teachers told me or it is something patterned on what they said." He leaned closer to me. "You may not believe this," he whispered, "but you and I are basically alike."

"In what way, Emilito?"

"We are both a bit insane," he said with a most serious face. "Pay close attention and remember this. In order for you and me to be sane, we have to work like demons at balancing, not the body or the mind, but the double."

I saw no point in arguing or agreeing with him. But as I sat down at the kitchen table again, I asked him, "How can we be sure that we're balancing the double?"

"By opening our gates," he replied. "The first gate is in the sole of the foot, at the base of the big toe."

He reached under the table and grabbed my left foot and in one incredibly swift maneuver, he removed my shoe and sock. Then using his index finger and thumb as a vise, he pressed the round protuberance of my big toe at the sole of my foot, and the toe joint at the top of my foot. The sharp pain and the surprise made me scream. I yanked my foot away so forcefully that I bumped my knee on the underside of the table. I stood up and yelled, "What the hell do you think you're doing!"

He ignored my angry outburst and said, "I'm pointing out the gates to you according to the rule. So pay close attention."

He stood up and moved around to my side. "The second gate is the area that includes the calves and the inner part of the knee," he said bending over and stroking my legs. "The third is at the sexual organs and tailbone." Before I could move away, he slid his warm hands into my crotch and lifted me up a bit as he gave me a firm squeeze.

I fought him off but he grabbed my lower back. "The fourth and the most important is in the area of the kidneys," he said. Unconcerned with my vexation, he pushed me down on the bench again. He moved his hands up my back. I cringed, but for Nelida's sake I let him. "The fifth point is in between the shoulder blades," he said. "The sixth is at the base of the skull. And the seventh is at the crown of the head." To isolate the last point, his knuckles descended hard on the very top of my head.

He moved back to his side of the table and sat down. "If our first or second centers are open, we transmit a certain kind of force that people may find intolerable," he went on. "On the other hand, if the third and fourth gates are not as closed as they are supposed to be, we transmit a certain force that people will find most appealing."

I knew for a fact that the caretaker's lower centers were wide open because I found him as obnoxious and intolerable as anyone could be. Half jokingly and partly out of guilt for feeling the way I did toward him, I admitted that people didn't take to me easily. I had always thought it was a lack of social grace, for which I felt I had to compensate by being extra accommodating.

"It's only natural," he said, agreeing. "You have had the gates in your feet and calves partially open all your life. Another consequence of those lower centers being open is that you have trouble walking."

"Wait just a moment," I said, "there's nothing wrong with the way I walk. I practice martial arts. Clara told me that I move smoothly and gracefully."

At that he burst out laughing. "You can practice whatever you please," he retorted, "you still drag your feet when you walk. You have an old man's shuffle."

Emilito was worse than Clara. At least she had the grace to laugh with me, not at me. He had absolutely no sympathy for my feelings. He picked on me the way older children pick on younger, weaker ones who have no defenses.

"You're not offended, are you?" he asked, peering at me.

"Me, offended? Of course not." I was seething.

"Good. Clara assured me that you have rid yourself of most of your self-pity and self-importance through your recapitulation. Recapitulating your life, especially your sex life, has loosened some of your gates even more. The cracking sound you hear at the back of your neck is the moment when your right and left sides have separated. This leaves a gap directly in the middle of your body where the energy rises to the neck, the place where the sound is heard. To hear that pop means that your double is about to become aware."

"What should I do when I hear it?"

"To know what to do isn't that important because there's very little we can do," he said. "We can either remain seated with our eyes shut or we can get up and move about. The important point is to know that we are limited because our physical body controls our awareness. But if we can turn it around so that our double controls our awareness, we can do practically anything we can imagine."

He stood up and came toward me. "Now, you're not going to trick me into talking about things the way you did Clara and Nelida," he said. "You can only learn about the double by doing. And I'm talking to you because your transition phase hasn't ended yet."

He took me by the arm and without another word, he practically dragged me to the back of the house. There he positioned me under a tree, with the top of my head a few inches below a low, thick branch. He said that he was going to see if I could project out my double again, this time in full awareness, with the help of the tree.

I seriously doubted I would be able to project out anything, and I told him so. But he insisted that if I intended it, my double would push out from inside me and expand beyond the boundaries of my physical body.

"What am I supposed to do, exactly?" I asked, hoping he would show me a procedure that was part of the sorcerers' rule.

He told me to close my eyes and concentrate on my breathing. As I relaxed, I was to intend a force to flow upward until I could touch the top branches with a feeling that came out of the gate in the crown of my head. He said that this was going to be fairly easy for me because I was going to use my friend the tree for support. The tree's energy, he explained, would form a matrix for my awareness to expand.

After a time of concentrating on my breath, I felt a vibrating energy rising up my back, trying to push out of the top of my head. Then something opened inside me. Every time I inhaled, a line elongated to the top of the tree; when I exhaled, the line was pulled down into my body again. The feeling of reaching the top of the tree became stronger with my every breath until I truly believed that my body expanded, becoming as tall and voluminous as the tree.

At one point, a profound affection and empathy for the tree enveloped me; it was at that same moment that something surged up my back and out my head and I found myself viewing the world from the top branches. This sensation lasted only an instant, for it was disrupted by the caretaker's voice commanding me to come down and flow inside my body again. I felt something like a waterfall, an effervescence flowing downward, entering the top of my head and filling my body with a familiar warmth.

"You don't want to stay mixed with the tree too long," he told me when I opened my eyes.

I had an overwhelming desire to embrace the tree, but the caretaker pulled me by the arm to a large boulder some distance away, where we sat down. He pointed out that aided by an outside force, in this case uniting my awareness with the tree, one can easily make the double expand. However, because it's easy, we run the risk of staying merged with the tree too long, in which case we might sap the tree of the vital energy it needs to maintain itself in a strong and healthy state. Or we might leave some of our own energy behind by becoming emotionally attached to the tree.

"One can merge with anything," he explained. "If whatever or whomever you merge with is strong, your energy will be enhanced, as it was whenever you merged with the magician, Manfred. But if it is sick or weak, stay away. In any case, you must do the exercise sparingly for, like everything else, it is a double-edged sword. Outside energy is always different from our own, often antagonistic to it."

I listened attentively to what the caretaker said. One thing stood out from everything else.

"Tell me, Emilito, why did you call Manfred a magician?"

"That's our way of acknowledging his uniqueness. Manfred to us can't be anything else but a magician. He's more than a sorcerer. He'd be a sorcerer if he'd lived among his kind. He lives among human beings, and human sorcerers at that, and he's par with them. Only a consummate magician could accomplish that feat."

I asked him if I would ever see Manfred again; the caretaker crossed his index finger over his lips in such an exaggerated fashion that I kept quiet and didn't press him for an answer.

He picked up a twig and drew an oval shape on the soft ground. Then he added a horizontal line that transected it midway. Pointing to the two partitions, he explained that the double is divided into a lower and an upper section, which correspond roughly in the physical body to the abdomen and chest cavities. Two different currents of energy circulate in these two sections. In the lower one circulates the original energy we had while still in the womb. In the upper section circulates the thought energy. This energy enters the body at birth with the first breath. He said that thought energy is enhanced by experience and rises upward into the head. The original energy sinks down into the genital area. Usually, in life, these two energies become separated in the double, causing weaknesses and unbalance in the physical body.

He drew another line, this time down the center of the elliptical shape, dividing it lengthwise into two, which, he stated, corresponds to the right and left sides of the body. These two sides also have two specific patterns of energy circulation. In the right side, energy circulates up on the frontal part of the double, and down on the back of it. On the left side, energy circulates down on the frontal part of the double, and up on the back.

He explained that the error many people make when trying to seek the double is to apply to it the rules of the physical body, training it, for example, as if it were made of muscle and bone. He assured me that there is no way to condition the double through physical exercises.

"The easiest way to resolve this problem is to separate the two," the caretaker explained. "Only when they are undeniably separate can awareness flow from one to the other. That is what sorcerers do. So they can dispense with the nonsense of rituals, incantations and elaborate breathing techniques that are supposed to unify them."

"But what about the breaths and sorcery passes that Clara taught me? Are they nonsense too?"

"No. She taught you only things that would help you separate your body and your double. Therefore they are all useful for our purpose."

He said that perhaps our greatest human fallacy is to believe that our health and well-being is in the realm of the body when, in essence, the control of our lives is in the realm of the double. This fallacy stems from the fact that the body controls our awareness. He added that ordinarily our awareness is placed on the energy that circulates in the right side of the double, which results in our ability to think and reason and be effective in dealing with ideas and people. Sometimes accidentally, but more often due to training, awareness can shift to the energy that circulates in the left side of the double, which results in behavior not so conducive to intellectual pursuits or dealing with people.

"When awareness is turned steadily to the left side of the double, the double is fleshed out and emerges," he went on, "and one is capable of performing inconceivable feats. This shouldn't be surprising, for the double is our energy source. The physical body is merely the receptacle where that energy has been placed."

I asked him if there are some people who can focus their awareness on either side of the double at will.

He nodded. "Sorcerers can do that," he replied. "The day you can do that, you'll be a sorceress yourself."

He said that some people can shift their awareness to the right or the left side of the double, after they have successfully completed the abstract flight, simply by manipulating the flow of their breath. Such people can practice sorcery or martial arts as readily as they can manipulate intricate academic constructs. He emphasized that the urge to turn awareness steadily to the left is a trap infinitely more deadly than the attractions of the world of everyday life because of the mystery and power inherent in it.

"The real hope for us lies in the center," he said, touching my forehead and the center of my chest, "for in the wall that divides the two sides of the double is a hidden door that opens into a third, thin, secret compartment. Only when this door opens can one experience true freedom."

He grabbed my arm and pulled me off the rock. "Your transition time is nearly up," he said, hurrying me back into the house. "No more time for explanations. We'll leave the transition phase behind us with one hell of a bang. Come, let's go to my room."

I stopped dead in my tracks. I was no longer merely ill at ease, I felt threatened. No matter how eccentric Emilito might be, and no matter how much he talked about the ethereal double, he was still a male, and the memory of his hand grasping my private parts in the kitchen was much too vivid. I knew that it hadn't been an impersonal touch merely for the purpose of demonstration, either; I had clearly sensed his lust when he touched me.

The caretaker peered at me with cold eyes. "What the hell do you mean that you sensed my lust when I touched you?"

I could only stare back at him with my mouth gaping. He had voiced my thought verbatim. A surge of shame went through me, accompanied by a cold shiver that spread over my entire body. I blurted out some lame apologies. I told him that I used to fantasize that I was so beautiful that all men found me irresistible.

"To recapitulate means to burn all that," he said. "You haven't done a thorough job. This, no doubt, is the reason you cracked while attempting the sorcerers' crossing."

He turned around and walked away from the house.

"It's not time yet to show you what I had in mind," he said. "No. You need to do much more work to clean up your act. Much more. And from now on, you'll have to be twice as careful, too; you'll have to run twice as hard, for you can't afford any more slip-ups."

21

My transition period ended right then as Emilito attacked me for having misread his thoughts. From then on he dropped his whimsical air of a prankster and became a most demanding taskmaster. There were no more lengthy explanations of the double or other aspects of sorcery, hence no more solace stemming from intellectual understanding. There was only work, pragmatic and demanding. Every day for months from morning until night, I would be steeped in activity until, exhausted, I went to sleep in the tree house.

Besides continuing to practice kung fu and working in the garden, I was put in charge of cooking lunch and dinner. The caretaker showed me how to light the stove and how to prepare some simple dishes, a thing that my mother had tried to do but had failed completely. Because I had other duties, I would usually put all the ingredients into one pot on the stove to cook, then come back later when it was time to eat. After several weeks of making the same stew, I got a perfect blend of flavors. Emilito said that I turned out to be, if not a fairly good cook, at least one whose food is edible. I took this as a compliment, because nothing I had made in my entire life, from poundcake to meatloaf, had been edible.

We ate our meals in total silence, a silence that he would break if he wanted to tell me something. But if I wanted to converse, he would tap his stomach to remind me of his delicate digestion.

Most of my time was still devoted to recapitulating. The caretaker had instructed me to go over the same events and people I had recapitulated before, except that this time I was to do it in the tree house. Hoisting myself up to the tree house every day made me lose my initial fear of heights. I relished being outdoors, especially in the late afternoons, the time I set aside for this particular task. Under Clara's supervision, I had recapitulated in a dark cave. The mood of that recapitulation was heavy, earthy, somber and often terrifying. My recapitulation under Emilito's guidance in the tree house was dominated by a new mood. It was light, airy, transparent. I remembered things with an unprecedented clarity. With my added energy, or the influence of being off the ground, I was able to remember infinitely more detail. Everything was more vivid and pronounced, and less charged with the self-pity, moroseness, fear or regret that had characterized my previous recapitulation.

Clara had asked me to write on the ground the names of each person I had encountered in my life, then erase it with my hand after I had breathed in the memories associated with that person. Emilito, on the other hand, had me write the names of people on dry leaves and then light a match to them after I had finished breathing in everything I had recollected about them. He had given me a special device to incinerate the leaves, a twelve-inch metal cube with neatly perforated, round, small holes on all sides. Half of one side of the box was fitted with a glass, like a tiny window. There was a sharp pin in the center of the underside of the lid. On the side with the window, there was a lever that slid in and out where one could fasten a match and strike it from the outside against a rough surface inside the box after the lid was closed.

"In order to avoid starting a blaze," Emilito explained, "you have to pierce the dry leaf with the pin on the lid so when you close the lid, it will be suspended in the middle of the box. Then look inside the box through its little glass window and, using the handle, strike your match and place it under the leaf and watch it burn to cinders."

As I gazed at the flames consuming each leaf, I was to draw in the energy of the fire with my eyes, always being careful not to inhale the smoke. He instructed me to put the ashes from the leaves into a metal urn and the used matches into a paper sack. Each of the matchsticks represented the husk of the person whose name had been written on the dry leaf that had been disintegrated by that particular match. When the urn was full, I was to empty it from the top of the tree, letting the wind scatter the ashes in all directions. I was instructed to lower the pile of burnt matchsticks in a paper bag on a separate rope and Emilito, handling the bag with a pair of tongs, would put it in a special basket he always used for that purpose. He was careful never to touch the matches or the bag. My best guess was that he buried them somewhere in the hills, or perhaps tossed them in the stream to let the water disintegrate them. Disposing of the matches, he had assured me, was the final act in the process of breaking the ties with the world.

After about three months of recapitulating in the afternoons, Emilito abruptly changed my work schedule.

"I'm tired of eating your boring stew," he said one morning as he hoisted up some food he had prepared for me.

I was overjoyed, not only because I might have extra time to spend in the tree house, but because I genuinely liked eating food cooked by someone else.

The first time I tasted his cooking, I had the total certainty that Clara had never cooked the food she had served me. The real cook had always been Emilito. He made things with a special zest that always made whatever he cooked a delight to eat.

Every morning around seven, Emilito would be standing at the foot of the tree ready to hoist up some food he had packed in a basket. After eating breakfast in the tree house, I usually went back to my recapitulation, which, once I had been freed from the dread of uncovering something unpleasant, was now more than ever like an exciting adventure of examination and insight. For the more of my past I breathed in, the lighter and freer I felt.

As I broke off old, past links, I began forming new ones. In this instance, my new links were with the unique being that was guiding me. Emilito, although stern and determined to make sure that I kept my nose to the grindstone, was in essence as light as a feather. At first, I was surprised that both he and Clara had claimed that I was like them. But upon a deeper examination, I had to agree that I was as ponderous as Clara and as flighty, if not as insane, as Emilito.

Once I became accustomed to his oddity, I found no difference between Emilito and Clara or the nagual or even Manfred. My feelings for them overlapped so that I began to feel affection for Emilito and very naturally one day began to rejoice in calling him Emilito. The first time we met, the caretaker had said to me that his name was Emilito—the Spanish diminutive for Emilio. It seemed ridiculous to me to call a mature man "little Emilio," so I did it reluctantly. But as I got to know him better, I couldn't conceive of addressing him in any other way.

Whenever I thought about the four of them, they merged in my mind. But I could never merge them with Nelida. She was special to me; I held her forever apart and above everyone else, even though I had seen her only once in the real world. I felt that the day I had focused my eyes on her, the bond that already existed between us became formalized. A single encounter in the daily world awareness, no matter how fleeting, had been enough to make that bond indestructible and everlasting.

One day after we had our lunch in the kitchen, Emilito handed me a package. As I held it against me, I knew it was from Nelida. I tried to find a return address on it but there was none. Attached to the package was a cartoon drawing of a woman puckering up her lips to kiss. Inside, written in Nelida's handwriting, were the words: "Kiss the tree." I ripped open the package and found a pair of soft leather ankle-high shoes that laced up the front. The soles were fitted with rubber cleats.

I held them up for Emilito to see. I couldn't conceive what they were used for.

"Those are your tree-climbing shoes," Emilito said, nodding in recognition. "Nelida knew you have an affinity for trees, in spite of your fear of falling. The cleats are made of rubber so you won't damage the tree bark."

The arrival of the package seemed to be the signal for Emilito to give me detailed instructions on tree climbing. So far, I had only used the harness to hoist myself up to the tree house. And sometimes I dozed off or slept in the harness as if I were lying strapped in a hammock. But I had never actually climbed the tree, except for one very low branch from which I had hung while propping my feet on another.

"Now is the time to find out what you're made of," he said in a no-nonsense tone. "Your new task won't be difficult, but if you don't give it your total concentration, it could prove to be fatal. You need to apply all your newly stored energy to learn what I have to show you."

He told me to wait for him by the grove of tall trees in front of the house. Moments later, Emilito met me, carrying a long flat box. He opened it and took out several safety belts and lengths of soft rock-climbing rope. He strapped a belt to my waist and affixed another, longer belt to it by means of safety hooks used in mountaineering. Putting a similar belt around himself, he showed me how to climb a tree by hooking the longer belt around the tree trunk and using it as a support to move up along the trunk. He climbed with swift and precise movements; along the way, he looped ropes on the branches to secure his position. The end result was a web of ropes that allowed him to move safely around the tree from one side to the other.

He came down as agilely as he had climbed up. "Be sure all the ropes and knots are secure," he said. "You can't have any major mistakes here. Little mistakes are correctable; big ones are fatal."

"My goodness, am I supposed to do what you just did?" I asked, really astonished.

It wasn't that I was any longer afraid of heights. I simply didn't feel I had the patience to tie all the hooks and ropes in place. It had taken me quite a while just to get used to going up and down the tree in the harness.

Emilito nodded and laughed cheerfully. "This is a real challenge," he admitted. "But once you get the hang of it, I'm sure you will agree it's worth it. You'll see what I mean."

He handed me a length of rope and patiently showed me how to tie and untie knots; how to use pieces of rubber hose with my climbing rope pulled through them in order not to bruise the tree bark when I looped a rope around a branch to set up a new rope line to climb; how to maneuver my feet to maintain my balance; and how to avoid disturbing birds' nests in the process of climbing.

For the following three months I worked under his constant supervision, confining myself to the lower branches. When I achieved a respectable control of the equipment, enough calluses on my hands so that I no longer needed to wear gloves and enough maneuverability and balance in my movements, Emilito let me venture into the higher branches. I meticulously practiced on them the same maneuvers I had learned on the lower branches. And one day, without even trying for it, I reached the top of the tree I was climbing. That day, Emilito presented me with what he told me was his most meaningful gift to me. It was a set of three green jungle camouflage overalls and matching caps, obviously bought in an army surplus store in the States.

Dressed in jungle fatigues, I lived in the grove of tall trees clustered by the front of the house. I came down only to go to the bathroom and, occasionally, to have a meal with Emilito. I climbed any tree I wanted, provided it was high enough. There were only a few trees I refused to climb; the ones that were very old and would find my presence an intrusion, or the really young ones that weren't strong enough to tolerate my ropes and movement.

I preferred youthful, vigorous trees, for they made me happy and optimistic. Yet some of the older ones were desirable too, for they had so much more to tell. But the only tree that Emilito allowed me to sleep in overnight was the one with the tree house in it, because it was fitted with a lightning rod. I slept on my platform bed or secured in the leather harness or even at times simply strapped to a branch of my own choosing.

Some of my favorite branches were thick and free from protuberances. I would lie on one face down. Resting my head on a small pillow I always brought up with me, I embraced the branch with arms and legs, maintaining a precarious but exhilarating balance. Of course I always made certain that a rope was tied to my waist and secured to a higher branch, just in case I lost my balance while asleep.

The feeling I had developed for the trees was beyond words. I had the certainty that I was able to absorb their moods, know their age, their insights and what they sensed. I could communicate with a tree directly through a sensation that came out from the inside of my body. Often, communication began with a spilling forth of pure affection, almost as intense as what I felt for Manfred, an affection that came out of me always unexpectedly and unsolicited. Then I could feel their roots descending into the earth. I knew whether they needed water and which roots were extending toward the underground water source. I could tell what it felt like to live seeking light, anticipating it, intending it, or what it felt like to feel heat, cold or be ravaged by lightning and storms. I learned what it was like never to be able to move off one's destined spot. To be silent, to sense through the bark, the roots and intake light through the leaves. I knew, beyond the shadow of doubt, that trees feel pain; and I also knew that once communication is engaged, trees pour themselves out in affection.

As I was seated on a sturdy limb with my back resting on the tree trunk, my recapitulation took on an altogether different mood. I could remember the minutest details of my life experiences without fear of any coarse emotional involvement. I would laugh my head off at things that at one time had been deep traumas for me. I found my obsessions no longer capable of evoking self-pity. I saw everything from a different perspective, not as the urbanite I had always been, but as the carefree and abandoned tree dweller that I had become.

One night, while we were still eating a rabbit stew I had made, Emilito surprised me by talking to me animatedly. He asked me to remain seated after dinner because he had something to tell me. This was so out of the ordinary that I grew excited with anticipation. The only beings I had talked to for months had been the trees and the birds. I prepared myself for something monumental.

"You've been a tree dweller for over six months now," he began. "It's time to find out what you've done up there. Let's go into the house. I have something to show you."

"What do you have to show me, Emilito?" I asked, remembering the time he had wanted to show me something in his room and I had refused to follow him.

The name Emilito suited him to perfection. He had become a most cherished being to me, just like Manfred. One of the lofty insights I had received while perched in the high branches of a tree was that Emilito was not human at all. Whether he had once been a human being and the recapitulation had wiped all that away, I could only speculate. His nonhumanness was a barrier that impeded anyone from crossing over to him for a subjective exchange. No average person could ever enter into what Emilito thought, felt or witnessed. But if he so desired, Emilito could cross over to any of us and share with us our subjective states. His nonhumanness was something I had sensed from the first time I encountered him at the kitchen door. Now I was able to be at ease with him; and although I was still separated by that barrier, I could marvel at his achievement.

I asked Emilito again, since he hadn't answered me, what he was going to show me.

"What I have to show is of ultimate importance," he said. "But how you will see it will depend on you. It'll depend on whether you have acquired the silence and balance of the trees."

We hurriedly walked across the dark patio to the house. I followed him through the hallway to the door of his room. It made me doubly nervous to see him stand there for a long moment and take deep breaths as if to compose himself for what was to come.

"All right, let's go in," he said, gently tugging the sleeve of my shirt. "A word of caution. Don't stare at anything in the room. Look at whatever you want, but scan the things lightly, using only quick glances."

He opened the door and we entered his extravagant room. Living in the trees had made me completely forget the first time I had walked into that room the day Clara and Nelida had left. Now I was again startled by the bizarre objects that filled it. The first things I saw were four floor lamps, one at the center of each wall. I couldn't even begin to conceive what kind of lamps they were. The room and everything in it was illuminated by an eerie, mellow amber light. I was familiar enough with electrical equipment to know that no standard light bulb, even if it were seen through a lampshade made of the most unusual tissue, could ever give off that kind of light.

I felt Emilito take my arm to help me step over a foot-high fence that parceled a small square area in the southwest corner of the room.

"Welcome to my cave," he said with a grin as we stepped into the partitioned area.

In that square there was a long table, half hidden by a black curtain and a row of four most unusual looking chairs. Each had a high solid oval back that curved around the body, and instead of legs, a seemingly solid round base. All four chairs were facing the wall.

"Don't stare," the caretaker reminded me as he helped me to sit down on one of the chairs.

I noticed that they were made of some sort of plastic material. The round seat was cushioned, although I couldn't tell how; it was hard as wood, but it had a springiness that gave way when I moved up and down on the seat. And it also swiveled as I moved sideways. The oval back, which seemed to wrap itself around my back, was also cushioned but equally hard. All the chairs were painted with a vivid cerulean blue.

The caretaker sat in the chair next to me. He swiveled his chair around to face the center of the room, and in an unusually strained voice, he told me to swivel around also. When I did, I let out a gutteral gasp. The room I had crossed a moment ago had disappeared. Instead, I was staring at a vast flat space, illuminated by a peach-colored glow. The room now extended out into seemingly infinite space right before my very eyes. The horizon in my view was jet black. I gasped again for I had a hollow feeling in the pit of my stomach. I felt the floor was moving out from under my feet and I was being pulled into that space. I no longer felt the swivel chair underneath me, although I was still sitting on it.

I heard Emilito say, "Let's swivel back again," but I had no strength to make the chair turn. He must have done it for me, for I suddenly found myself looking at the corner of the room again.

"Incredible, wouldn't you say?" the caretaker asked, smiling.

I was incapable of uttering a single word or asking questions I knew had no answers. After a minute or two, Emilito made my chair swivel around once more, to give me another eyeful of infinity. I found the immensity of that space so terrifying that I closed my eyes. I felt him turning the chair around again.

"Now get off the chair," he said.

Automatically I obeyed him and stood there shaking involuntarily, trying to get my voice back. He bodily turned me around to make me face the room.

Gripped with fear, I stubbornly or wisely refused to open my eyes. The caretaker gave me a sound rap on the top of my head with his knuckle, which made my eyes pop open. To my relief, the room was not black endless space, but the way it had been when I walked in. Discarding his admonitions to only look in glances, I stared at every one of those unidentifiable objects.

"Please, Emilito, tell me, what is all this?" I asked.

"I am merely the caretaker," Emilio said. "All this is under my care." He swept his hand over the room, "But I'll be damned if I know what it is. In fact, none of us knows what this is. We inherited it with the house from my teacher, the nagual Julian, and he inherited it from his teacher, the nagual Elías, who had also inherited it."

"This looks like some sort of backstage prop room," I said. "But this is an illusion, isn't it, Emilito?"

"This is sorcery! You can perceive it now, because you've freed enough energy to expand your perception. Anyone can perceive it, provided he has stored enough energy. The tragedy is that most of our energy is trapped in nonsensical concerns. The recapitulation is the key. It releases that trapped energy and *voilà!* You see infinity right in front of your eyes."

I laughed when Emilito said *voilà*, because it was so incongruous and unexpected. Laughing alleviated some of my tension. "But is all this real, Emilito, or am I dreaming?" was all I could say.

"You are dreaming, but all this is real. So real that it can kill us by disintegrating us."

I couldn't rationally account for what I was seeing, thus there was no way I could either believe or doubt my perception. My dilemma was insurmountable and so was my panic. The caretaker moved closer to me.

"Sorcery is more than black cats and naked people dancing in a graveyard at midnight, putting hexes on other people," he whispered. "Sorcery is cold, abstract, impersonal. That's why we call the act of perceiving it the sorcerers' crossing, or the flight to the abstract. To withstand its awesome pull we have to be strong and determined; it's not for the timid or weak-hearted. This is what the nagual Julian used to say."

My interest was so intense that it forced me to listen with unequalled concentration to every word Emilito was saying; all the while, my eyes were riveted to those objects in the room. My conclusion was that none of them was real. Yet since I was obviously perceiving them, it made me wonder if I too wasn't real, or if I was concocting them. It was not that they were indescribable, they were simply unrecognizable to my mind.

"Now prepare yourself for the sorcerers' flight," Emilito said. "Hold on to me for dear life. Grab my belt if you have to or climb on my back piggyback fashion. But whatever you do, don't let go."

Before I could even ask him what he intended next, he maneuvered me around the chair and made me sit down facing the wall. Then he swiveled the chair ninety degrees so that I was once again looking at the center of the room at that terrifying infinite space. He helped me stand up by holding my waist and made me take a few steps into infinity.

I found it almost impossible to walk; my legs seemed to weigh a ton. I felt the caretaker pushing and lifting me up. Suddenly an immense force sucked me in and I was no longer walking but gliding in space. The caretaker was gliding alongside me. I remembered his warning and grabbed onto his belt. In the nick of time too, for just then another surge of energy made me accelerate at top speed. I yelled at him to stop me. Quickly he eased me onto his back and I held on for dear life. I squeezed my eyes shut but it made no difference. I saw the same vastness before me whether my eyes were; open or closed. We were soaring in something that wasn't air; it wasn't over the earth, either. My greatest fear was that a monumental burst of energy was going to make me lose my hold on the caretaker's back. I fought with all my might to hang on and maintain my grip and my concentration.

It all ended as abruptly as it had begun. I was jolted by another blast of energy and I found myself drenched in perspiration, standing by the blue chair. My body trembled uncontrollably. I was panting and gasping for air. My hair was over my face, damp and tangled. The caretaker pushed me onto the seat and swiveled me around to face the wall.

"Don't you dare to piss in your pants while sitting on this chair," he warned harshly.

I was beyond bodily functions. I was empty of everything including fear. It all had drained out of me while soaring in that infinite space.

"You are able to perceive as I do," Emilito said, nodding. "But you don't have any control yet in the new world you are perceiving. That control comes with a lifetime of discipline and storing power."

"I'll never be able to explain this to myself," I said, and swiveled on my own to face the center of the room, to take another peek at that pinkish infinity. Now the objects I saw in the room were tiny, like chess pieces on a chess board. I had to deliberately seek them out to notice them. On the other hand, the coldness and awesomeness of that space filled my soul with unmitigated terror. I remembered what Clara had said about seers that had sought it; how they had stared at that immensity and how it had stared back at them with a cold and unyielding indifference. Clara never told me that she herself had stared at it, which now I knew she had. But what would have been the point of telling me then? I would only have laughed or found her fanciful. Now it was my turn to stare at it with no hope of comprehending what I was looking at. Emilito was right, it would take me a lifetime of discipline and of storing power to understand that I'm gazing at the boundless.

"Now let's look at the other side of infinity," Emilito said, and gently made my chair swivel to face the wall. He ceremoniously lifted the black curtain while I stared vacantly, trying to control my chattering teeth.

Behind the curtain there was a long narrow blue table; it had no legs and seemed to be attached to the wall, although I couldn't see any hinges or braces holding it up.

"Prop your forearms on the table and rest your head on your fists by placing them under your chin the way Clara showed you," he ordered me. "Put pressure under your chin. Hold your head gently and don't become tense. Gentleness is what we need now."

I did as he instructed. Instantly a small window opened on the black wall, about six inches away from my nose. The caretaker was sitting to my right, apparently also looking through another small window.

"Look inside," he said. "What do you see?"

I was looking at the house. I saw the front door and the dining room on the left side of the house, which I had glanced into briefly as I had passed it with Emilio the first time I used the main entrance. The room was well lit and filled with people. They were laughing and conversing in Spanish. Some of them were helping themselves to food from a sideboard set with an assortment of tempting dishes, beautifully laid out on silver platters. I saw the nagual and then

Clara. She was radiant and happy. She was playing the guitar and singing a duet with another woman who could easily have been her sister. She was as large as Clara but dark complected. She didn't have Clara's fiery green eyes. Hers were fiery, but dark and sinister. Then I saw Nelida dancing by herself to the hauntingly beautiful tune. She was somehow different from the way I remembered her, although I couldn't pinpoint what the difference was.

For a while I watched them, enchanted as if I had died and gone to heaven; the scene was so ethereal, so joyous, so untouched by daily concerns. But I was suddenly jolted out of my enjoyment when I saw a second Nelida entering the dining room from a side door. I couldn't believe my eyes; there were two of them! I turned to the caretaker and confronted him with a silent question.

"The one that's dancing is Florinda," he said. "She and Nelida are exactly alike, except that Nelida is a bit softer looking." He peered at me and winked. "But far more ruthless."

I counted the people in the room. Besides the nagual, there were fourteen people; nine women and five men. There were the two Nelidas; Clara and her dark sister; and five other women who were unknown to me. Three were definitely old, but like Clara, Nelida, the nagual and Emilito, they were of an indeterminate age. The other two women were only a few years older than I, perhaps in their midtwenties.

Four of the men were older and looked as fierce as the nagual, but one was young. He had a dark complexion; he was short and seemed very strong. His hair was black, curly. He gesticulated in an animated way as he talked, and his face was energetic, full of expression. There was something about him that made him stand out from all the rest. My heart leaped and I was instantly drawn to him.

"That one is the new nagual," the caretaker said.

As we looked into the room, he explained that every nagual imbues his sorcery with his particular temperament and experience. The nagual John Michael Abelar, being a Yaqui Indian, had brought to his group the pathos of the Yaquis as a characterizing mark of all their actions. Their sorcery, he said, was soaked in the somber mood of those Indians. And all of them, myself included, were bound by the rule to familiarize ourselves with the Yaquis, to follow their ups and downs.

"This perspective will prevail for you until the new nagual takes over," he said in my ear. "Then you will have to soak yourself in his temperament and experience. That is the rule. You will have to go to college. He's lost in academic pursuits."

"When will this take place?" I whispered.

"Whenever all the members of my group together face that infinity in the room behind us, and allow it to dissolve us," he replied softly.

A cloud of fatigue and desperation was beginning to envelop me. The strain of trying to understand the inconceivable was too great.

"This room, of which I am the caretaker, is the accumulated intent and range of temperament of all the naguals that preceded John Michael Abelar," he said in my ear. "There is no way on earth I can explain what this room is. To me, just as it is to you, it's incomprehensible."

I moved my eyes away from the dining room with all its ebullient people and looked at Emilito. I wanted to weep, for I had finally understood that Emilito was as solitary as Manfred; a being capable of inconceivable awareness, yet burdened by the solitude that that awareness brings. But my desire to weep was momentary for I realized that sadness is such a base emotion when in its place I could feel awe.

"The new nagual will take care of you," Emilito said, pulling my attention back into the dining room. "He is your final teacher, the one who will take you to freedom. He has many names, one for each of the different facets of sorcery he is involved with. For the sorcery of infinity, his name is Dilas Grau. Someday you will meet him and the others. You couldn't do it the day you were with Nelida in the left hallway, nor can you do it now, here with me. But you will cross over soon. They are waiting for you."

A nameless longing took hold of me. I wanted to slip through that viewing hole into the room to be with them. There was warmth and affection there. And they were waiting for me.

FOR THE BEST IN PAPERBACKS, LOOK FOR THE

In every corner of the world, on every subject under the sun, Penguin represents quality and variety—the very best in publishing today.

For complete information about books available from Penguin—including Penguin Classics, Penguin Compass, and Puffins—and how to order them, write to us at the appropriate address below. Please note that for copyright reasons the selection of books varies from country to country.

In the United States: Please write to *Penguin Group (USA), P.O. Box 12289 Dept. B, Newark, New Jersey 07101-5289* or call 1-800-788-6262.

In the United Kingdom: Please write to *Dept. EP, Penguin Books Ltd, Bath Road, Harmondsworth, West Drayton, Middlesex UB7 0DA*.

In Canada: Please write to *Penguin Books Canada Ltd, 90 Eglinton Avenue East, Suite 700, Toronto, Ontario M4P 2Y3*.

In Australia: Please write to *Penguin Books Australia Ltd, P.O. Box 257, Ringwood, Victoria 3134*.

In New Zealand: Please write to *Penguin Books (NZ) Ltd, Private Bag 102902, North Shore Mail Centre, Auckland 10*.

In India: Please write to *Penguin Books India Pvt Ltd, 11 Panchsheel Shopping Centre, Panchsheel Park, New Delhi 110 017*.

In the Netherlands: Please write to *Penguin Books Netherlands bv, Postbus 3507, NL-1001 AH Amsterdam*.

In Germany: Please write to *Penguin Books Deutschland GmbH, Metzlerstrasse 26, 60594 Frankfurt am Main*.

In Spain: Please write to *Penguin Books S. A., Bravo Murillo 19, 1° B, 28015 Madrid*.

In Italy: Please write to *Penguin Italia s.r.l., Via Benedetto Croce 2, 20094 Corsico, Milano*.

In France: Please write to *Penguin France, Le Carré Wilson, 62 rue Benjamin Baillaud, 31500 Toulouse*.

In Japan: Please write to *Penguin Books Japan Ltd, Kaneko Building, 2-3-25 Koraku, Bunkyo-Ku, Tokyo 112*.

In South Africa: Please write to *Penguin Books South Africa (Pty) Ltd, Private Bag X14, Parkview, 2122 Johannesburg*.